Thackeray

IRAN

**Recent Titles in
Contributions in Political Science**

A Staff for the President: The Executive Office, 1921–1952
Alfred D. Sander

Hungary and the USSR, 1956–1988: Kadar's Political Leadership
Andrew Felkay

Trotsky and Djilas: Critics of Communist Bureaucracy
Michael M. Lustig

Isolation and Paradox: Defining the "Public" in Modern Political Analysis
Frank Louis Rusciano

The President and Civil Rights Policy: Leadership and Change
Steven A. Shull

Nominating Presidents: An Evaluation of Voters and Primaries
John G. Geer

A Right to Bear Arms: State and Federal Bills of Rights and Constitutional Guarantees
Stephen P. Halbrook

The Politics of Economic Adjustment: Pluralism, Corporatism, and Privatization
Richard E. Foglesong and Joel D. Wolfe, editors

Policy Through Impact Assessment: Institutionalized Analysis as a Policy Strategy
Robert V. Bartlett, editor

Behind the Uprising: Israelis, Jordanians, and Palestinians
Yossi Melman and Dan Raviv

From Feudalism to Capitalism: Marxian Theories of Class Struggle and Social Change
Claudio J. Katz

The Challenge of the Exception: An Introduction to the Political Ideas of Carl Schmitt between 1921 and 1936, Second Edition
George Schwab

The Demobilization of American Voters: A Comprehensive Theory of Voter Turnout
Michael J. Avey

IRAN

From Royal Dictatorship to Theocracy

MOHAMMED AMJAD

CONTRIBUTIONS IN POLITICAL SCIENCE, NUMBER 242
Bernard K. Johnpoll, *Series Editor*

GREENWOOD PRESS
New York • Westport, Connecticut • London

Library of Congress Cataloging-in-Publication Data

Amjad, Mohammed.
    Iran : from royal dictatorship to
theocracy / Mohammed Amjad.
      p. cm.—(Contributions in political science, ISSN 0147–1066
  no. 242)
    Bibliography: p.
    Includes index.
    ISBN 0–313–26441–4 (lib. bdg. : alk. paper)
    1. Iran—History—Revolution, 1979—Causes. 2. Social classes—
Iran—History. 3. Iran—Economic conditions—1945– 4. Iran—
Politics and government—20th century. 5. Islam and state—Iran.
I. Title. II. Series.
DS318.825.A45   1989
955.05′4—dc20   89–11746

British Library Cataloguing in Publication Data is available.

Copyright © 1989 by Mohammed Amjad

All rights reserved. No portion of this book may be
reproduced, by any process or technique, without the
express written consent of the publisher.

Library of Congress Catalog Card Number: 89–11746
ISBN: 0–313–26441–4
ISSN: 0147–1066

First published in 1989

Greenwood Press, Inc.
88 Post Road West, Westport, Connecticut 06881

Printed in the United States of America

The paper used in this book complies with the
Permanent Paper Standard issued by the National
Information Standards Organization (Z39.48–1984).

10 9 8 7 6 5 4 3 2 1

Contents

Preface	vii
1. State and Revolution	1
2. The History of Iranian Political Economy	9
3. Islam and Revolution in Iran	33
4. The Struggle for Democracy and the Triumph of Dictatorship (1941–1960)	47
5. Crisis of the State (1960–1963)	69
6. Socioeconomic Development of Iran (1963–1977)	81
7. The Revolution	103
8. Toward the Creation of a Theocracy	131
9. State and Theocracy in Iran	147
Glossary	157
Bibliography	159
Index	173

Preface

The Iranian revolution surprised everyone. The country, which was assumed to be the most stable regime in the region, became the scene of mass uprising against the Shah's regime. The outcomes of the revolution have not been less surprising. The monarchy was replaced by a theocracy, and the secular forces were pushed aside. Domination of the state power by the religious hierarchy (popularly known as mollahs) resulted in clashes between them on the one hand and their secular allies and opponents on the other. The latter groups, however, failed to generate popular support in order to assert their authority in the country. The focus of this work is to analyze the structure of the Iranian political economy, the transformation of the state role of religion in the political process, and the socioeconomic developments that resulted in the overthrow of the monarchy and the creation of theocracy in Iran.

I visited Iran in 1979–1980 to collect data for the present research. During that time I was able to obtain first-hand information from the people who had participated directly in the revolution. These people came from all walks of life. They included young as well as old, members and supporters of underground political organizations who had surfaced after the overthrow of the monarchy, bazaaris, students, workers, and university professors. I am indebted to all of them for sharing their experiences, insights, and information with me. My main interest was to find out why a country that was assumed to be one of the most stable governments in the world crumbled so quickly. Several factors, including a corrupt regime, a dictatorship, the alienation of the people from the regime, economic mismanagement, and an economic crisis in the mid–

1970s after a period of economic development, provided the situation for a revolution.

Destruction of all political organizations by the regime allowed the religious hierarchy, which had daily contacts with the people throughout the country, to dominate the struggle against the monarchy. Shi'a style militancy accompanied by rituals that glorified martyrdom and sacrifice were utilized effectively to mobilize the masses against the regime. The six-month-long strike of the workers and government employees also played a crucial role in paralyzing the Shah's regime. By the end of 1978 the overthrow of the monarchy was only a matter of time. February 1979 marked the end of the monarchy and the creation of the Islamic Republic of Iran.

During the long journey that resulted in the creation of the present work, I benefited from the assistance and encouragement of many scholars and friends. I am especially indebted to Fred Halliday, James Bill, Michael Fischer, and Maxime Rodinson whose comments in early stages of this work were crucial for reorganizing and formulating my thoughts. I am grateful to many friends, especially Michael Kearney and Richard Lowey, for their encouragement and comments. Abdo Basklini also read the entire work and made useful comments, which were seriously taken into consideration.

I also would like to thank the staff of Greenwood Press, especially Mildred Vasan and Alicia Merritt, who worked closely with me and patiently participated in the production of the book.

I think it is appropriate to mention that despite the assistance I received from many people, I am solely responsible for the errors and shortcomings of the book.

IRAN

1 State and Revolution

The Iranian revolution took almost everyone by surprise. Social scientists were no less surprised about the mobilization of the people against the monarchy than the CIA or the Shah. This was probably due to the general misconception about the power and effectiveness of the Shah and the weakness and fragmentation of the opposition. The aim of this study is to investigate the socioeconomic and political factors that led to the Iranian Revolution and the transformation of the Iranian state from a royal dictatorship to a theocracy.

This study will try to answer the following questions: (1) What was the nature of the Iranian state in both pre- and postrevolutionary periods? (2) What kind of transformation took place in Iran during its transition to capitalism? and (3) Why did Islam play such an important role in the revolution?

Although class is an economic concept, it must not be reduced to the relations of production. Social classes, in fact, must be studied on their political and ideological levels as well. As Nicos Poulantzas indicates, "A social class can be identified either at the economic level, at the political level or at the ideological level, and thus can be located with regard to a particular instance" (Poulantzas 1979a:63).

Relations between the state and social classes is very complicated. Contrary to what instrumentalists such as Ralph Milliband argue, the state is not merely an instrument of the ruling class (Milliband 1969:5). The state is rather the condensation of class relations and a structure within which class conflict takes place. The state has relative autonomy vis-à-vis social classes, and its major function is to create cohesion within the social formation (Poulantzas 1979b:18–35). As prominent Italian

Marxist Antonio Gramsci notes, the state is the arbitrator between the different groupings within the ruling class. "The state's function is to find juridical settlement to internal class disputes, to clashes between opposed interests; thereby it unifies different groupings and gives the class a solid and unified external appearance" (Gramsci 1977:40).

I will utilize concepts such as hegemony, the power bloc (sometimes referred to as the ruling bloc), and relative autonomy of the state to explain the relationship between the state, class, and revolution. Poulantzas defines the power bloc as "a specific alliance of several classes and fractions" (Poulantzas 1979b:71). The concept of hegemony, on the other hand, will be utilized to show the relationship between the Iranian ruling bloc and the ruled masses. Gramsci defines hegemony as consent given by the ruled masses to the ruling bloc, differentiated from domination, which is accompanied by coercion. Gramsci argues that it is the "spontaneous" consent and confidence given by the ruled masses to the power bloc that allows it to depend on its hegemony rather than domination (Gramsci 1971:12). He also emphasizes that the ruling bloc must depend on its "intellectual and moral" leadership to make the masses accept its worldviews (Gramsci 1971:57).

A power bloc is successful in so far as it can depend on the consensus of the ruled masses. If it fails in this respect, a crisis of authority or hegemony will result. The crisis of authority emerges as the result of the inability of the ruling bloc to cope with the socioeconomic transformation of the society. It signals the end of the consensus period and the need for the reorganization of the ruling bloc (Gramsci 1971:210–12, 275–76).

REVOLUTION

Revolutions do not occur overnight. They come as the results of class conflict, crisis of hegemony, failure of the ruling bloc to cope with the increasing opposition of the masses, and crisis within the ruling bloc itself. Despite this, these factors by themselves do not result in the overthrow of the old regime and the creation of a new order. A revolution also requires organization, effective leadership, and ideology in order to succeed (Rejaii 1977:28–36).

Theories of revolution fall within five categories: psychological, psychoeconomic, sociological, multiple sovereignty, and Marxist. Psychological theories of revolution are based on the hypothesis that the motives of individuals are the root cause of revolutions (Gurr 1970; 1972; Feierabend et al. 1972; Schwartz 1972). According to this approach, the social conflict takes place in the minds of individuals. Schwartz, for example, contends that revolutions originate in the minds of people (1972:58). Gurr, the most prominent proponent of this approach, contends that discontent, anger, and frustration result in the aggressive behavior (Gurr 1970:9–57).

Ted Robert Gurr sees frustration as the major cause of political violence (i.e, revolution). In *Why Men Rebel* (1970), Gurr emphasizes "the greater the frustration, the greater the quantity of aggression against the source of frustration" (Gurr 1970:9). He then moves on to conclude that "the greater the intensity of deprivation, the greater the magnitude of violence" (1970:9). Gurr equates frustration with relative deprivation and defines it as a perceived discrepancy between men's value expectations and their value capabilities (Gurr 1972:37). Gurr's theory of revolution could be summarized thus: relative deprivation results in discontent, and the discontented people become angry and resort to violence against the regime.

Alexis de Tocqueville, Crane Brinton, and James Davies view the psychological impact of economic development and political liberalization as the major cause of revolution. Their approach may be categorized as the psychoeconomic theory of revolution. This theory is based on the hypothesis that a long period of economic development followed by a sharp reversal results in a revolution (Tocqueville 1955:174–80). Tocqueville bases his theory on the French revolution and tries to apply it to other societies. His theory could be summarized as follows: First, rapid economic development results in rising expectation among the people. Second, a sharp reversal in economic conditions results in popular discontent. Third, political liberalization after a long period of repression contributes to the mobilization of the masses against the regime. Finally, the social groups that were better off during the economic growth will participate in the revolution more actively (Tocqueville 1955:169–86).

The major contribution of Brinton is the idea that revolutions occur in crisis-ridden societies where the ruling group has lost its legitimacy and does not enjoy support among either privileged or nonprivileged groups (Brinton 1952:34–35). The economic crisis will make all social classes withdraw their support from the regime and will result in a political crisis. This will eventually lead to a revolution that aims to create a state that is more compatible with the needs of the society (Brinton 1952:54–87).

Another contributor to this approach is James Davies. Davies attempts to modify Marx's argument regarding worsening economic conditions and Tocqueville's approach about the improvement of economic conditions as the cause of revolution. He stipulates that he has found a short cut between the two: "Revolutions need both a period of rising expectations and a succeeding period in which they are frustrated" (Davies 1962:17).

Davies basically reinterprets the findings of Tocqueville by emphasizing that "revolutions ordinarily do not occur when a society is generally impoverished. . . . [E]vils that seem inevitable are patiently endured, . . . because the physical and mental energies of people are totally employed in the process of staying alive" (Davies 1962:7). He indicates that "revolutions are most likely to occur when a prolonged period of objective economic and political development is followed by a short period of sharp reversal" (p. 6), calling this process a J-curve of rising expectations and their effective frustration.

Sociological theories of revolution are based on systems theory and structural-functionalism. Chalmers Johnson presents a very sophisticated version of the sociological approach. He is very much interested in the maintenance of equilibrium within the environment (Cohan 1975:120–24). According to Johnson, equilibrium in a society is maintained so long as the values of the society are in harmony with its division of labor. A discrepancy between the values of a society and the existing conditions of life will result in "dys-synchronization" of the society. When the values of a society are dys-synchronized, a crisis develops. At this point, a revolution will occur in order to resynchronize those values. "Revolution is a response to a particular crisis in a political system. The fundamental factor which gives rise to a variation among revolutions is the type of systems in which they occur and the conditions of systemic disequilibrium that they seek to overthrow" (Johnson 1982:53–60, 94–129).

Multiple sovereignty theory was developed by Charles Tilly as a reaction to the reductionism and ideological conservatism of psychological and sociological approaches (Tilly 1975:490–95). In his celebrated work *From Mobilization to Revolution* (1978), Tilly argues that revolutions are the result of power struggles, or multiple sovereignty. The aim of the revolution, then, is to create a single sovereignty polity. "Multiple sovereignty is . . . the identifying feature of a revolutionary situation. A revolutionary situation begins when a government previously under the control of a single sovereignty polity becomes the object of effective, competing, mutually exclusive claims on the part of two or more distinct polities. It ends when a single sovereignty polity regains control over the government" (Tilly 1978:191).

For Marx, revolutions must be studied in light of the mode of production. Instead of emphasizing the "motives of individuals," "frustration," or "political conflict," Marx regards the structural changes in the society as the root cause of revolution. According to Marx, each mode of production gives rise to a particular class structure. Social classes in a mode of production are engaged in a political class struggle for the ownership of the means of production and the seizure of state power (Marx 1983:12). The intensification of class struggle will result in a revolutionary situation. The new class within a mode of production (i.e., bourgeoisie in feudalism and proletariat in capitalism) will oppose the ruling class. Class struggle itself is a result of the contradiction between the social relations of production (i.e., property relations) and the productive forces (i.e., workers in capitalism). The consequence of this development is a social revolution.

At a certain stage of their development the material forces of production in society come in conflict with the existing relations of production, or—what is but a legal expression for the same thing—with the property relations within which they had been at work before. From forms of development of the forces of production these relations turn into their fetters. Then comes the period of social revolution. (Marx 1911:12)

Within the same framework, Marx contends that a revolution occurs when the self-conscious revolutionary class leads the movement. The class-conscious bourgeoisie in feudalism led the bourgeois revolution. Through this process feudalism was destroyed and capitalism was born. So far as the bourgeoisie was struggling against the feudal mode of production and "revolutionizing" the means of production, it was a revolutionary class. The development of capitalism, however, opens the way for the creation of the revolutionary working class, which opposes the capitalist mode of production. The class-conscious proletariat will eventually lead the socialist revolution against capitalism.

The key concept in the Marxist approach is social revolution. "Social revolutions are rapid, basic transformation of a society's state and class structures; and they are accompanied and in part carried through by class-based revolts from below" (Skocpol 1979:4). In political revolutions, on the other hand, the regime changes while the class structure of the society remains the same.

CONCLUSION

As Theda Skocpol notes, present social science theories fail to explain revolutions (Skocpol 1979:25). But this does not mean that these theories are totally invalid. I believe that class analysis, crisis and transformation of the state, and the concept of hegemony should be the focal points for studying revolutions. Despite this, social scientists should not neglect studying psychological, cultural, and ideological factors within any given society. Consequently, I propose a multidimensional approach that combines class analysis and the role of hegemony, and the crisis of the state with the culture and political structure as well as the psychological impact of social and economic development on the formation of revolutionary movements. Gurr and his colleagues are mainly interested in the study of violence as the manifestation of anger and frustration of individuals. Chalmers Johnson, on the other hand, deals with the system maintenance and equilibrium. Charles Tilly tries to move away from the reductionism of both approaches but fails to look at the root cause of the revolutions (i.e., structural transformation of the society) and busies himself with the struggle for power. Tocqueville and Brinton come closer to grasping the roots of revolution, but fail to present a concrete formula because of their misconceptions about the role of the classes involved in the revolution. Marxist theorists, except Gramsci, put too much emphasis on the role of economics and the mode of production. As a result, they tend to become economistic and deterministic.

What students of revolutions can learn from the psychological and multiple-sovereignty approaches is not the causes of the revolution (that they do not explain), but what happens during the process of revolution. That is, the role of violence and destruction in the psychological approach as well as the struggle for the seizure of state power in the multiple-sovereignty approach can be utilized to analyze what happens during the process that (in successful revolutions) ends with the overthrow of the old regime. During the initial stages of revolution until the creation of a new order, the revolutionaries are engaged in "collective violence" against the old regime (Tilly 1978:172–93). The sociological approach plays down the role of economic and political crises and the necessity for change in human societies. Despite this, it helps the student of social conflict to look seriously at the reaction of traditional societies to modernization and its impact on the revolutionary process. For example, in analyzing the Iranian revolution, it is necessary to study the reaction of bazaaris, mollahs, and the other conservative groups to the secularization of the society and the increasing influence of Western culture, which they viewed as a threat to their power and prestige. Yet it would be simplistic to equate the Iranian revolution with a movement to resynchronize the society through imposing Islamic values, since the values that are imposed on Iran at the present time were not predominant in prerevolutionary Iran. The hegemony of Islamic ideology and the domination of the movement by the hierarchy of mollahs was mainly due to the absence of nationwide political organizations.

The psychoeconomic theories have great explanatory power if they are modified and combined with class analysis. They show the impact of economic development on peoples' modes of thought and consciousness about the conditions of their lives. That is, the change of economic structure of the society makes the social classes more conscious of their interests. Also, the argument that political liberalization after a long period of repression will result in revolution has a certain validity. Political liberalization, however, should not be abstracted from class antagonism and social inequality. Rather, it must be studied in light of the crisis of the state and class antagonism within each given society.

Political liberalization and economic crisis by themselves do not result in revolutions. For example, liberalization policies in Iran during the 1960–1963 period and liberalization policies in Brazil since 1979 did not result in revolutions. What must be taken into consideration is that repressive states during economic crises will resort to liberalization policies in order to achieve some sort of legitimacy and reorganize themselves to crush the opposition. Relaxation of repression, however, gives an opportunity to the opposition to organize itself against the state. If the opposition succeeds in organizing its forces and is armed with effective leadership and a popular ideology (i.e., an ideology which is shared or at least understood by the majority of people) it has a good chance of overthrowing the old regime and creating a new order.

Taking theories of revolution into consideration, the Iranian revolution might be summarized as follows: A combination of socioeconomic factors including mismanaged economy, failure of agriculture, inflation, decline of oil revenues, and political repression resulted in a crisis of the state. By late 1976, not only had the situation become intolerable for the masses, but also the regime had become incapable of running the state as before. The liberalization policies of the Shah (starting in early 1977) and the removal of Amir Abbas Hoveyda premiership (in the summer of 1977), proved that the situation was getting out of hand for the Shah. The liberalization policies after a long period of political repression provided favorable conditions for the opposition to organize its forces against the regime.

The effective leadership of Ayatollah Rouhollah Khomeini, the vacillation of the Shah, mass demonstrations and strikes—followed by a military showdown between the demoralized army of the Shah on the one hand and the armed masses and guerrilla organizations on the other—brought down the monarchy on February 12, 1979. Seizure of state power by mollahs, however, did not allow the movement to mature into a social revolution. The struggle of the masses against the monarchy remained a political revolution in which state power was transferred from the hands of the Shah to a power bloc composed of traditional bourgeoisie, traditional petty bourgeoisie, and liberal bourgeoisie. Liberal bourgeoisie, whose class base was among the remnants of national bourgeoisie (i.e., owners of textile factories and cement plants) and middle class, was in favor of a Western-style democracy and reorganization of the old bureaucracy. The traditional bourgeoisie and petty bourgeoisie composed of the merchants and shopkeepers of Iranian marketplaces (bazaar), on the other hand, were against the Western-style institutions and favored the creation of a theocracy. Within a few months after the overthrow of the monarchy, the traditional bourgeoisie and petty bourgeoisie represented by mollahs were able to do away with the liberal bourgeoisie and create a theocracy.

2 The History of Iranian Political Economy

The objective of this chapter is to investigate the obstacles to capitalist development and formation of a strong bourgeoisie in Iran. This chapter demonstrates that until the nineteenth century the nature of the state and social classes and property relations did not provide the conditions for the growth of capitalism. That is, the constant interference of the state in commercial activities, lack of a hereditary nobility, and a weak bourgeoisie obstructed the growth of capitalism in Iran. Penetration of British and Russian capital and manufactured goods during the nineteenth century added to these unfavorable conditions, resulting in the destruction of Iranian crafts and manufactures. The combination of these domestic and external factors created unfavorable conditions for capitalist development in Iran.

The key to understanding Iranian political economy lies in its precapitalist social formation. Contrary to the Western societies, Iran did not have a feudal system. What existed was very close to what Marx referred to as the Asiatic Mode of Production (AMP). The state theoretically owned the land and water and the individuals were propertyless (Bashirieh 1984:7). Ownership of land and the arbitrary use of power by the state obstructed the growth of a unified and strong landowning class. The same situation continued during the transition to capitalism. The state was the organizer of the political economy, and the modern bourgeoisie was, in fact, created by the state; hence it was dependent on the state.

The history of Iranian political economy is the subject of controversy. One view contends that Iran had a feudal system and its political economy should be studied in the light of feudalism and general laws pertaining to the development of both feudalism and its transformation into capitalism (Fashahi 1979; Pigulovskaya 1975; Sodagar 1979). The opposing view rejects this argument and sees the Asiatic Mode of Production as the only way of explaining the tenets of the Iranian history and political economy (Hosseiny 1983).

The majority of scholars, both Marxist and non-Marxist, argue that Iran had a feudal system. These scholars fall into two groups: first, the Soviet Iranologists and traditional Iranian Marxists, and second, non-Marxist scholars. The first group divides Iranian history into four stages: primitive communism, slavery, feudalism, and capitalism (Atighpour 1979:29–70; Pigulovskaya 1975:60–131). For these scholars, Western and non-Western societies have had the same precapitalist mode of production. As a result, they underestimate the structural differences between Western and non-Western societies. This approach sees history as a process of unilinear development commencing in primitive communism and terminating in mature communism.

The non-Marxist scholars do not stress the periodization of Iranian history, but they argue that Iran had a feudal system. Concentration of land in the hands of landlords, periodic decentralization of the state, and the existence of toyoul lands (lands assigned to individuals by the ruler) are regarded as the proof of the existence of feudalism in Iran (Cahen 1953:20–43; Christensen 1944:12–45). Despite this, some scholars are aware of the structural differences between the feudal West and precapitalist Iran. They see the existence of large cities and a money economy, the residence of Iranian landlords and the kings in the cities, and the lack of a hereditary nobility as the major differences between Iranian "feudalism" and its Western "counterparts" (Keddie 1960; Lambton 1953:53–74; 1967:45–50). Keddie shows the sharp distinction between the feudal West and precapitalist Iran very clearly: "Iranian features not found in Western Feudalism include the lack of a serfdom; or personal bondage; the fact that the Iranian ruling classes lived in the cities rather than on manors, the prevalence of nomadic tribes, leading to frequent wars and destructive raids; and the importance of water control and irrigation" (Keddie 1960:3).

Marx and Engels recognized that the socioeconomic formations of non-European societies were structurally different from the feudal West. They referred to these socioeconomic formations as the Asiatic Mode of Production. They suggested that the aridity of land necessitated a strong state for the organization of the irrigation systems. This in turn resulted in the lack of private property and the organization of political economy by the state. Based on the reports of the British authorities in India, they concluded that one of the major characteristics of these societies was the existence of immutable, self-sufficient village systems (Marx 1969:89–95).

Marx's treatment of the AMP can be categorized as follows: First, in the Asiatic societies the individual is propertyless, and the property belongs to the state and more accurately to the despot (i.e., head of the state) (1965:69). He further notes: "Here the state is the supreme overlord" (Draper 1978:570). Second, Asiatic societies are composed of self-sufficient small communities, which survive despite the change and division of empires (Marx 1969:92–93). Third, the despot appears as the father of the smaller communities: "The despot here appears as the head of all the numerous lesser communities, thus realizing the common unity of all . . . [T]herefore the surplus product . . . belongs to this highest unity" (Marx 1965:70). Fourth, the Asiatic societies are change-resistant and their socioeconomic foundations could only be destroyed from without. Based on this hypothesis, Marx expected that the British rule in India would destroy the Asiatic nature of the Indian society and would provide the condition for a rapid capitalist development.

After Marx, discussion about the AMP disappeared from Marxist analysis, and it was Karl Wittfogel who revived the debate about oriental despotism. In his voluminous and controversial work, *Oriental Despotism* (1957), he based his argument on the aridity of land and the existence of water supply as the raison d'être of oriental despotism. He referred to non-European societies and states as "hydraulic states," "hydraulic despotism," "agromanagerial society," and "hydraulic regimes" (1957:60–125). His major argument was that the general aridity of land required a centralized state for the management of the economy. This resulted in a legal system in which private property was subjected to arbitrary confiscation by the state (p. 72).

It is not the intention of this study to go into much detail about the validity of the AMP and oriental despotism, but it must be realized that what Marx and Engels were trying to prove was that first, property relations in Eastern societies were fundamentally different from those in the West, hence leading to different forms of socioeconomic developments. Second, lack of private property was the major obstacle to the growth of capitalism in these societies. Although Marx was right about the different nature of the socioeconomic foundation of these societies, he overemphasized the universality of this socioeconomic formation. There are ample documents that prove the existence of private property in both ancient and modern Iran (Lambton 1967:41–50; Nomani 1979:146–70). Besides that, the hydraulic works and the aridity of land that were emphasized by Marx, Engels, and Witfoggel were not applicable to all parts of Iran. Some parts of Iran—for example the southern, western, and central parts—were dry, while northern parts had adequate rainfall. In the above-mentioned regions, public hydraulic systems were rare. Moreover, the predominant hydraulic systems were underground water supplies called Qanat that were either privately owned or communal.

My own view is that Iran did not have a feudal system because the precapitalist social formation of Iran was not preceded by slavery, did not have a manorial system, and peasants were not serfs (Hosseiny 1983; Katouzian 1981:14–15). Despite this, it would be simplistic to label the precapitalist mode of production in Iran as Asiatic. First, all aspects of the AMP did not exist in Iran. Second, the precapitalist social formation of Iran was not destroyed following the penetration of foreign capital (as Marx had anticipated). Third, if we assume that the AMP existed in Iran, we will face the problem of periodization. That is, we should answer the question, At what point in history was the AMP replaced by feudalism or capitalism? For example, should we regard the Constitutional Revolution (1905–1911), in which the security of life and property was guaranteed by law, a bourgeois revolution which ended the AMP? Then the question would be, Why should a bourgeois revolution strengthen the position of the landlords?

Even if we agree that the 1911–1963 period was one of feudalism (because the landlords were the dominant class), the question of arbitrary and absolute use of power by the Shahs and the control of the economy by the state would still make the society more Asiatic than feudal. It is worth noting that even after the transition to capitalism in the mid–1960s the state played a dominant role in shaping the political economy.

What is further lacking in Marx's argument about Iranian society is the importance of tribes and religious institutions on the structure of the state and social classes. Also, despite restrictions, private property existed in Iran. The conclusion of this argument is that the Iranian society was not purely Asiatic despite the existence of strong elements of the Asiatic Mode of Production in it. I believe that despite the arbitrary use of power by the head of the state and the management of the political economy by the state, it would be misleading to brand the Iranian state as Asiatic. Consequently, in this study the Iranian state will simply be referred to as precapitalist and capitalist.

Based on the theoretical aspects of this chapter, the history of Iranian political economy could be summarized as follows: First, the state controlled the political economy. Second, arbitrary confiscation of private property by the state prevented the growth of genuine and unified landholding and bourgeois classes. Even during the period of weakness of the central government, the governors of the provinces tightly controlled land distribution and confiscated the private property of both landlords and merchants at will (Ashraf 1971:14).

Third, as a result, the state remained stronger than the civil society, and the social classes did not develop into strong, unified entities. Fourth, tribes played a significant role in the formation and the structure of the Iranian political economy and the state. On the one hand, they repeatedly attacked the cities and villages and disrupted normal life and production. On the other hand, they constituted the backbone of the Iranian army. Hence the state's dependence on tribes. This situation continued until the 1920s, when Reza Shah (1925–1941) subdued the tribes, ending their crucial role in the development of the Iranian state. Fifth, penetration of foreign capital since the nineteenth century and the introduction of European manufactured goods destroyed Iranian crafts and weakened the Iranian traditional bourgeoisie, and thus obstructed the development of the traditional Iranian bourgeoisie into a modern bourgeoisie.

Sixth, as the result of the weakness of the traditional bourgeoisie, the central role of the state in the economy, and the penetration of foreign capital, capitalist development took place under the auspices of the state and foreign capital. Consequently, the majority of Iranian merchants were kept out of the industrialization efforts. The only segment of the commercial bourgeoisie of Iran that was able to play an important role in the modernization of the country was composed of the big merchants who had connections with both the state and foreign capital. As a result, the Iranian modern bourgeoisie (industrial bourgeoisie) from the beginning had a dependent nature. Seventh, by the late nineteenth century, the penetration of foreign capital and the introduction of industry weakened the state but strengthened the landlords, merchants, and the Iranian clergy (mollahs). Lastly, the combination of all of these factors prevented the growth of a genuine capitalist development in Iran.

The Iranian political economy can be divided into three distinct periods: precapitalism (which lasted until the mid–nineteenth century), the transition to capitalism from the 1850s to 1963, and the capitalist period thereafter. During the precapitalist period Iran was predominantly an agrarian society, and the Iranian industries were primitive. Even the efforts of the Safavid kings in the sixteenth century for the industrialization of the country did not change the structure of the economy (Banani 1978:93). Commercial activities took place in the bazaar. The domination of landownership by the state and interference of the state in commercial activities obstructed the growth of both sectors. There was no hereditary nobility, and landownership had a bureaucratic nature (Lambton 1967:41–50).

In general, five types of landownership existed in Iran: crown lands (khaleseh); state lands assigned to the government officials in lieu of service or salary (toyoul); lands belonging to the charitable organizations (ouqaf); private landownership (malekkiat-e-arbaby); and peasant holdings and small holdings (malekkiat-e-dehghani and khordeh maliki respectively). Landownership, however, did not remain constant, and usually with the fall of a dynasty or even the death of a king, a new landowning class emerged. The monarch also confiscated the lands he liked with no regard to whom they belonged. These types of landownership were also interchangeable. For example, Nader Shah (Afshar) took over a considerable number of ouqaf lands and made them state lands.

The toyoul land was mainly assigned to the military officers and tribal leaders in lieu of salary or services (Lambton 1953:110; Khosrawi 1977:91). Toyoul land was also assigned to the members of the royal family. The possessors of toyoul had absolute power in their domain, which sometimes included several villages. They were, however, responsible for providing the government with soldiers and collecting taxes from the peasants. Toyoul land could be granted to the individuals for a short or long period of time. It could also be given on a lifetime or hereditary basis (Issawi 1971:221). The general tendency of toyoul land was that it was hereditary (Lambton 1953:250–63).

Khaleseh or crown land was owned by the state. Khaleseh lands were originally confiscated from their owners or retaken from the toyoul possessors by the state. By the late nineteenth century, three types of khaleseh lands could be identified. Raqabat-e-Naderi were mainly ouqaf lands confiscated by Nader Shah of Afshar (1736–1747); Mohammad Shahi Land Register, confiscated by Agha Mohammad Khan Qajar (1796–1797); and Nasser-od-Din Shahi Register, expropriated during Nasser-od-Din Shah's reign (1846–1894). Lord Curzon, who had visited Iran in the mid–nineteenth century, notes that the crown lands were acquired by the government through the confiscation of private property, semicompulsory donation to the monarch, or disgrace of the owner (Curzon 1966:489). Another document written in the early twentieth century also shows that most of the crown lands werre acquired by compulsory confiscation of the private and ouqaf lands (Kermany 1972:108–9).

Khaleseh lands were operated in three different ways. First, they were partly utilized directly by the state. These were called khaleseh-e-divani. Second, some khaleseh lands were assigned to the military personnel or tribal leaders in lieu of salary. These were called toyoul lands. Third, khaleseh-e-inteqali lands were rented temporarily to the individuals. Khaleseh lands were the main source of economic power for the state and especially for the monarch (Lambton 1953:117–19). The king could confiscate lands, assign them to those serving him, and retake them again. This illustrates why there was no hereditary aristocracy in Iran. It also demonstrates the instability of the political power of the landed aristocracy. Considering the monopolization of economic and political power by the king, Sismondi wrote in the mid–nineteenth century that "the shah of Persia esteems himself rich, because he reckons as his wealth all inhabitants of his vast empire, who are his slaves, and all their goods, which he can take from them whenever he chooses" (Sismondi 1966:125).

Ouqaf land has usually been called charitable land. Ouqaf land, however, could be charitable or private. Charitable ouqaf was utilized for religious purposes (i.e., supporting seminaries) or helping the poor. Private ouqaf, on the other hand, was dedicated to the descendants or relatives of the owner. The main purpose behind ouqaf was to make it a public institution and as a result protect it from confiscation by the state or usurpation by powerful tribal khans or individuals. Despite this, on some occasions even ouqaf lands were confiscated by the state. For example, Nader Shah confiscated the ouqaf lands dedicated by the Safavid dynasty to the shrine of Imam Reza (the eighth shiite Imam) and turned them into crown lands (Kermany 1972:108).

Both private and charitable ouqaf needed the guidance of the mollahs. The person in charge of ouqaf land was called Motavali. Motavali had the responsibility of spending the income of the ouqaf for due purposes. The administration of ouqaf lands by mollahs gave them considerable power vis-à-vis the state (Keddie 1981:17). The existence of this kind of ownership relieved the mollahs from depending on the government for financial reasons. The government document shows that by the early 1960s, out of 50,000 Iranian villages, 713 belonged to the ouqaf institutions.

Private lands were either former toyoul lands, which eventually became the property of their possessors, or were acquired by direct usurpation or fraud (Kermany 1972:100–109). In general, there were three types of private land ownership, large landownership (omdeh maliki), small holdings (khordeh maliki), and jointly owned estates (mosha'a). Large land proprietors owned between one and sixty villages, while khordeh maliks had shares in one or more villages. Those khordeh maliks with shares in several villages can be categorized as large landowners. Like large landowners, these khordeh maliks lived in towns. Khordeh maliks with shares in only one village, however, lived mainly in that village. Some peasants also owned a piece of land that they tilled. Their land was very small (i.e., less than five hectares), and they had to work for landlords as well. This kind of land ownership was called peasant ownership (malekkiat-e-dehghani). Mosha'a lands were owned by several owners. The difference between mosha'a land and small ownership was that in mosha'a the land was undivided and usually owned by the members of a family or by relatives.

Big landowners lived in town and in fact were absentee landlords. They managed their estates through hired overseers called mobashers (McLachlan 1968:685). Mobashers also lived in town and went to the villages only to inspect the productivity of lands or to collect taxes. Chiefs of the villages, or kadkhodas, were also chosen by the government or by the landlords and lived in the village. They were the official representatives of both the government and the landlords in the village. As a result of the formal and actual responsibilities of the kadkhodas, the inhabitants of the villages regarded them as the guardians of the interests of the landlords (Lambton 1953:90).

Regardless of the type of ownership, the peasants had to shoulder the burden of the tax and the hard work. They had to deal with the cruelty of the landlords, the mobashers, the kadkhodas, and the other government officials. They were also often attacked by wandering tribes who looted the villages and stole the herds. James Fraser, who had visited Iran in the early nineteenth century, explains the miserable life of the Iranian peasants this way:

> There is no class of men whose situation presents a more melancholy picture of oppression and tyranny than the farmers and cultivators of the ground in Persia. They live continually under a system of extortion and injustice . . . , [and] every tax, every present, every fine, every bribe, from whomsoever received, or demanded in the first instance, ultimately falls on them. (Fraser 1825:195)

The village population was composed of two distinct groups. Those who had cultivation rights were called nasaghdaran. Landless peasants, money lenders, oxen owners (gavbands), millers, blacksmiths, coppersmiths, peddlers, and craftsmen were referred to as khoshneshinan (happy squatters). A 1960 government study shows that the village population was composed of 60 percent nasaghdaran and 40 percent khoshneshinan (Iran Almanac 1963:388).

Nasaghdaran were composed of three strata: First, a small group of rich peasants (6 percent) who had connections with the landlords. Despite their small numeric size, this group was very powerful in the village (Kazemi 1980:32). Second, middle peasants, comprising 10 percent of the village population. The largest group, however, was composed of poor peasants who did not have any lands. The same relation was reproduced after the land reform. The rich peasants acquired big pieces of land (i.e., more than 10 hectares). The poor peasants received less than 5 hectares, and middle peasants acquired between 5 and 10 hectares.

Khoshneshins also consisted of three groups. About 80 percent of khoshneshins were landless peasants. This group was composed of agricultural workers who tilled the lands of the landlords or rich peasants. When there was no job in the country, this group went to town and took seasonal jobs or worked as construction laborers. About 10 percent of the khoshneshinan was composed of artisans and nonagricultural workers such as blacksmiths, goldsmiths, coppersmiths, and millers. The remaining 10 percent was composed of a privileged group of moneylenders, gavbands (oxen-owners), shopkeepers, and traders.

The sharecropping system was based on five vital inputs: land, water, seed, oxen, and labor. Depending on how many shares were provided by the landlord, peasant, and/or privileged khoshneshin, each of these people received his benefits accordingly. Generally, the landlords owned the land and water and automatically received two shares of the crops (Alvandi 1982:405). The peasants received one-fifth because of their labor. Usually gavbands provided the oxen, hence receiving one-fifth (in some areas, instead of gavbands, the landlords or peasants provided this input and received another one-fifth). The seed could also be provided by peasant, landlord, or privileged khoshneshin. Whoever provided this input received another share.

Agricultural production was based on a system called boneh, sahra, tagh, or haraseh. Boneh was composed of teams of four to sixteen peasants who tilled the lands (Safinejad 1977:2–21). Bonehs were engaged in different activities such as maintenance of water supplies (i.e., ditches and qanats), rotation of crops, and leaving the land fallow (Katouzian 1981:299; Najmabadi 1987:133). The landlords were not directly connected to the bonehs. Instead, they sent the mobashers to represent them in the decisions made by the boneh's members. Bonehs eventually became institutions that gave a sense of identity to their members and affected every aspect of their lives.

Despite the harsh conditions of life in the rural areas and the unbearable exploitation of both peasants and agricultural workers by the landlords, the rich peasants, and the rural bourgeoisie (i.e., privileged khoshneshins), the Iranian rural areas before the 1979 revolution did not witness widespread rebellions. However, fragmentation of the rural population did exist. First, the agricultural workers were the most underprivileged group, shuttling between town and country to earn a living. As a result, they were opposed to both the landlords and Nasaghdaran (Momeni 1983). Second, the rich peasants were the natural allies of the landlords and were very powerful, despite their small numeric size (Kazemi 1980:32). Third, the poor peasants were exploited by the landlords, the rural bourgeoisie, and rich peasants. Fourth, the Iranian villages were self-sufficient communities with very little contact with the outside world; hence there was a lack of solidarity with the neighboring rural areas. Fifth, the sanctity of private property, which was preached by rural mollahs, also contributed to the passivity of Iranian peasantry.

MERCANTILIST ACTIVITIES

The study of cities and bazaars is very important for the understanding of mercantilist activities and the lack of a strong bourgeoisie in Iran. Iranian cities have always been the center of political, economic, and social activities. Each city had three component parts: Arg (government citadel), Mosque, and the bazaar. The kings, the government officials, the landlords, the influential ulema, and some of the tribal khans lived side by side with bazaaris in the cities. The bazaaris paid taxes and dues to both the government and the religious hierarchy. Because of their economic ties with the bazaaris and their traditional opposition to temporal authority, the mollahs supported bazaaris in their disputes against the state (see chapter 3).

The bazaars were divided into different quarters. Each quarter was named after the craftsmen working there. For example, Bazaar-e-Bazzazha (weavers bazaar), and Bazaar-e-Sarrafha (moneylenders market), and Bazaar-e-Tala Foroushha (goldsmith market) were the locations where the weavers, moneylenders, and goldsmiths did business (Kuznetsova 1963:310). Merchants, artisans, craftsmen, peddlers, and shopkeepers all worked in the bazaar. The merchants, as wholesalers, however, had extensive influence and power in the bazaar. Iranian kings chose leaders of guilds and merchants. The representative of the merchants was called Malek-ol-Tojjar (i.e., chief of the merchants) and was a liaison between the state and the merchants. The most important bazaars were Bazaar-e-Bazzazha (for their connection with the numerous textile manufactures) and Bazaar-e-Sarrafha (because both the government and the other merchants lent money from this bazaar).

TRANSITION TO CAPITALISM (1850–1963)

In Europe the crisis of feudalism, growth of commerce, and need for exports, plus technological innovations resulted in the decline of feudalism and the growth of capitalism (Dobb 1947; Wallerstein 1979). Craftsmen and merchants lived in towns, while the kings and landlords lived in their fortified castles in the country. The autonomy of the city from the country and the division of labor between the town and country played a significant role in the growth of capitalism in Europe. In Iran, on the contrary, the presence of the landlords and kings in the city, lack of security for private property, and constant interference of the state in commercial activities prevented the Iranian traditional bourgeoisie from developing into a modern bourgeoisie.

In Western Europe, the favorable conditions and internal factors resulted in the growth of capitalism. Capitalist development in Iran, however, was the by-product of the need of the European markets for Iranian goods, on one hand, and the import of European manufactured goods into Iran, on the other. Although European capital and goods at first resulted in the growth of commerce, trade, and industry, they eventually became the major obstacles to capitalist development in Iran. First, the European manufactured goods destroyed the Iranian crafts and manufactures (Curzon 1966:405–60; Issawi 1971:56). Second, the competition of European merchants with each other and with Iranian merchants stifled the growth of capitalism in Iran (Djamalzadeh 1956:20–85). Third, the intention of the European entrepreneurs was not the industrialization of Iran. What they wanted was to turn Iran into the importer of manufactured goods and the exporter of raw materials. Fourth, the two powerful European countries, Britain and Russia, turned Iran into a battleground to impose their economic, political, strategic, and cultural domination. As a result, Iran became a buffer state, with a semicolonial position between Russia and Britain. Thus, capitalist development in Iran was a result of the political, economic, and strategic needs of Europe. Bazaaris and the state were two domestic factors which contributed to the growth of capitalism in Iran. Because of the control of the political economy, the state was in a position to invest in industrial planning. The bazaaris faced the restrictions imposed on them by the state and the competition of foreign capital and manufactured goods. Consequently, the Iranian bazaaris could not play a significant role in the reorganization of the political economy. As a result, capitalist development took place under the auspices of foreign capital and the state. The following discussion will examine the roles of bazaaris, the state, and foreign powers and capital in the industrialization efforts and their impact on Iranian political economy.

THE BAZAARIS

The existence of the bureaucracy of the state in the cities and the arbitrary use of power by the Shahs prevented the natural growth of bazaaris into a strong, unified class. The Shahs and the governors of the provinces confiscated the property of the bazaaris at will. The insecurity of property dissuaded the bazaaris from investing in industry wholeheartedly. Fraser notes the negative impact of insecurity and the arbitrary use of power by the state on capitalist development in Iran: "The direct check to improvement and prosperity in Persia is the insecurity of life, limb, and property. This must always repress the efforts of industry; for no man will work to produce what he may be deprived of the next hour" (Fraser 1825:190).

Despite these unfavorable conditions, the bazaaris struggled very hard to create a socioeconomic system in which the private property and life and limb of the people were protected by the rule of law. The first organized effort of the bazaaris was the establishment of the Council of the Representatives of the Merchants (Majlis-e-Vokalaye-e Tojjar) in 1884. Through the council, the merchants demanded that the government guarantee the private property and the security of life of all citizens. They argued that lack of security of private property and the competition of European-made products were the major obstacles toward a genuine economic development (Adamyyat 1976:299–320). Nasser-od-Din Shah (1848–1896) accepted these demands and issued a decree regarding his approval. Etemad-os Saltaneh, Nasser-od-Din Shah's Minister of Publication, however, notes that the decree was simply issued to silence popular opposition against the corrupt officials (Etemad-os Saltaneh 1971:568).

The industrialization efforts of the Iranian merchants in the latter part of the nineteenth century is worth mentioning. The leading merchants were Hadj Hassan Amin-oz-Zarb and his son, Hadj Hossein. They established several factories, including a glass factory, an electric power plant, and a brick-making factory in Tehran. In addition to Amin-oz-Zarbs, other merchants were involved in industrial planning in this period. For example, Mohammad Hassan Khan Nasser-ol-Molk built a spinning mill in 1885, Mohammad Mohsen Rashty built a silk-reeling factory in Guilan (Northern Iran). A toilet-soap factory was built by Rabi'a Zadeh and his partners, and Hadj Mirza Hossein Sepah Salar established a gas company in Tehran (Djamalzadeh 1956:93–96). Because of foreign competition and the lack of government support, most of these factories stopped operating shortly. The only factories that continued operating were those that were complementary to the European products (Ashraf 1980:82–86). The Iranian bazaaris saw the arbitrary use of power by the head of the state, intervention of the state in economic affairs, and foreign interests as the main obstacles to economic development. The active participation of the bazaaris in the Tobacco Movement (1891) and the Constitutional Revolution (1905–1911) demonstrated the class consciousness of the bazaaris and their eagerness for changing the socioeconomic conditions of the country.

The Tobacco Movement was a struggle against foreign domination. It followed the granting of the monopolization of production and sale of tobacco to a British merchant, Major Talbot. The victory of the Tobacco Movement, in which the bazaaris in alliance with the mollahs were able to organize the people against this concession, paved the way for the Constitutional Revolution. The Constitutional Revolution limited the power of the monarch. According to the Iranian Constitution signed by the ailing Mozaffar-od-Din Shah in August 1906, the legislative, judicial, and executive powers were separated. Most of the responsibilities and duties of the monarch—including having final determination over all laws, decrees, treaties, budgets, monopolies, and concessions—were given to the Iranian parliament or Majlis. The most important achievement of the Constitutional Revolution was guaranteeing the sanctity of private property and freedom of press, speech, and assembly.

The bazaari members of the Majlis had a major impact on the reforms for economic developments and guaranteeing national sovereignty. They recommended economic, financial, and political reforms for the modernization of the country, refused to grant any concessions to foreign countries, and requested the government to establish the National Bank (Bank-e-Melli) to replace Russian and British banks. They also passed laws to reduce the salary of the royal family and to abolish the toyoul system (Adamyyat 1976:433–99). The presence of the landlords in the Majlis, however, had a negative impact on the reform measures and the freedom of activity of the bazaari deputies. The immediate result of this condition was that, while a land reform was necessary for rapid economic development, it was not introduced in the Majlis. The position of the landlords became stronger in the Majlis following the bloody coup of Mohammad Ali Shah in 1911. The landlords and tribal khans stabilized their position at the expense of the bazaaris. While in the First and Second Majlis the landlords and tribal khans constituted about 25 percent of the deputies, their number increased to 55 percent after the Third Majlis (Shajii 1965:178). Following the Third Majlis, independent bazaaris and guild members did not play a significant role in the Majlis and were replaced by the dependent merchants and bureaucrats. Even the abrogation of the toyoul system by the first Majlis mostly benefitted the former toyoul possessors, tribal khans, and bureaucrats who took over these lands (Momeni 1978; Sodagar 1979).

The increasing role of the landlords and later the accession of Reza Shah to the Iranian throne in 1925 put the bazaaris in check. Reza Shah created a centralized state that was directly involved in economic planning and capitalist development. The bureaucratic capitalism of Reza Shan weakened the position of bazaaris and prevented them from emerging as a strong class. The groups benefiting from the capitalist development in this period were contractors, the bazaaris who had connections with the court, and bureaucrats (Ashraf 1971:79–81). The bazaaris, as a result, were kept out of the industrialization efforts. It was only after the fall of Reza Shah that the bazaaris started growing stronger. The weakness of the state was the major factor that contributed to this new development.

The growth of the bazaaris and the national bourgeoisie reached its peak during the Mossadegh period (1951–1953). His policy was to reduce the power of the Shah, strengthen the bazaaris and the national bourgeoisie, and end the dependence of Iran on foreign capital (Mazdak 1982:288–300; Nirumand 1969:41–55, 70–94). The economic blockade of Iran following the nationalization of the oil industry helped the Mossadegh government to pursue this policy more boldly. An import substitution sector was created to reduce the dependence of Iran on foreign products and resist the economic blockade. Mossadegh's policies, while benefiting the national bourgeoisie and the bazaaris, undermined the court, the comprador-bourgeoisie, the landlords, and the influential mollahs. It was not surprising that the former group supported him wholeheartedly while the power bloc opposed him. The power bloc, with the support of Britain and the United States, overthrew Mossadegh and put the national bourgeoisie and the bazaaris in check again. The fall of Mossadegh was a major blow to both the national bourgeoisie and the bazaaris. The comprador-bourgeoisie and the landlords, however, grew stronger following the coup.

THE STATE

Some Iranian politicians were aware that the arbitrary use of power by the head of the state, lack of the security of private property, and foreign economic and political domination were detrimental to the modernization of Iran. These politicians argued that the state should provide the conditions for the industrialization of the country instead of obstructing the efforts of the Iranian bazaaris for modernization. Among the reform-minded politicians who had a major impact on economic developments of Iran before the Constitutional Revolution, Qaem Maqam and Amir Kabir are worth mentioning. They realized that without reforming the structure of the state and civil society, Iran was doomed to remain weak, backward, and dependent on foreign powers. Qaem Maqam (Mohammad Shah's prime minister) cut the lavish spending of the court, curtailed power of the royal family, and invested most of the government revenues in industrial planning. He also forbade making any economic or political concessions to Britain or Russia (Nashat 1982:149). Amir Kabir (Nasser-od-Din Shah's prime minister) had more ambitious plans for the industrialization of the country. He founded a military-technical high school called Dar-ol-Fonoon. He hired European teachers to train the students in areas such as mining, engineering, and military sciences. He also established textile, sugar, china, paper, and metal factories (Adamyyat 1976:354–89).

The efforts of these modernizing prime ministers were obstructed by their respective kings. Both Qaem Maqam and Amir Kabir were executed for interfering in the royal domain. Failure of the reform-minded politicians to provide favorable conditions for the growth of national bourgeoisie and bazaaris opened the way for the emergence of Reza Shah. Reza Shah pursued a vigorous industrialization policy under tight state control. Although his policies obstructed the growth of national bourgeoisie and the bazaaris, he laid down the foundation of state capitalism in Iran. Within twenty years, power of the tribal khans and the landlords was broken and a state capitalism emerged by the side of the precapitalist social formation. The state also separated itself from the religious hierarchy. The pre-Islamic Iranian culture was revived and the educational and judicial systems that were administered by the mollahs became secularized. Hence the alienation of the Ulema from the state and their increasing animosity toward it.

Under Reza Shah, Iran became more centralized and the power of tribal khans and landlords was eliminated (Wilber 1975:220–60; Zirinsky 1986:281). The army was also reorganized and disciplined. Plans for the industrialization of the country were started with the building of roads and railroads. By 1938, approximately 14,000 miles of new roads had been built. The Trans-Iranian Railway (TIR) was also completed by 1938, connecting 287 miles of railway in the north and 575 miles in the south (Bharier 1971:196). The TIR was financed by special taxes on tea and sugar and also a loan from the National Bank of Iran. Because tea and sugar were two important items in the national diet, the tax burden was mainly shouldered by the poor (Keddie 1981:100). The road construction, however, was mainly strategic, had no economic benefits, and did not connect major cities (Banani 1961:134–35; Key Ostovan 1948:175–78).

The overall government policy for industrialization was to create an important substitution sector. The industries established by the state during this period included cotton, silk, wool, and textile factories; chemicals; oil processing; sugar refineries; and match and cement plants. Foreign trade was also nationalized, which put this sector under the total control of the state (Motamedi 1971:68). The oil revenues were the major financial source for the state. The oil revenues, however, were not stable and were subject to the fluctuation of the international market. For example, in 1919 the annual income from the oil revenues was $649 million, but it fell to $310 million a year in 1930 as a result of the international economic crisis. In 1931, Reza Shah's powerful court minister, Teimour Tash, proposed increasing Iran's share from oil revenues as a means to finance the industrialization efforts. The British government, however, refused to consider this demand. Following this development, Reza Shah abrogated the D'Arcy concession (Rezun 1980:128). Later on, however, Reza Shah realized that Iran had neither the expertise nor the market for its oil and agreed to extend the former concession for another sixty years.

The terms of the new agreement were even less favorable than the old one and put Iran at the mercy of the British government. According to Article 15 of the old D'Arcy Concession: "On the expiration of the term of the present concession, all materials, buildings, apparatuses thus used by the company for the exploitation of its industry should become the property of the said government" (Hershlag 1980:361). In the new contract, however, the tools and machinery were to remain the property of the company after the expiration of the concession in 1993 (Madany 1982:117). Katouzian also comments that "the basis of the revenue payment was changed from the previous 16 percent of the company's annual net profit to 4 shillings per barrel produced: It was by no means certain that this would improve over the concession period" (1981:118).

The state capitalism of Reza Shah further weakened the position of bazaaris. As a result, the state and the merchants who had connections with the court became the proponents of capitalist development. The monopolization of foreign trade by the state put the control of the economy under its tutelage. A significant step toward the sanctity of private property taken during this period was the Law for the Registration of Private Property. This law theoretically protected private property against arbitrary confiscation by the state, but it did not prevent Reza Shah and his powerful generals from confiscating the lands of many landlords. By 1941, Reza Shah, who did not have any property before coming to power, possessed 2,670 villages.

By the late 1930s the inefficient and corrupt state capitalism of Iran had collapsed. The fall of Reza Shah in 1941 relieved the Iranian merchants and national bourgeoisie from the total control of the state. The weakness of the state between 1941 and 1953 resulted in the rapid growth of national bourgeoisie and the bazaaris. The semidemocratic political apparatus imposed by the Allies on the power bloc prevented the state from direct control of the political and economic institutions. A measure taken by the state to reverse the situation and make the economic growth contingent upon its policy was the First Seven-Year Plan (1949–1956) and the creation of the Plan Organization. The First Seven-Year Plan was drawn up during the premiership of Ahmad Qavam-os Saltaneh in 1946. Qavam-os Saltaneh notes that the Shah put forward the idea of the Plan Organization (Shafaq 1951:142). A significant aspect of the creation of the Plan Organization was the increasing role of the United States in Iran (Lotz 1950:102–3). American firms and capital, as a result, had a crucial role in the formation of the Plan Organization. As an American scholar notes, "The World Bank, the American embassy in Tehran, two American consultant firms, and Max Thornburg played a crucial role in the foundation of the Plan Organization" (Baldwin 1967:25). Max Thornburg, head of Overseas Consultants, Inc., however, had the most impact on the structure and responsibilities of the Plan Organization (Elwell-Sutton 1955:271). The aim of the government in the establishment of the organization was to channel the oil revenues for economic development (Looney 1977:43).

The First Seven-Year Plan emphasized the infrastructure. The same trend was followed by the Second Seven-Year Plan (1955–1962), in which most of the budget was spent on building dams and highways. The Third (1963–1967), Fourth (1968–1972), and Fifth (1973–1978) were directed more toward rapid industrialization. Despite the efforts of the state, the Plan Organization was not able to provide the necessary change in the society for a genuine economic development. First, the aim of the planners was not to reduce economic inequality or create more jobs. Therefore, the emphasis was placed on the establishment of capital-intensive industries. Second, the economic modernization was not accompanied by modernization of the political machinery. As a result, while economic growth between the 1950s and the 1970s was impressive, the political apparatus of the state remained underdeveloped and incapable of coping with the needs of a modern society.

The Mossadegh period (1951–1953), was a very important stage in the Iranian political economy. The nationalization of the oil industry, preventing the royal family from intervention in economic and political affairs, and a land reform were the major tenets of Mossadegh policies (Mazdak 1982:286–350). An import substitution sector was also created to reduce dependence on European-made products (Bharier 1971:184). Under Mossadegh, the bazaaris and the national bourgeoisie grew stronger and, as a result, lent their support to him. While the national bourgeoisie and the bazaaris were growing stronger, the power bloc composed of the comprador-bourgeoisie, the landlords, the army generals, and the court suffered a major setback (Ashraf 1971: 157–215; Bill 1972:138–39). The fall of Mossadegh reversed the situation. The power bloc emerged stronger and the national bourgeoisie and the bazaaris were pushed aside. The post-Mossadegh governments pursued a policy of attracting foreign capital to Iran. In 1957, the Majlis passed a legislation for Attraction and Protection of Foreign Investment in Iran. This legislation guaranteed protection of foreign capital, gave a five-year exemption from the tax and custom duties, and allowed foreign investors to repatriate the profit earned in the original currencies. The injection of large sums of foreign capital since the mid-1950s provided the conditions for rapid growth of the dependent capitalism in Iran (Brown 1959:157–215). The cabinet of Dr. Manouchehr Eqbal followed the Open Door Policy which encouraged foreign investment and imports. Foreign goods soon filled the Iranian market, and many Iranian merchants went bankrupt (Jazani 1978:123–28). By 1960, the overheated economy of Iran was out of control. Rising inflation, recession, and unemployment resulted in tightening economic and credit policies.

The growth of industries and the banking system since the mid-fifties made the state less dependent on the landlords. The absence of a strong bourgeoisie and the control of the economy by the state allowed the latter to become the champion of capitalist development. As a result, the Iranian state played the same role that the European bourgeoisie had during the transition to capitalism. The difference was that, first, while the European bourgeoisie created a democratic order, the state-sponsored transition to capitalism in Iran resulted in the creation of a more authoritarian political order, and second, the bourgeoisie created the state in Europe, but in Iran it was the state that created the modern bourgeoisie; hence, the dependence of the latter on the former.

ROLE OF FOREIGN CAPITAL

Penetration of foreign capital and the import of European products started in mid-nineteenth century. This new condition initially helped economic growth but deprived the country of genuine capitalist development. Hobsbawm notes that European capitalism forcibly held the economy of the Third World backward, for its own growth (Hobsbawm 1976:163–64). Foreign trade did not pave the way for the industrialization of the country. It mainly increased the volume of foreign trade, which was to Iran's disadvantage. In 1880 the volume of import and export was £2,500,000, but it rose to £20,500,000 by 1914. Iran's main export items were carpets, cotton, silk, opium, and livestock. The imports included textiles, hardware, glass, silver, gold, sugar, and tea (Safavi 1929:160–61). The volume of imports rose from £2,000,000 in 1880 to £11,767,000 by 1914. The volume of exports rose from £2,000,000 to £8,288,000 within the same period (Issawi 1971:130–31). Iran's foreign trade was mostly with Russia and Britain. At the turn of the century, more than 50 percent of the trade was with Russia, 25 percent with Britain, and the remaining 25 percent with Turkey, France, Austria, Germany, and other nations (Djamalzadeh 1956:9).

The integration of the Iranian economy into the international market had the following negative effects. First, fluctuations in the international market deeply affected the Iranian economy. In this respect, the falling price of silver in the international market devalued Iranian currency, which was based on silver (Avery and Simmon 1974:259–65). Second, the Iranian power bloc became dependent on foreign capital instead of reorganizing the political economy for genuine economic development. In the late nineteenth century big pieces of land were dedicated to the cultivation of cash crops such as opium, cotton, and rice for export. As Keddie notes, the revenues of exported cash crops were spent on European luxury items rather than invested in agriculture or industry (Keddie 1972:67–68). Another negative aspect of the penetration of foreign capital was that the Iranian factories soon had to close down as the result of foreign competition (Djamalzadeh 1956:70–123).

The weakness of the Iranian state opened the country for foreign domination (Nashat 1982:11–14). The Russo-Iranian wars of 1801 and 1828, in which the tribal army of Iran was badly defeated, resulted in the humiliating treaties of Golistan (1813) and Turkoman Tchai (1828). According to these treaties, Iran lost Armenia, Georgia, and Caucasia and had to accept the Caspian Sea as a Russian lake (Kazemzadeh

1968:5). Iran was also forced to grant capitulation rights to the Russian subjects and pay an indemnity of £3,000,000 to Russia. Later Britain followed suit to acquire the same concessions. In 1854, Britain attacked Southern Iran and retreated only after securing the Treaty of Paris (1857), according to which the Iranian government accepted the cessation of Afghanistan and granted capitulation rights to the British subjects.

The capitulation rights gave an advantageous position to the European merchants. They were exempt from custom duties and many taxes that Iranian merchants had to pay. Furthermore, European merchants had the protection of their government in disputes with the Iranian government. This was in sharp contrast to Iranian merchants, whose property was subject to arbitrary confiscation by the state. After the penetration of foreign countries in Iran, several Iranian merchants chose Russian or British nationality in order to protect their property against arbitrary confiscation by the state. Lambton mentions the case of Hadj Abdul-Karim, who chose British nationality in order to get back the money he had loaned to the government (Lambton 1971:331–60). Among the economic concessions made to the British subjects the following are worth mentioning: Baron Julius de Reuter obtained a contract for the establishment of the Imperial Bank of Iran (1889). The tobacco concession was also made to Major Talbot in the same year. This treaty was abrogated following a popular uprising against it (Teimouri 1982:10–40, 50–70). In 1901 William Knox D'Arcy was granted a contract for the production and export of oil throughout Iran, except the provinces bordering Russia. This concession was obtained for the sum of £20,000 in cash and £20,000 in shares (Fateh 1926:137–38). The concessions made to Russia included the establishment of the Banque de Pretes (1890), monopoly of the fishing industry in the Caspian Sea (1888), and a contract for administration of the telegraph lines in the northeastern part of the country (Djamalzadeh 1956:103).

In 1900 Mozaffar-od-Din Shah's reform-minded prime minister Amin-od-Dowleh hired a Belgian named Monsieur Naus to manage the custom and finance departments. Monsieur Naus's policies increased the efficiency of the collection agencies of the government. Naus, however, extended his duties and took over the ministry of finance. The policies of Naus in general hurt the Iranian merchants, who complained he had discriminated against them in favor of the European and non-Muslim merchants (Algar 1969:226). Many Iranian merchants regarded Naus as the instrument of Russian policy in Iran (Cottam 1979:161). The increasing influence of the Western political and economic power in general and the policies of Naus in particular triggered the Mashruteh Revolution (i.e., Constitutional Revolution).

The Mashruteh Revolution was a genuine popular movement against the arbitrary use of power by the Shah and his entourage and the lack of security of life and property, and also a struggle against foreign domination (Adamyyat 1976:240–60; Katouzian 1981:215). It is worth mentioning that the interests of Britain and Russia on several occasions coincided with those of the Iranian people. In the Tobacco Movement, Russians supported the Iranian protests against Britain. During the Mashruteh Revolution, the situation was quite different. Like Iranian merchants, the British government believed that the purpose of Naus's policy was to enhance Russian interest in Iran. Britain also supported the Mashruteh Revolution, in order to prove that it favored democracy everywhere (Katouzian 1981:59). It was not surprising that the demonstrators took refuge in the British legation during the Mashruteh Revolution (Browne 1966:119).

The interventionist policy of Britain and Russia in Iran took yet another turn in 1907, when these two foreign powers secretly divided Iran into their spheres of influence. Northern and central provinces, including Tehran and Isfahan, came under the sphere of influence of Russia. A buffer zone was also assigned between these two states. Following this treaty, these two countries obstructed any attempt to establish a centralized government or any economic reform. The most significant aspect of their intervention reached a climax when they prevented the Iranian government from reforming its finance department. In 1911, the Iranian government hired an American economist, Morgan Shuster, to reform its finance department. Claiming that the operation of the Iranian government in northern and southern provinces required their approval, Britain and Russia forced the Iranian government to dismiss Shuster (Kazemzadeh 1968:548–644).

The Russian Revolution (1917) changed the situation dramatically. The Soviet government on January 1918 renounced all the unequal treaties between the two countries, including the Russian sphere of influence (Lenckzowski 1949:48). The British government, as a result, changed its former policy of obstructing reform, enticing tribal skirmishes, and weakening the central government. The new British policy was to reorganize the Iranian political economy, integrate it with British capital, and encourage the establishment of a strong centralized government in Iran (Katouzian 1981:78–81).

The notorious Vosough-od-Dowleh treaty was the result of this new policy. In 1919, the British government signed a treaty with the Vosough-od-Dowleh cabinet to grant economic aid, reorganize the army, develop communication and transportation services, and provide technicians and advisers for the reorganization of the Iranian administration. Keddie notes that this agreement would have turned Iran into a British protectorate (Keddie 1981:81–82). This treaty was cancelled under pressure from popular protests.

During the Reza Shah period, neither the Soviet Union nor Britain had any direct influence in Iran. Both countries welcomed Reza Shah's policies. The Soviet Union regarded Reza Shah as the leader of the national bourgeoisie and went so far to ask all opposition forces to support Reza Shah. The immediate result of this policy was the withdrawal of Soviet support from the Jangali movement, which was struggling to establish a socialist republic in Northern Iran. Britain also concluded that her interests would be more secure under Reza Shah. As a result, Britain withdrew its support from the governor of Khuzistan, Sheikh Khaza'l, who with British support was planning to announce Khuzistan as an independent state.

After the fall of Reza Shah, Britain, the Soviet Union, and the United States competed to get the upper hand in Iran. The instrument of the Soviet policy was the Red Army and the Tudeh Party (see chapter 4). Britain had a vested interest with the power bloc and as a result was in a stronger position than both the Soviet Union and the United States. The United States was a newcomer and wanted to appear as the protector of Iran's independence, economic growth, and territorial integrity. The U.S. military and economic advisers under General Norman Shwartskopf and Arthur Millspaugh, respectively, played a crucial role in preparing the condition for an active U.S. role in Iran. While the military presence of the United States in Iran remained unheeded by many Iranians, the increasing role of Millspaugh in economic affairs was so overwhelming that Mohammad Mossadegh (a Majlis Deputy from Tehran who later became prime minister) and the Tudeh Party demanded his dismissal (Kambakhsh 1972:91–92; Key Ostovan 1948:254–55).

The U.S. role in Iran increased following the Soviet Union's refusal to withdraw from Iran and the Azerbaijani crisis (see chapter 4). U.S. diplomatic pressure and its military aid on both occasions helped the Iranian state to resolve these crises (Sanghavi 1966:116–35). U.S. policy altogether was to strengthen the Shah, stabilize the economy, and gradually get an upper hand in the economic activities of Iran. The Plan Organization was the result of this policy. First, the Plan Organization was created with direct assistance from American economic institutions; second, the Organization was run by U.S.-educated economists, who saw the American model of economic development as the ideal.

With the nationalization of the oil industry in 1950 and the decline of the Tudeh Party in 1953, the position of Britain and the Soviet Union weakened, but the position of the United States became more stabilized. Following the CIA-engineered coup of August 1953, the United States granted an emergency loan of $40 million which was followed with more economic and military assistance. The growth of capitalist relations of production since the mid–1950s was made possible by the injection of American dollars. The influence of the United States since Mossadegh's overthrow was so great that the Shah had to base his crucial policies on

U.S. recommendations. The land reform programs of 1960 and 1962 were the direct result of the U.S. pressures. The White Revolution and the state-sponsored rapid capitalist development of post–1963 also reflected the U.S. influence and interests.

STATE AND CAPITALIST DEVELOPMENT (1963–1979)

The White Revolution was the beginning of a new era in Iranian history. The precapitalist economic formation of Iran was effectively broken and a rapid industrialization policy was put into effect (see chapter 6). The old class structure of Iran was dismantled and the landlords disappeared from political and economic scenes. Through the state bank, rural cooperatives, and mechanized agriculture, capitalism penetrated the villages. The old class alliance composed of the court, the landlords, the comprador-bourgeoisie, and the mollahs was broken and replaced by a new power bloc consisting of the court, the comprador-bourgeoisie, and the rural bourgeoisie. The state also added the former landlords to the new power bloc by the sale of the government-owned factories to them.

The modern bourgeoisie of Iran is a creation of the state (Rah-e Kargar 1983). The only sector of the modern bourgeoisie that has bazaar background is the segment that was dependent on the state. The modern bourgeoisie was also composed of former landlords who sold their lands to the state and bought the state-owned factories following the White Revolution. In this regard, when the bureaucratic landownership was transformed into the bureaucratic capitalist system, the former landlords and dependent bazaaris became the entrepreneurs of the new socioeconomic formation. Furthermore, the oil revenues provided the state with liquid assets to invest directly in industrial planning and subsidize the "private sector" (see chapter 6).

Despite the dependence of the modern bourgeoisie on the state, these entrepreneurs struggled for autonomy. They formed associations to cope with the pressures of the state through organizations such as Syndicate of Textile Owners, Syndicate of Metal Industries, Syndicate of Sugar Industries, and the Association of Commerce, Industry and Mines (Ashraf 1971:285; Bashirieh 1943:42). The economic journals such as *Bours* and *Tehran Economist* voiced the disagreements of the industrialists with government policies. *Tehran Economist* went so far as to request the government to sell the state-owned factories to the private sector (*Tehran Economist*, June 14, 1966).

The industrialization program was financed by the oil revenues. The oil revenues rose from $817 in 1968 to $5.6 billion in 1973 and $22 billion in 1974. The state policy was to distribute the oil revenues among the industrialists in order to enhance the industrialization efforts. The Plan

Organization (now renamed Plan and the Budget Organization) and the Pahlavi Foundation determined the share of each industry from the oil revenues. The Pahlavi Foundation was established by the Shah as a "charity organization." The foundation, however, became the largest industrial group, with shares in most industries. It received large sums of money from the oil revenues and controlled the private sector and the bazaar through the Omran Bank and the Industrial Bank of Iran.

While the modern bourgeoisie was benefitting from the easy state credits, low interest rate, and protectionist policies, the bazaar was left out of this sphere. The growth of banks also took away the money-lending functions of the bazaar. The state wanted to weaken the bazaaris (because of their traditional autonomy from the state) and replace them with the modern bourgeoisie. The antiprofiteering campaign of 1975–1976 was also aimed at weakening bazaaris. During this period more than forty thousand shops were closed and eighty thousand bazaaris were imprisoned or exiled. It is not surprising that bazaaris participated in the 1979 Revolution wholeheartedly.

Government policy toward the modern industries was to resort to protectionism and subsidization. Tax exemption was yet another factor helping the modern bourgeoisie grow at the expense of the consumers. Easy credits, tax exemptions and protectionist policies against foreign competition were the major steps taken by the state to support modern industries (Ashraf 1971:262). The growth of industries speeded up following the quadrupling of the oil revenues in the 1973–1974 period. The oil revenues emboldened the Shah to launch more ambitious industrialization planning. The budget of the Fifth Plan (1974–1978) was doubled overnight from $60 billion to $120 billion.

The quadrupling of the oil revenues made the Shah dream of transforming Iran into the fifth industrialized nation of the world in less than twenty years. The result of this policy was rapid industrial growth, destruction of the village system, and migration of millions of the peasants to the cities. This royal whim concerning industrializing the country without taking into account the low productivity, lack of skilled personnel, shortages of port facilities, and other economic bottlenecks eventually turned into a nightmare (see chapter 6). By 1975, the economy was out of control. The drop of international demand for Iranian oil was the major reason for this new situation. Iran soon started borrowing from the World Bank, a sharp contrast with the period from 1973 to 1975, when Iran loaned to several countries including Britain, France, Egypt, and Senegal.

The overthrow of the monarchy brought a new power bloc into power composed of the liberal bourgeoisie (i.e., remnants of the national bourgeoisie), the bourgeoisie of bazaar, and the traditional petty bourgeoisie (i.e., shopkeepers). The liberal bourgeoisie lost the power struggle to the traditional bourgeoisie and petty bourgeoisie, represented by the fundamentalist mollahs. This strengthened the position of the fundamentalist mollahs in the power bloc.

The fundamentalist mollahs, who have strengthened their position since the ouster of liberals in 1981, are divided over the issues of private property and the role of the state in regard to economic planning. A conservative group led by Ayatollah Ali Kani, Sheikh Mahmoud Halabi, and Abolghasem Khazali believes in the sanctity of private property and emphasizes that the state should leave economic planning to the industrialists and big merchants. The radical faction, led by Hojjatolislam Akbar Rafsanjani (the Majlis speaker), Ali Khamenei (the president), and Hossein Moosavi (prime minister), is in favor of extensive government intervention in economic planning and improving the conditions of life for the poorest strata of the society. Although the power struggle among the radicals and conservatives continues, the radical faction has the upper hand. This faction has been able to execute a land reform and nationalize foreign trade and major industries. Two economic organizations were founded after the overthrow of the monarchy that have helped the government to control the economy: Construction Crusade and Foundation of the Poor. The Construction Crusade (Jahad-e Sazandegi) has reorganized the political economy of the rural areas and has been constructive in executing new land distribution. The Foundation of the Poor (Bonyad-e Mostazafin) has confiscated the properties of the Pahlavi family and the factories of the industrialists who fled the country during the revolution. Directors of these two organizations have a coalition with the radical mollahs. The conservative mollahs, who are against land reform and the nationalization of industry, have been greatly weakened and do not seem to be able to play a crucial role in the future of Iran.

3 Islam and Revolution in Iran

Islam, and more specifically Twelver Shiism, is deeply rooted in Iranian culture and social life. As a result, studying Shiism is necessary for understanding the Iranian Revolution. The aim of this chapter is to study the development of Shiism, its relation to the state, and its impact on social movements. In Islam, politics and religion are intertwined. Prophet Mohammad was both the head of the state and the administrator of religious affairs. Following Mohammad's death in A.D. 632 Moslems were divided into two groups. The majority argued that Mohammad's successor should be selected by the Islamic community (Ommah) (Jafri 1979:13).

This group is called Sonnis, or follower of the tradition (Sonnat) of the Prophet. A minority, called Shi'a, argued that Mohammad had already appointed his cousin and son-in-law, Ali, to take the leadership of the Ommah following his death. Shi'as also believe that Imamate (i.e., political and religious leadership) is the right of the male descendants of Ali. Imamate, however, ends with the Twelfth Imam Mahdy, who lives in occultation (Ghayba) (Hussain 1982:22). According to the Shi'a doctrine, the only legitimate ruler after Mohammad was Ali. Ali, however, did not become Caliph immediately after Mohammad's death, but was selected the fourth Caliph in A.D. 657. Ali's rule was short and ended in 661, when he was assassinated by a political opponent. Ali's son, Hassan, failed to consolidate his power and was outmaneuvered by the governor of Sham (Syria), who founded the Omayyid Dynasty (661–749). This new development ended control of the state power by Ali's family. Martyrdom (Shahadat) is a very important aspect of Shiism. None of the Imams (except the Twelfth Imam Mahdy who according to

Shi'a doctrine lives in occultation) died of a natural cause. Ali was assassinated in a mosque by a political opponent. Imam Hossein (the Third Imam and Mohammad's grandson) was killed in a battle against the army of the Ommayid Caliph Yazid in Karbala (Iraq). The rest of the Imams were poisoned by their respective caliphs. The martyrdom of Imam Hossein, however, illustrates the most emotional and heartrending aspect of Shiism. Hossein and seventy-two of his followers rebelled against the injustice and tyranny (Zolm) of the Omayyid Caliph Yazid, but fell in the battle in A.D. 683.

Hossein's martyrdom is commemorated throughout the year especially during the holy month of Moharram. The first ten days of Moharram are very important in this respect. The ninth day of Moharram (Tasu'a) is when Hossein's small camp was surrounded by the army of Yazid and Hossein was asked to surrender and save his life, but he refused to do so by saying "Death is better than life under oppressors" (Fischer 1980:129). On the 10th of Moharam (Ashura) Hossein and his disciples (As'hab) were massacred, and their wives and children became captive.

Shi'as believe that crying for the plights of Hossein's family in Karbala provides the condition for the salvation of the faithful. Hossein is also the symbol of resistance against oppression (Fischer 1980:104). He is referred to as the Seyyed-ol Shohada (Master of the martyrs) of all time. The martyrdom of Imam Hossein and his followers is glorified by emphasizing the necessity of sacrifice for the sake of freedom and the creation of justice in society (Shariati 1972:30–67), hence the slogan Kol-o Yawm-en Ashura, Kol-o Arz-en Karbala (everyday is Ashura and the whole earth is Karbala).

The events of Karbala are immortalized through rituals such as narrating the tragedy of Karbala (Rowz-e Khani), passion plays (Ta'azieh), wailing songs (Noh-e Khani), beating on the bare chest (Seen-e Zani), and beating oneself with chains on the back (Zanjir Zani). In Rowz-e Khani, a Rowz-e Khan (preacher) narrates the story of Karbala and asks his audience to cry for the plight of Hossein's camp. Ta'azeihs recreate the story of Karbala (Baktash 1979:183).

Noh-e Khani and self-flagellation (Seen-e Zani and Zanjir Zani) go together. In this regard, a large group of Seen-e Zan and Zanjir Zan march in lines of four to ten to mosques or other religious institutions called Hosseinieh (after the name of Imam Hossein). A Noh-e Khan leads the marchers and stops them frequently to sing wailing songs. The marchers composed of Noh-e Khan and Seen-e Zan repeat the verse after the Noh-e Khan and beat on their chests and backs. Noh-e Khani and self-flagellation are effective means of organizing people for demonstrations. During the revolution, it was not difficult for the mollahs to lead the marchers and have them repeat antigovernment slogans.

Another important aspect of Shiism is the question of Mahdy. He is the son of the Eleventh Imam Hassan Askari. Mahdy is referred to as the Vally-e Asr (Ruler of the Time) and Saheb-e Zaman (the Lord of the Time). According to the Shi'a doctrine, he lives in occultation and will emerge only after the God orders him to take over his duties as the just ruler and true successor of Ali. When Mahdy emerges, "he will fill the earth with equity and justice as it was filled with oppression and tyranny" (Tabatabaii 1975:211). Algar notes that the most important duty of a Shi'a (after believing in God and the prophecy of Mohammad) is total obedience to the Imam-e Zaman (Algar 1969:6).

Mahdy's occultation is divided in two periods. After his father's death in A.D. 874, Mahdy went in lesser occultation (Ghaibat-e Soghra). During this time he was connected to his followers through four successive representatives (Naebs). Naebs were responsible for collecting religious taxes such as Khoms and Zakat, keeping the hideout of Mahdy secret, and delivering his messages to the faithful. This is called Velayat-e Khaseh (specific agency), in that Mahdy had handpicked four deputies to give guidance to the people. After the death of the last Naeb in A.D. 940, Imam-e Zaman started his greater occultation (Ghaibat-e Kobra) (Hussain 1982:83). During this period his duties, including interpretation of Qoran and Hadith (narrations of the Prophet), collection of religious taxes, and distribution of money among the poor, are delegated to the ulema or mojtaheds (the learned scholars of Islamic jurisprudence) (Bill 1982:22–23). This is called Velayat-e Ammeh (General Agency), in which theoretically anyone can become a representative of the Imam-e Zaman (i.e., a mojtahed).

Mojtaheds use their independent judgement for the interpretation of Islamic laws (Shari'a). The rest of the society are called moghalid or imitators. They must follow the rulings of living mojtaheds. Becoming a mojtahed is a long process. Those who wish to gain this title begin by studying in the seminaries (Houzeh-e Elmieh). These students, called Talabehs, live in seminaries (Houzeh-e Elmieh). A majority of Talabehs leave seminaries after a few years of education and become prayer leaders (Pishnemaz) or preachers (Rowz-e Khan). After many years of education, a small group of Talabehs reach the rank of mojtaheds. Mojtaheds are divided into three categories. A large section of mojtaheds become Hojjatolislam (Manifestation of Islam). Hojjatolislams, although capable of interpreting Qoran, are not specialized in any branches of Islamic Jursiprudence (Figh). The number of the Hojjatolislams in Iran at the present time is estimated to be about five thousand (Irfani 1983:12). Yet a smaller group (about fifty) have reached the rank of Ayatollah (sign of the God).

An Ayatollah is specialized in Islamic laws. He writes a book called *Resaleh-e Touzihol Massael* (*Book of Explanation of the Problems*) in which he provides answers regarding the application of Shari'a to everyday life. The highest ranking mojtaheds are called Ayatollah-ol Ozma (Grand Ayatollah) or Marj'a-e Taghlid (Source of Imitation). A Marj'a-e Taghlid (pl. Maraje-a Taghlid) has many followers and is known for his piety and knowledge of Shari'a. Currently, there are only four Maraje-a Taghlid in Iran.

The choice of a Marj'a-e Taghlid is not based on election or referendum, but on the acceptance of each Marj'a-e Taghlid by the Moghalids. Marjayyat is decentralized, and no Marj'a-e Taghlid has a right to interfere in the rulings of another Marj'a-e. Each Marj'a-e is connected to his followers through the network of Ayatollahs, Hojjattolislams, Talabehs, Pishnemazes, and Rowz-e Khans. As a result, the Maraje-a Taghlid are closely connected to the general public and are aware of their needs and grievances. Maraje-a Taghlid have traditionally had immunity, and their houses were refuges (Bast) for the people against the excesses of the government. The 1906 Constitution recognized the immunity of the Maraje-a Taghlid and gave them a veto power over the laws they deemed contradictory to Islam.

Shiism became the official state religion in 1501 following the establishment of the Safavid dynasty. Before then Shi'as were a minority in Iran. Hassan Nasr reports that more than two-thirds of the population of Tabriz (the capital) in 1501 were Sonnis (Nasr 1974:273). The majority, as a result, were forced to convert to Shiism. In order to provide an ideological basis for their rule, the Safavid kings did two things. First, they forged a document that traced their lineage to the Mousa-ye Kazem (the seventh Shi'a Imam), hence implying that they were the only legitimate rulers of Iran in the absence of Imam-e Zaman. Second, many Shi'a mollahs were imported from Bahrain, Iraq, and Lebanon in order to generate ideological support for their rule and indoctrinate people to Shiism (Banani 1978:86). The mollahs were given toyoul lands and a share of political power in return for providing ideological support for the Safavid dynasty (Arjomand 1984:123–40). The power and prestige of the Ulema increased throughout the Safavid period, The decomposition of the Safavid dynasty early in the eighteenth century and the instability that followed created unfavorable conditions for mollahs. Consequently, a majority of them migrated to Iraq, where they lived a secure and peaceful life.

It was during the reign of the Qajar dynasty (1796–1925) that mollahs became powerful and played a significant role in Iranian politics. The weakness of the Qajar state, the penetration of foreign capital, and the political domination of Iran by European powers gave mollahs an opportunity to establish themselves as the defenders of nationalism and the independence of Iran. During the Russo-Iranian Wars, the mollahs tasted their power by calling for Jihad (holy war) against Russia. The result of these interventions was catastrophic and Iran lost more lands. The constant interference of mollahs in the political process made some reformer politicians such as Abbas Mirza (Fath Ali Shah's heir apparent), Qaem Maqam, and Mirza Hossein Sepah Salar (Mohammad Shah and Nasser-od-Din Shah's prime ministers respectively), decide to curb their influence.

Despite the efforts of these politicians, the influences of Ulema increased following the intervention of European powers in the political and economic activities of Iran. The penetration of European capital and manufactured goods resulted in the decline of Iranian crafts and manufactures, hurting the bourgeoisie and petty bourgeoisie of the bazaar (merchants and shopkeepers respectively). The cultural impact of Western penetration also started a trend toward the secularization of the society, and undermined the position of Ulema and the Islamic culture. Mollahs and bazaaris saw the domination of the country by the West as detrimental to economic development, independence, and the traditional culture of Iran. This resulted in an alliance between the two parties. The best manifestation of this alliance during the Qajar period was the Tobacco Movement and the Mashruteh (Constitutional) Revolution.

The Tobacco Movement started in 1889 upon granting the monopolization of tobacco in Iran to a British merchant, Major Talbot (Teimuri 1982:24–29). According to this contract, the monopolization of the production, sale, and export of tobacco was granted to Talbot for fifty years. This contract put the Iranian merchants and shopkeepers at the mercy of a foreign company. They protested against this concession, which they felt was against the public interest and a total sellout to foreigners (Adamyyat 1976:36). This feeling was shared by the majority of the people, who saw this contract as evidence of the corruption of the government and the government's disregard for national interests (Adamyyat 1977:36–50; Teimouri 1982:20–46, 52–90).

The Iranian merchants and shopkeepers turned to the Ulema for support. This act was the beginning of an alliance between the bazaaris and Ulema which was manifested in the forthcoming Mashruteh Revolution (1905–1911) and the 1979 revolution. The active participation of Ulema in this movement played a crucial role in the abrogation of the tobacco concession.

The victory of the Tobacco Movement opened the way for the Mashruteh Revolution. The Mashruteh Revolution started in 1905 as a result of the political dictatorship, lack of security of life and property, and the increasing influence of European countries in Iran. The economic hardship and the increasing price of sugar that resulted from the Russo-Japanese war of 1905 greatly contributed to popular discontent against the regime. The incident that triggered the revolution was the flogging of two respected members of the bazaar on the false charges of speculation (Ehtekar) on sugar trade. The popular response was not to support the government but to demonstrate against this unfounded allegation.

The leadership of the revolution was composed of four distinct groups: Ulema, bazaaris, landlords, and intellectuals. The intellectuals were affected by the democratic values of the West and saw constitutional democracy as the best way of ending despotism and the separation of the state from religion (Kermany 1967:87). Bazaaris and landlords, on the other hand, wanted autonomy from the state and security of life and property. Ulema, however, did not know much about the constitutional form of government. Their main aim was to monopolize the leadership of the revolution (Adamyyat 1976:4).

Faced with mass demonstrations and the support of the British legation for these demands, Mozaffar-od-Din Shah granted Edalat Khaneh to the people. Witnessing the growth of the movement, the continuous British support, and the weakness of the government, the intellectuals rejected the vague Edalat Khaneh and demanded the creation of a Mashruteh (i.e., constitutional) system. Mashruteh in Arabic means conditioned or constrained. By this token, the demand of the intellectuals was for the creation of a system that was based on the constrained power of the king (Katouzian 1981:56). The change of the name from Edalat Khaneh (which has an Islamic overtone) to Mashruteh made the Ulema feel uneasy about the future of their position in the political process. As a result they requested that the Iranian parliament be named Majlis-e Shoray-e Islamy (the House of the Islamic Council). A majority of the people, however, rejected this name and suggested Majlis-e Shoray-e Melli (the House of the National Council). They were worried that by giving an Islamic name to the parliament, people could be prosecuted for their religious beliefs (Kasravi 1983:10).

This was the beginning of a rift between the secular forces and the Ulema. The most outspoken mojtahed who turned against Mashruteh soon after its implementation in 1906 was Sheikh Fazlollah Noori. Noori argued that freedom of the press, equality of all people before the law, and the replacement of the Islamic laws (Shari'a) by civil codes were contrary to the principles of Islam (Haeri 1977:329; Noori 1984:100–125). In general, Noori and his supporters were against the political, economic, and social changes promised by the constitution. They also argued that sovereignty belonged to God, the prophet, and the Ulema, and as a result the masses had no right to exercise sovereignty (Akhavi 1980:26–35). Noori suggested that Mashruteh should be replaced by Mashru'eh (i.e., theocracy). The Mashru'eh was to impose Islamic laws (Shari'a) and forbid Western-style institutions and laws (Noori 1984:120–60).

As an Iranian scholar notes, a significant impact of the Mashru'eh would be the restoration of despotism (absolute dictatorship of the Shah) with the leading role of Ulema in the political process (Katouzian 1981:59). Sheikh Fazlollah publicly denounced the Mashruteh Revolution and encouraged the Shah to abrogate the constitution (Hosseiny 1972:158). Encouraged by the conservative Ulema, the king decided to do away with the Mashruteh (Kermany 1972:263; Milani 1988:55). In June 1908 Mohammad Ali Shah, with the help of the Russian-led cossack brigades, staged a coup against the Mashrutiat. The Majlis was bombarded, many deputies were arrested, and some of them were executed. Among those executed were Jahangir Sur Israfil and Malekol-Motakkalemin (two famous journalists) and also a fiery preacher named Seyyed Jamal od-Din Isfahani. Some deputies managed to go underground, and some were able to leave the country.

Mohammad Ali Shah's coup was defeated by the civil war that followed. He was dethroned, and Sheikh Fazlollah Noori was executed. Despite this, the coup and the legacy of Noori and his conservative associates left a deadly impact on the Mashruteh. First, the active participation of tribal khans in the civil war resulted in strengthening their economic and political power. Second, in the amendment which was added to the constitution, the Ulema were given a veto power over the laws which they deemed contrary to the principles of Islam. This allowed many Ulema to oppose reforms when they felt they were anti-Islamic. The opposition of Ulema to land reform and equal rights for women (in the 1960s) was expressed in the guise of defending principles of Islam and Mashruteh.

During the Reza Shah period, the role of mollahs in the political process was substantially reduced. Secularization of the society took the judicial and educational functions of the mollahs away. The late Iranian essayist and novelist Jalal-e Al-e Ahmad notes that mollahs complained that with the secularization of the judicial system there was nothing left for them to do (Al-e Ahmad 1981: 45–47). Rowz-e Khanis and religious processes were banned and the mollahs were forced into silence.

It was only after Reza Shah's abdication in 1941 that mollahs emerged as a powerful political entity. The class alliance that ensued included the mollahs as well as the landlords, army generals, and the court. The alliance between the court and the religious hierarchy continued until late 1959, when the government pushed for a series of reforms and for the secularization of the society. To begin with, Prime Minister Manuchehr Eqbal proposed a land reform to the Majlis in 1959. The Land Reform Bill became a dead letter under the pressure of the landlords (who constituted 60 percent of the Majlis seats) and the mollahs. Ayatollah Hossein Borujerdi, the then Marj'a-e Taghlid, issued a Fatva (proclamation) in which he announced that land reform was against the principles of Islam and should not be carried out (Lambton 1964:118).

The most important factor that made mollahs oppose land reform was not their opposition to the betterment of the condition of lives of the peasants. It was rather the changes that would be associated with land reform. Lambton notes:

> The opposition of the religious classes was probably due not only, or even mainly, to obscurantism and reaction but rather to an instinctive feeling that the whittling away in one field by the temporal Government... of personal rights guaranteed by the divine law and the Constitution is likely to weaken their position all along the line. (Lambton 1961:82)

The term "instinctive" here is the key word. The mollahs were aware that land reform and the modernization of society would result in secularization of society and the reduction of their influence and power; hence their opposition to the reform measures of 1960s.

The death of Ayatollah Borujerdi in March 1961 left a vacuum in the Shi'a hierarchy. There was not an influential Marj'a-e Taghlid to replace him. Ayatollah Kazem Shariatmadary and Ayatollah Ruhollah Khomeini in Qom, Ayatollah Hossein Mahallati in Mashhad, and Ayatollah Mohsen Hakeem in Najaf (Iraq) were among those mentioned as Borujerdi's successor. Noticing the crisis of authority in the Shi'a hierarchy, the Shah attempted to move the center of gravity of the Shi'a leadership from Qom to Najaf. In order to do so, the Shah sent a telegram of condolence to Ayatollah Hakim in Najaf by referring to him as Marj'a-e Taghlid. This implied that Ayatollah Hakim was the successor of Ayatollah Borujerdi.

The first unified action of Ulema against the government was reflected in their reaction to the granting of voting rights to women in 1962. The fierce opposition of the Ulema to this issue forced the Shah to withdraw his proposal (Madany 1982:12–15). A year later, the Shah had consolidated his power and was ready to end his alliance with the Ulema. In January 1963, he announced his six-point reform program known as the White Revolution, which granted (among other things) voting rights to women and a land reform. This new development ended the alliance that had existed between the Shah and the mollahs since 1941 (Akhavi 1980:60–79). Maraje-a Taghlid in general opposed the White Revolution, but Khomeini played a crucial role in labeling it as an antidemocratic and anti-Islamic measure.

Between March and June 1963 Khomeini delivered several fiery speeches in the Faizieh seminary of Qom against the White Revolution and attacked the Shah for violating the principles of Islam and the 1906 Constitution (Khomeini 1981:169–80). On March 22, 1963, following Khomeini's speech against the White Revolution, the Faizieh seminary was attacked by the army. Several Talabehs were killed and many others were wounded. Khomeini's June 5 (15 of Khordad on the Iranian calendar) speech was even more dramatic. In this speech, Khomeini compared the Shah to Yazid and by implication himself to Imam Hossein. He asserted that, like Yazid, the Shah wanted to destroy Islam and weaken the position of Ulema who were defending Islam. Khomeini also threatened that if the Shah continued his anti-Islamic activities, he would ask the people to expel him from the country (Khomeini 1981:177–80). The government's reaction was harsh and quick. The next day the Faizieh seminary was closed down and Khomeini was arrested.

Khomeini's arrest resulted in an angry reaction from the other Maraje-a Taghlid such as Shariatmadary, Qomi, and Milani, who argued that the government had violated the immunity of the Marj'a-e Taghlid that had been recognized by the 1906 Constitution (Rouhani 1977:337). On June 5, 1963, thousands of people in Qom and other major cities including Tehran, Tabriz, and Mashhad demonstrated against the government. The National Front and the university students also called for demonstrations against the regime. Witnessing the formation of an alliance between secular and religious forces, the Shah decided to suppress the demonstrations before the situation got out of hand. The army was sent to suppress the demonstrations at any price. The June 5 upheaval was brutally suppressed, leaving thousands dead and wounded.

Ayatollah Khomeini was released from jail in August, but he continued to criticize the regime. This time, however, he chose to attack the regime not only for the implementation of the White Revolution, but also for violation of the constitution, injustice, corruption, subservience to the United States, and for establishing diplomatic and economic relations with Israel (Khomeini 1981:177–201). To make the situation worse, in October 1964, the Shah had the Majlis pass a bill to grant diplomatic immunity to U.S. military personnel. Following this new development, Khomeini delivered another fiery speech against the Shah, criticizing him for being subservient to the United States. "The government has sold our independence, reduced us to the level of a colony.
... They have reduced the Iranian people to a level lower than that of an American dog" (Khomeini 1981:182). Following this speech, he was arrested again and sent to exile in Turkey. A year later, he was allowed to move to Iraq, where he resided in the holy city of Najaf.

The White Revolution and the suppression of the June 5 (15 of Khordad, Iranian calendar) uprising had a major impact on the religiously oriented intellectuals and bazaaris. The former saw the White Revolution as a major step toward the creation of a dependent capitalist state. The bazaaris felt that rapid industrialization and the growth of banks would undermine their economic activities even further. The bazaaris could not depend on the National Front for support, since it had stopped all of its activities after the June 1963 massacre. As a result, they decided to organize their resources, build closer ties with the mollahs, and support Islamic intellectuals in challenging the regime. In this regard, bazaaris did two things: first, they organized Islamic cultural and financial institutions to strengthen their position against the regime, and second, they provided material and moral support to the underground Islamic political organizations.

With the help of bazaaris, the Fedayan-e Islam (whose members were mostly bazaaris) was reorganized. This group assassinated premier Hassan Ali Mansur, who was responsible for granting diplomats immunity to the American advisers in Iran (Savory 1972:300). Several Islamic underground political organizations were created following June 1963. Some of these organizations, such as Jamiathay-e Moatalef-e Islami (the Coalition of Islamic Societies), Hezb-e Melal-e Islami (the Party of the Islamic Nations), and Hezb-ol Lah (the Party of God), were created by bazaari members. The aim of these political organizations was to create an Islamic government based on the tradition of the Prophet and Ali's governments. Other groups such as Jonbesh-e Enghelabi-e Mardom-e Iran, usually known by its acronym JAMA (Revolutionary Movement of the Iranian People), Jonbesh-e Mosalmanan-e Mobarez (the Movement of the Militant Moslems), and the Sazman-e Mojahedin-e Khalq Iran (People's Mojahedin Organization of Iran) were created by Islamic intellectuals and had socialist tendencies. These latter groups were independent from the bazaaris but received financial support from them.

Among these Islamic institutions and groups only Mojahedin and Shariati (as the main speaker of the Hosseinieh Ershad) gained prominence. Ali Shariati, a Sorbonne-educated sociologist and a proponent of the revival of Islam in Iran, returned from France in 1961 and taught in the University of Mashhad (capital of Khorasan Province). Later he moved to Tehran, where he founded the Hosseinieh Ershad in 1967.

Shariati believed that Islam was against exploitation, injustice, backwardness, ignorance, class differences, and imperialism (Shariati 1977:380–400). He argued that Iranian intellectuals should liberate Islam from the dogmatism of the mollahs and turn it into a powerful weapon against imperialism and exploitation (Shariati 1978:24). He also argued that Islam was more progressive than Marxism and quite capable of creating a just society in Iran (1979:97–98). Shariati's ideas attracted many young people to his interpretation of Islam. Shariati popularized the concepts of martyrdom as an act of liberation and a necessary step towards the creation of a just society. Fischer notes: "It was particularly Shariati who managed to instill an enthusiasm among the youth of Iran for an Islamic ideological revolution and liberation" (1980:183). Another scholar also notes that Shariati played a crucial role in raising the political consciousness among the people (Irfani 1983: 125–35).

His popularity caused concern among the conservative mollahs and the regime. The regime tried to silence him, first, by closing down the Hosseinieh Ershad (1972), and then by imprisonment (1973). He remained in jail for two years and went to England in 1977, where he died mysteriously. Many believed that he was murdered by the Shah's secret police, SAVAK.

The Mojahedin-e Khalq Organization was founded by Mohammad Hanif Nejad, Said Mohsen, and Ali asghar Badi Zadegan in 1965. The organization was clandestine and recruited its members from religiously oriented university students. Its base of support was the bazaar, the religiously oriented students, Talabehs, and Ulema. The basic ideology of Mojahedin was very close to that of Shariati. Mojahedin, however, blended Marxism and Islam in their analysis of the Iranian society. Their aim was to organize masses for armed propaganda against the regime (Mohsen 1978:11–25). Mojahedin initially attracted some of the influential mojtaheds to their cause, among whom the following are worth mentioning: Ayatollah Hossein Ali Montazeri (Ayatollah Khomeini's former successor), Hojjatol Islam Ali Akbar Rafsanjani (Majlis speaker), Ayatollah Morteza Mottahari (a close associate of Ayatollah Khomeini who was assassinated by a terrorist Islamic group named the Forghan in 1979), Ayatollah Hossein Beheshti (founder of the Islamic Republican Party), and Ayatollah Mahmud Taleghany.

Although Shariati and Mojahedin were able to give a new consciousness to the Iranian masses, they were not able to organize them against the regime in the period 1977–1979. The reasons for this were the death of Shariati in 1977, the crackdown on Mojahedin by the regime, and a split within the Mojahedin organization in 1975. As a result, when the mass mobilization of 1977–1979 started, neither Mojahedin nor supporters of Shariati were in a position to lead the movement. Consequently, the mollahs were able to monopolize the leadership of the revolution.

Following the White Revolution the Shah speeded up the secularization and westernization of the society, emphasized the pre-Islamic culture of Iran (in order to provide an ideological basis for the monarchy), and attempted to control the religious institutions. In 1967, the Shah had the Majlis pass the Family Protection Law, according to which women were given more equal rights with men in regard to marriage and divorce. The civil courts were also to take the place of mollahs in these matters. In 1971, a religion corps was created and attempts were made to establish an Islamic university to replace the Hozeh-e Elmiehs (seminaries). To make the situation worse, in 1975 the Hejira (Islamic) calendar was replaced by a royal calendar. All of these measures were attacked by the Ulema, who saw them as a conspiracy to undermine their power and destroy Islam (Milani 1988:117). Khomeini, however, played a crucial role and championed the struggle of the mollahs against the regime. He attacked the Family Protection Law as anti-Islamic by arguing that women divorced under this law were still married and if remarried they were committing adultery. He concluded that the children of the new marriage were illegitimate and had no inheritance rights (Ferdows 1986:130). Ayatollah Khomeini also criticized the creation of the religion corps as an imperialist plot to undermine Islam and Ulema (Madany 1982:192–93). Khomeini's attack on the change of calendar, however, was harsher. He regarded it as a clear sign of the animosity of the regime towards the prophet and Qoran (Mottahari 1982:42).

The uncompromising position of Khomeini against the Shah enhanced his popularity (Algar 1972:254). Ayatollah Khomeini's position was contrasted with that of moderate Maraje-a Taghlid such as Shariatmadary and Qomi, who kept the channel of communication with the Shah open (Rouhani 1977:20–55). Consequently, militant Talabehs and Ulema accepted Khomeini as their sole leader. The popularity of Khomeini was also based on his sympathy with the poor and destitute and his call for the betterment of the condition of lives of this group. Throughout the 1960s Khomeini was a constitutionalist who saw no role for the Ulema but to advise the government to follow the Islamic principles in passing laws. In his *Kashf-ol Asrar* (Revelation of Secrets), published in 1943, he had argued that the Ulema had always cooperated with the temporal rulers and had no intention of creating an Islamic government. He further asserted that the mollahs should only supervise the laws passed by the Majlis, to be certain they were not contrary to the principles of Islam (Khomeini 1943:240–41). Until the 1970s, he constantly referred to the Iranian Constitution in order to criticize the Shah, but did not ask for the abolition of the monarchy.

By 1970, he had changed from a constitutionalist to a proponent of Mashru'eh (theocracy). In 1971, he delivered a series of speeches about the nature of government in Islam. These lectures were later published under the title of the *Velayat-e Faghih* (Government of the Jurisprudence). In this book, for the first time, he announced that Islam was against the monarchy (Khomeini 1981:31). He suggested that just Fughaha (Jurisprudence) should create an Islamic state and rule the country based on the tradition of Mohammad and Ali. "The just Fughaha must be leaders and rulers, implementing divine ordinance and establishing the institutions of Islam" (1981:79).

Despite Khomeini's call for the creation of an Islamic government, his idea was not fully accepted by his supporters, and even his most ardent supporters did not take the book very seriously. The incident that brought name of Khomeini to the fore and helped his cause was the mysterious death of his first son Mostafa in Najaf (Iraq) and its consequences. Commemoration of Mostafa Khomeini's death throughout the country frightened the Shah and made him worried about a religiously inspired upheaval like that of 1963.

In order to defuse the situation, the Shah unsuccessfully tried to ban the commemoration of Mostafa Khomeini and then discredit Ayatollah Khomeini. In January 1978, the Shah had the semi-official newspaper *Ettella'at* publish a slanderous article against Khomeini. The article accused Khomeini of being a reactionary and an agent of British imperialism. This article infuriated Khomeini's supporters. About four thousand Talabehs demonstrated in Qom against it and demanded dissolution of the Rastakhiz Party, reopening of Tehran University, the return of Khomeini to Iran, and reinstitution of the 1906 Constitution (Fischer 1980:194). The police opened fire on the demonstrators, killing several Talabehs and wounding many others (Parsons 1984:61). Ayatollah Shariatmadary, a moderate and quiet Ayatollah, played a crucial role at this stage of the movement. Overwhelmed by the atrocities committed by the police, he issued a proclamation (fatva) in which he called the Shah's regime non-Islamic, denounced the massacre, and asked the people to participate actively in the commemoration of the fallen Talabehs (Fischer 1980:194; Madany 1982:245–47). The regime, which had miscalculated the popularity of Khomeini and was counting on the moderation and restraint of Shariatmadary, now was put in check on two fronts.

The traditional Islamic public mournings are held on the third, seventh, and fortieth day of a death. When Shariatmadary made the commemoration of those slain in Qom a religious duty, he put an Islamic stamp on the movement (Saedi 1983:9). Bringing the tradition of mourning for the dead and the other Islamic rituals into the political struggle, a new era in the movement started (Sheikholeslami 1986:246–47). From the incident of Qom, the death of every person at the hand of police was followed by public mourning and protest against the regime (Shivers 1980:69).

This gradually gave the movement a religious coloring and made the mollahs de facto leaders of the revolution. Moreover, the movement grew so rapidly after January of 1978 that the existing political organizations both underground and open, could not keep up with it. This gave the hierarchy of the Shi'a mollahs, which was operating through the network of 80,000 mosques and 180,000 mollahs, the chance to dominate the leadership of the revolution.

Mollahs were already trained for mobilizing masses through leading Seen-e Zanis, Rowz-e Khanis, and other religious processions. By the end of the summer, government employees and workers joined the movement. Their demands were both economic (i.e., wage increases) and political (unionization, freedom of political prisoners). The six-month strike of workers and government employees broke the back of the regime. These strikes combined with a brief armed insurrection on February 12, 1979, resulted in the overthrow of the monarchy. With the collapse of the old regime, Ayatollah Khomeini announced the creation of the Provisional Islamic Government on February 13, 1979.

4 The Struggle for Democracy and the Triumph of Dictatorship (1941–1960)

In this chapter I shall discuss the transformation of the Iranian state from the constitutional monarchy to a royal dictatorship. This period witnessed a struggle between the power bloc, on one hand, and the national bourgeoisie, the middle class, and the working class, on the other hand. The 1953 coup signaled the triumph of the dictatorship and end of the democratic process. The 1940s and 1950s can be divided into four periods: constitutional monarchy (1941–1949), the emergence of dictatorship (1949–1950), the popular movement (1951–1953), and the absolute dictatorship of the Shah (1953–1960).

The first period (1941–1949) was marked by major socioeconomic changes that left their trademark on the Iranian history. First, the dictatorship of Reza Shah was replaced by a semidemocratic monarchy in which the Shah was reduced to a figurehead. Second, political prisoners were released from jail and political parties and newspapers mushroomed overnight. Third, a new power bloc composed of the court, the landlords, the tribal khans (chiefs), the comprador-bourgeoisie, the army generals, and the mollahs emerged and lasted until early 1960s. Third, the occupation forces influenced the political process and struggled to enhance their interests in Iran through some of the political parties and the power bloc. Fourth, nationality movements grew strong in Kurdistan and Azerbaijan but were eventually defeated in 1946. Fifth, by the end of this period, the Shah's position was strengthened to such an extent that he was able to restrict the democratic process and push for the creation of a dictatorship. In the following sections I will discuss the impact of domestic forces and foreign powers on the socioeconomic development of this period.

THE ALLIES

Iran was divided into three zones. British forces occupied the south, the Red Army occupied the north except the holy city of Mashhad, and central Iran remained unoccupied. In January 1942, the Soviet and British governments signed an agreement with Iran according to which they promised to respect the independence and territorial integrity of Iran and not to intervene in internal affairs of the country. They also promised to grant economic aid to Iran to solve the problems caused by the occupation. Both countries also promised to withdraw their troops from Iran within six months after the war. Iran, on the other hand, was to hand over the control of its means of communication such as roads, railroads, ports, pipelines, telephones, telegraph, and radio stations to the Allies (de Villiers et al. 1976:101–3). The Iranian government was also responsible for providing food and raw materials for the occupation forces.

The Allies arranged to pay for their expenses in the Iranian currency, the rial. This was to Iran's disadvantage, since it could not get hard currency to pay for its imports. Moreover, the allies forced the Qavam-os Saltaneh government to print an extra 700 million rials (about £100 million) in order to pay for their expenses in Iran. As a result, the cost of living went up 20 percent. This trend continued later, and by 1942 the cost of living rose 400 percent (de Villiers et al. 1976:104–5). The Iranian currency was also devalued by more than 100 percent, from 68 rials to 140 rials to the pound sterling (Katouzian 1981:142). These factors reduced the buying power of the ordinary people and the government's capacity for paying its employees or carrying out development plans. Soon after the occupation, most of the products (especially foodstuffs) were black marketed. This trend hurt the poor to a great extent but made those in charge of black markets rich quickly.

POWER BLOC

Contrary to Reza Shah's period, the Shah did not have much power and was reduced to a figurehead. Despite this, he had one winning card: the army. The army had traditionally been a royal domain and the Shah was impatiently waiting to use this winning card. With military assistance from the United States, the Shah was able to reorganize and modernize the Iranian army. Four years later, the Iranian army had adequate training to suppress the autonomy movement in Azerbaijan and Kurdistan. This new development provided the conditions for the Shah to create a dictatorship in Iran. Among the social forces of the power bloc, the mollahs and the landlords had suffered under the Reza Shah. They much preferred to see the power of the Shah limited. Despite this, they stood staunchly behind him for the following reasons: First, the fragile democracy imposed by allies in Iran had allowed the newspapers and political parties which advocated social reform, equality of all people (including women), reduction of the power of the Shah, land reform, and noninterference of mollahs in the political process, hence endangering privileges of these groups. Second, the economic dislocation of the country had created a volatile situation that could only be handled by a repressive political system. Third, by supporting the Shah, they could create a more formidable alliance for the preservation of the existing political economy.

POLITICAL PARTIES

After the abdication of Reza Shah in September 1941, three groups of political parties emerged and vied for political power. The conservative parties supported the existing political economy and demanded the revival of Islamic values. Another group supported the national bourgeoisie of Iran and founded political organizations that eventually made a coalition known as the National Front. A group of liberal and radical intellectuals founded the Tudeh (Masses) Party. The latter eventually was transformed into a Marxist-Leninist party.

The conservative parties aimed to safeguard the existing political economy of the country, strengthen the embattled monarchy, and impose Islamic values in society. Seyyed Zia'a od-Din Tabatabaii, the coauthor of the 1921 coup, was the pillar of conservatism. His National Will party soon attracted the attention of the court, the landlords, some factions of the religious hierarchy, and the more conservative faction of the bazaar. In his newspaper *Ra'ad-e-Emrooz* (Today's Thunder), he denounced the control of economy by the state, supported private property, and asked for the revival of Islam. The party was staunchly against the Tudeh Party, the Social Democratic parties, and intellectuals. Mohammad Mossadegh (a respected Majlis deputy from Tehran) and the Tudeh Party in turn attacked Seyyed Zia'a and his party as the supporter of British imperialism (Key Ostovan 1948:214–19; Fatemi 1980:57). The Edalat Party was another conservative party founded by Ali Dashti (Reza Shah's chief of censorship) and Dadgar (the Majlis speaker under Reza Shah).

Some intellectuals who had social democratic tendencies presented an alternative to the conservative parties. Their main goal was the reduction of the shah's power, the restoration of the 1906 constitution, a land reform, the reorganization of political economy, and a nonaligned foreign policy. The most popular party of this group was Iran Party. This party was founded by some engineers, doctors, lawyers, and university professors such as Allah Yar Saleh, Ahmad Zirak Zadeh, and Jahangir

Hagh Shenas. The party called for a land reform and a rapid industrialization of the country by the state (Sharifi 1983).

In 1948, the social democratic parties founded the National Front. Although Mossadegh did not officially belong to any political parties, he was very close to the Iran Party (Sharifi 1983). The political parties that constituted this new organization were the Iran Party, the Toilers Party, and the Party of the Iranian People. Ayatollah Abol Qasem Kashani and Fedayan-e Islam later joined the National Front. The National Front had three principles: nationalization of the oil industry, political independence, and reducing the Shah to a figurehead.

The Iran Party and the Party of the Iranian People represented the secular middle class and the national bourgeoisie. The Toilers Party (founded by Mozaffar Baghaii) was the party of the small shopkeepers and the traditional working class. In late 1948, the Khalil Maleki group (a splinter group from the Tudeh Party) joined the Toilers Party and gave it a more socialist outlook. This alliance was ended in 1952 when the original body of the Toilers Party broke away from the National Front and supported the court. The Fedayan-e Islam group was an Islamic fundamentalist group that intended to create an Islamic government. Its main base of support was among the petty bourgeoisie of the bazaar. Relations between the secular parties of the National Front and the Fedayan-e Islam were not very cordial, and this group eventually pulled away from the National Front in 1952 and supported the court against Mossadegh (Rahaii 1982:116–21). The Tudeh Party was founded in 1941. Initially the party was not a Marxist organization. As one of the former leaders of the Tudeh Party, Anwar Khameii, reports, the party was a democratic front composed of social reformers who demanded the reorganization of the political economy within the context of the constitutional monarchy (Khameii 1983:20–25). Ten years later, the Tudeh Party announced that it was the Communist Party of Iran. The party soon attracted many intellectuals, workers and civil servants. The party from the beginning looked to the Soviet Union for guidance. In fact, the organization of the party, its structure, its strategy, and its tactics reflected Soviet foreign policy. Bijan Jazani, a prominent Iranian Marxist (who was killed by the Shah's security forces in 1975) comments that "the recommendations and advice of the Soviet Union played a crucial role in shaping the Tudeh Party" (Jazani 1978:20–21).

The Tudeh Party gradually came under the control of a Stalinist faction led by Abdol Samad Kambakhsh and Nourod-Din Kianouri. Kambakhsh was a member of a small Marxist group known as the Group of 53. This group was founded in early 1930s by Taghi Arani, a professor of chemistry at Tehran University. Kambakhsh had reportedly cooperated with the police for the arrest of the Group of 53. As Feridoun Keshavarz, a former member of the central committee of the Tudeh Party (who resigned in 1959 to protest against the domination of the party by the Kambakhsh-Kianouri faction and its subservience to the Soviet interests), comments, Kambakhsh was imposed on the party by Baghirov, the then secretary general of the Communist Party of the Soviet Azerbaijan (Keshavarz 1982:56). Kianouri was grandson of the infamous Sheikh Fazlollah Noori (who plotted with the Mohammad Ali Shah against the Constitutional Revolution) and the brother-in-law of Kambakhsh. The Kianouri-Kambakhsh faction suggested that the party members should do anything (including spying) to protect the interests of the Soviet Union in Iran (Elm Va Jameech, May 20, 1982, pp. 2–5; Keshavarz 1982:77–85. Subservience of the Tudeh Party to the Soviet Union resulted in a split within the party in 1947. The most prominent members of this group were Khalil Maleki and Anwar Khameii, both of whom were among the original members of the Group of 53 and the Tudeh Party. This group joined the Toilers Party in 1948. In June 1942, the party convened its first provisional conference in Tehran. Eighty-seven delegates from Tehran and thirty-three delegates from the provinces attend the meeting. The conference selected a fifteen-member central committee. The conference asked for the distribution of lands among the peasants, an eight-hour work-day for workers, cheap housing and free clinics for the poor, recognition of trade unions, and equality for women (Kambakhsh 1972:152–58). The party also recommended the adoption of the newspaper *Rahbar* (Leader) as the party's central organ and participation in the forthcoming election for the Majlis (Abrahamian 1982:285; Kambakhsh 1972:51–55).

TRADE UNIONS

After the fall of Reza Shah the workers struggled for unionization. More than eight hundred unions emerged throughout the country. The Tudeh Party's strategy was to monopolize the unions as its major base of support. From 1941, the party started uniting these unions under its leadership. Reza Radmanesh, a member of the central committee of the Tudeh Party, did astonishing work among the workers and was able to organize the majority of them in the Central Council of the Federated Union of Workers and Toilers (CCFTU). Although the CCFTU members were not obliged to join the party, they had to follow the policy of the party without reservation. This fact gave much power and influence to the party, but deprived the workers of developing into a class with specific demands and interests. As a result, when the Soviet Union demanded an oil concession in northern Iran, the CCFTU (following the Tudeh Party's policy) demonstrated en masse to support his demand (Al-e Ahmad 1981:344; Katouzian 1981:154).

THE FOURTEENTH MAJLIS

The election for the fourteenth Majlis was the first honest election since the Pahlavi dynasty came into power. The Majlis was dominated by the landlords and the comprador-bourgeoisie (Parsa Benab 1982:107). Despite this, the Tudeh Party and the Social Democratic Parties were able to send twenty deputies to the Majlis. The Tudeh Party had eight deputies in the Majlis who acted as a bloc. Social Democrats gathered around Mossadegh. The Tudeh Party and Social Democrats cooperated in the Majlis around issues such as reducing power of the Shah and genuine economic development that would benefit the majority of the people; they attacked the conservative deputies such as Seyyed Zia'a od-Din Tabatabaii as the supporters of British interests in Iran (Parsa Benab 1982:105–6).

Mossadegh, as the spokesman of the Social Democratic forces, proposed that the Iranian economy and politics should be based on the mobilization of internal resources and the elimination of dependence on foreign powers. He suggested that Iran should not make any economic or political concessions to foreign countries (Key Ostovan 1949:55–89). This program, known as the "neutral balance," gave Mossadegh and the Social Democratic forces credibility in their struggle against the Shah and his conservative allies.

THE ROLE OF FOREIGN POWERS IN IRAN

Britain, the United States, and the Soviet Union competed with each other for the domination of Iran. Britain's position was initially secure because of its long-term alliance with the power bloc, especially the landlords, the tribal khans, and the court. Its major concern was to keep its privileges (i.e., control of the oil industry) and prevent the growth of American and Soviet influence in Iran. The position of the United States and the Soviet Union was different. They both wanted an oil concession in Northern Iran and were interested in Iran's logistical location. The United States could rely on some factions of the power bloc such as the court, the army, and the comprador-bourgeoisie. The Soviets, on the other hand, had the total support of the Tudeh Party and the CCFTU.

The Shah and some politicians such as Ahmad Qavam-os Saltaneh and Ahmad Soheili (two prime ministers of this period) were the proponents of involving the United States in Iran. The Shah was very eager to establish close ties with the United States and to reorganize the army and the economy with American assistance. This was in line with U.S. policy, which was based on modernizing the Iranian economy in order to contain communism in this country (Ashraf 1971:124). Arthur Millspaugh, the American finance expert who had served in Iran in the 1930s, was recalled to reorganize the economy (Millspaugh 1946:45–59). The U.S. military presence was quite visible. The number of American troops in Iran had reached thirty thousand by 1944. As an Indian scholar notes, during the 1940s U.S. influence had increased in Iran to a great extent and many Americans had advisory positions in strategically important fields such as the economy, the army, the police, and the gendarmerie (Singh 1980:54). In the late 1940s the Point Four program was established by the United States to give financial assistance to Iran. General Hassan Arfaʿ, Iran's former chief of staff, explains why the Shah was so anxious to involve the United States in Iran as follows:

An agreement was to come (*sic*) between the Iranian and the USA governments for the engagement of a U.S. military mission headed by General Ridely for advice on the working of the administrative section of the army, and another with Colonel Schwartskopf for the reorganization of the Gendarmerie. Already since November 1942, Dr. Arthur Millspaugh had again been engaged by the Iranian government for the supervision of the financial administration of the country. Our policy was to bring as many Americans as possible to Iran, to be witness of the Soviet political encroachments and by their presence act as a deterrent for the more open violations of our independence and interference in our internal affairs. (Arfaʿ 1964:272)

The Social Democratic forces and the Tudeh Party favored sweeping reforms and national independence. While for the Social Democratic forces national independence meant eliminating the influence of all foreign powers in Iran, the Tudeh Party regarded the Soviet Union as an ally of the Iranian people in their struggle against imperialism. This caused friction between the two groups when the Soviet Union demanded an oil concession in northern Iran in 1944. The Tudeh Party immediately organized thirty-five thousand workers to support this demand.

Mossadegh's position based on his "negative equilibrium" was that granting concessions to any foreign power was contrary to the interests of the Iranian people and must be rejected (Fatemi 1980:66–68). In dealing with the problem of oil concessions to the Soviet Union, Mossadegh did two things. In a letter to the Soviet ambassador in Iran, Alexander Maximov, he praised the Soviet Union as a friendly neighbor who had helped Iran on many occasions. In the same letter, he indicated that despite his respect for the Soviet Union, he favored selling oil to that country but he was against granting concessions to all foreign countries (Key Ostovan 1948:244–47). Mossadegh also introduced a bill into the Majlis according to which granting any concession to foreign countries was a punishable crime (Marlowe 1963:76). This bill played a crucial role in rejecting the Soviet demand for an oil concession in the Fifteenth Majlis.

THE AUTONOMY MOVEMENTS IN AZERBAIJAN AND KURDISTAN

Iran is composed of different nationalities such as Kurds, Turks, Baluchis, Arabs, and Persians. Although Persians constitute only 40 percent of the total population of Iran, they dominate the country politically, economically, and culturally. As a result, the Persian language (Farsi) is the official language of the country and the other nationalities are deprived of practicing their languages and cultures. With the fall of Reza Shah, these nationalities expected to be free from the repression of Persian chauvinism and achieve autonomy in their region. Among these nationalities Azerbaijanis and Kurds were better organized and had developed genuine political organizations to struggle for autonomy in their regions. The Azerbaijani and Kurdish autonomy movements were also supported by the Soviet Union.

The leader of the autonomy movement of Azerbaijan was Seyyed Ja'far Peeshevary. Peeshevary was a veteran of the communist movement of Iran and a member of the short-lived (1920–1921) Soviet Republic of Gilan (Ramazani 1986:112). Following the disintegration of the Jangali movement in 1921 he went to the Soviet Union. Later, in 1929, he escaped from the Stalin's purges and went back to Iran. He was arrested and jailed by the Iranian government and released only after the occupation of Iran by the Allies. He did not join the Tudeh Party and published his own newspaper, *Azhir* (Alarm), in Tehran. In 1945 he and some of the survivors of the Khiabani Movement (1919–1921) founded the Democratic Party of Azerbaijan for the realization of autonomy in that region (Abrahamian 1982:217). The program of the Democratic Party of Azerbaijan included the promulgation of a land reform, reforming the tax system, and teaching the Turkish language in schools (Keddie 1981:119–120).

In Kurdistan, the autonomy movement was led by the Democratic Party of Kurdistan (KDP). The KDP was founded by Qazi Mohammad who also saw the solution of the socioeconomic problems in the realization of its autonomy from the central government. The party created women, youth, and peasant organizations for the mobilization of the people (Eagleton 1963:102). In December 1945 the party announced the establishment of the Autonomous Republic of Kurdistan with Qazi Mohammad as its president.

The Red Army shielded the autonomy movement in both Azerbaijan and Kurdistan against the central government (Eagleton 1963:59; Sanghavi 1966:116). This allowed the Democratic parties of both regions to disarm the military garrisons in their regions without suffering from any casualties. The direct intervention of the Soviet Union in the area made many people suspicious about its intentions in Iran. As a result, the autonomy movement was regarded as a pawn in the Soviet political chess game. This prevented the autonomy movement from gaining support from the majority of Iranians, giving the central government an opportunity to crush the autonomy movement when the Soviet Union withdrew its troops from Iran in late 1945.

With the end of the war in sight, the Hakimi government in May 1945 demanded the withdrawal of the Allied forces from Iran. British and Soviet troops were scheduled to evacuate the occupied zones by March 2, 1946. Britain started withdrawing its forces from Iran before the set deadline. The Soviet Union, however, withdrew only from Tehran, but remained in northern regions of the country. This Soviet move gave the United States the best opportunity to present itself as the savior and protector of the independence and territorial integrity of Iran (Rubin 1980:30–45). To start with, the United States encouraged the Hakimi government to submit its grievances against the Soviet Union to the United Nations. It also sent an ultimatum to Stalin that if the Soviet troops did not withdraw from the Iranian territory, he would be responsible for the consequences. This ultimatum played a crucial role in the Soviet's decision to withdraw from Iran. On January 30, 1946, the United Nations Security Council recommended that both countries resolve their differences through direct negotiations. The same day the Tudeh Party organized demonstrations in Tehran and other cities against the Hakimi government and requested Hakimi's resignation. Aware of the hostility of the Soviet Union to the Hakimi government, the Shah dismissed Hakimi and replaced him with Qavam-os Saltaneh. Qavam-os Saltaneh was a landlord from the northern province of Guilan who had good relations with both the Soviet Union and the Tudeh Party. Qavam was against the absolute monarchy and his aim was the restoration of the 1906 Constitution (Abrahamian 1982:22). His policy could be explained as initially making concessions to all parties involved and eventually turning against all of them. In dealing with the problem of oil concessions to the Soviet Union, the presence of the Red Army in the northern regions, and the autonomy movement, he pursued a complicated policy that could be summarized as follows: First, in order to prove his good intentions to the Soviet leaders, he gave three cabinet posts to Tudeh members. The Iran Party, an ally of the Tudeh Party, also received one post. Second, he suggested direct negotiations between the leaders of the autonomy movement and the central government and a peaceful settlement. Third, he offered an oil concession to the Soviet

Union in return for withdrawal of the Red Army from Northern Iran. Finally, he established the Democratic Party of Iran to counterbalance the influence of the Tudeh Party.

Before his trip to Moscow, Qavam took yet another step to assure the Soviets about their interest in Iran by removing pro-British chief of staff General Hassan Arfaʿ and replacing him with General Hadj Ali Razm Ara. Razm Ara was an independent and ambitious general who, like Qavam, had good relations with the Soviet Union and the Tudeh Party. In Moscow Qavam signed an agreement with the Soviet leader for the withdrawal of the Red Army from Iranian soil in return for an oil concession in the North and a peaceful settlement of the Azerbaijani and Kurdish problem (Marlowe 1963:80–81). Whether the Soviets were aware that by withdrawing from Iran they had given a free hand to the Iranian government to crush the autonomy movement is debatable. Despite this, it is clear that the Soviet Union was more concerned about obtaining an oil concession than about the future of the autonomy movement in Azerbaijan and Kurdistan. Having achieved the neutrality of the Soviet Union in the autonomy movement, the Qavam government decided to crush the movement decisively. In December 1946, under the pretext of guaranteeing the safe conduct of the upcoming election for the Fifteenth Majlis in Kurdistan and Azerbaijan, Qavam-os Saltaneh sent the Iranian army to those regions to crush the autonomy movement. The unprepared and untrained militia of both regions put up a stiff resistance against the army but were eventually defeated. The army was aided by the armed forces of the landlords in the region (Jazani 1978:74). Katouzian explains the behavior of the invading forces this way: "There was a wholesale killing, burning, looting and rape" (Katouzian 1981:155). The number of civilians killed by the armed forces was estimated to have exceeded 16,000 (Keshavarz 1982:63–64). After crushing the autonomy movement, it was time to turn against the Soviet Union. In October 1947, with United States' encouragement, Qavam had the new Majlis (which was dominated by his Democratic party) reject ratification of the oil agreement with the Soviet Union (Marlowe 1963:83).

Crushing the autonomy movement was a great victory for the Shah. As the commander-in-chief of the armed forces, the Shah had organized the attack. In the aftermath of this bloody "victory," the army was strengthened and the Shah's position within the power bloc improved. In the next few years, he gradually moved forward to establish a dictatorship by filling the Majlis with his men, putting pressure on the Tudeh Party and the Social Democratic parties, and harassing the independent journalists.

During the Second Period (1949–1950), the Shah succeeded in establishing a dictatorship and forcing the opposition out of the political scene. He had struggled for eight years to defeat the opposition unsuccessfully.

An incident in 1949 gave him an opportunity to move quickly against the democratic achievement of the post–Reza Shah period. In February 1949, when the Shah was visiting Tehran University, a Tudeh Party member, Nasser Fakhr Araii, tried to assassinate him. The Shah was slightly injured, and the assassin was killed by the security forces. As was revealed later, the Kambakhsh-Kianouri faction, without consulting the other members of the central committee of the Tudeh Party, had arranged for this act of terrorism (Keshavarz 1982:40–70). Using the assassination attempt as an excuse, the Shah immediately restricted the activities of the opposition and pushed for the creation of a dictatorship. In order to intimidate the opposition, he imposed martial law throughout the country, outlawed the Tudeh Party, closed down all of the newspapers that were critical of the court, and confined Mossadegh to his estate in Ahmad Abad (near Tehran). He also accused Ayatollah Kashani of involvement in the plot and exiled him to Lebanon (Madany 1982:175).

With martial law in effect, the Shah pushed for more political power. Under his order, a Constituent Assembly was convened. It provided for the establishment of an upper house (Senate), and also granted the Shah power to dismiss both houses at any time he deemed necessary. He scored more political gains following these events. The royal estates, which were made public property after the abdication of Reza Shah, were now returned to the Shah again. This new development gave the Shah an economic base for meddling in politics.

During this period, the nationalization of oil put forward by the National Front was a hot issue. As an Iranian scholar notes, "The principles of social justice and national sovereignty formed the basis of Mossadegh's drive towards the nationalization of the oil industry" (Diba 1986:91). There were numerous demontrations in favor of oil nationalization throughout the country. The Shah tried to discourage the opposition by appointing a military government. General Ali Razm Ara was appointed prime minister in May 1950. Razm Ara was an intelligent and capable general who did not have much respect for the Shah and had plans to seize the state power (Nejati 1986:158). The Shah was aware of the ambitions of Razm Ara, but decided to rely on him for the time being. Despite the animosity between the two men, they were both against the nationalization of the oil industry and the popularity of Mossadegh (Rahaii 1982:76–90). Like the Shah, Razm Ara believed that Iran was not capable of running its oil industry and should reach an agreement with the Anglo-Iranian Oil Company (AIOC) instead of nationalizing the oil industry (Madany 1982:182–85). Razm Ara, however, was assassinated by a member of Fedayan-e Islam before the realization of his dream of seizing the state power or the Shah's dream of crushing the nationalization movement.

Following Razm Ara's assassination, on March 8, 1951, Hossein Ala became prime minister. Despite the opposition of both the Shah and Ala, the Majlis approved the proposal of the National Front for the nationalization of the oil industry on March 20. Faced with popular demonstration in favor of the Nationalization Act, Ala resigned in mid-April. The same day, the Majlis voted in favor of selecting Mossadegh as prime minister (Abrahamian 1985:127).

The Third Period started with Mossadegh's premiership (1951) and ended with his overthrow in August 1953. This period witnessed a popular movement for national sovereignty, democratization of the political order, and a popular struggle for the reorganization of the political economy. The 1951–1953 period is a very important phase in Iranian history. First, the National Front as the representative of the national bourgeoisie struggled to put the power of the Shah and the influence of the foreign powers in check. Second, despite the fact that the National Front was in power, it did not have the state power in control. The Shah remained the commander-in-chief of the armed forces, the power bloc kept its deputies in Majlis, and the landowning class was not touched until late 1952. Third, the weakness of the national bourgeoisie prevented it from transforming the Iranian political economy. Fourth, the National Front was under fire not only from the power bloc and its Western allies, but also from the Tudeh Party, which accused Mossadegh of being an agent of U.S. imperialism. Consequently, before the start of the social revolution, the power bloc and its foreign allies organized their forces against the Mossadegh government and restored absolute monarchy.

With the nationalization of the oil industry, the name of the Anglo-Iranian Oil Company was changed to the National Iranian Oil Company (NIOC). The British government, however, did not recognize the nationalization act and was determined to use all of its power to reverse the situation. The battleship Mauritius was sent to Abadan (in the Persian Gulf) as the first step toward the military occupation of the oil fields. This gunboat diplomacy, however, failed because of U.S. opposition and fear of possible Soviet intervention (Tarzi 1982:246). Having failed to harass Iran militarily, British imposed economic sanctions against it. These economic sanctions hurt Iran very badly, since no foreign country was allowed to buy its oil. As a result, Iran was deprived of the revenues it needed for the reorganization of its political economy.

Britain's next step was to isolate Iran internationally by referring the case to the International Court of Justice (ICJ) at the Hague. In July 1952, the ICJ ruled in favor of the AIOC. Mossadegh rejected the court's decision by arguing that it had no jurisdiction in a dispute between a private company and a sovereign state. This development weakened Iran's position internationally and allowed the oil companies to justify boycotting Iranian oil. One year later, at Iran's request, the ICJ reviewed the case again. This time the ICJ confirmed Mossadegh's position that it had no jurisdiction, implying that Iran had used its legitimate right to nationalize the oil industry.

At the first stage of the nationalization movement, the United States took a conciliatory position between the British and the Iranian governments. Following this policy, President Truman sent Averell Harriman to Iran on January 25, 1951, to mediate between the two parties. In his discussion with Harriman, Mossadegh announced Iran's willingness to reach a settlement with Britain provided that the latter accepted the following:

1. If the British government, as the authorized representative of the company, acknowledges the legality of the nationalization of oil industry, the Iranian government is willing to enter into negotiations with Great Britain.
2. The British government must officially acknowledge nationalization before sending its representative.
3. "Nationalization" is defined as the measures passed by the Majlis on March 20, 1951, as the Nationalization Law. (Nirumand 1969:53)

These demands were delivered to the British government by Harriman. A delegation headed by Richard Stokes, a member of the British cabinet, was sent to Iran to negotiate about the future of the cooperation of Iranian and British personnel in the oil industry (Diba 1986:125–30). This initiative, however, failed because the British side insisted on keeping the management of the oil industry in its hands. Stokes argued that British nationals would not work under Iranian management (Nirumand 1969:53). Following this unyielding position of Britain, the British employees were asked to leave the country and an Iranian board of directors was selected to take over the management of the oil industry. Iran also cut off diplomatic relations with Britain.

In order to combat the problem created by the British economic sanction against Iran, Mossadegh tried to secure economic and political support from the Soviet Union and the United States. The Soviet Union was asked to pay its wartime debts to Iran, including eleven tons of gold and $8 million. The Soviets were also asked to buy Iranian oil and agricultural products in order to help the nationalization movement survive the economic blockade. The Soviet Union, however, failed to support the movement either morally or materially (Mazdak 1982:361). U.S. policy was different. The popular movement was initially supported as the only alternative to communism (Nirumand 1969:73). There was yet another reason behind U.S. support: it wanted to end the monopolization of the Iranian oil by Britain and include American oil companies as well.

By October 1952, Britain was able to convince the U.S. government that Anglo-American cooperation against Iran would be more beneficial to both countries (Eden 1960:227–30). Consequently, U.S. policy toward Iran became hostile and it cooperated with Britain in imposing a worldwide boycott of the Iranian oil (Bergsten 1978:323). The United States also rejected Iran's request for a loan. The convergence of the Anglo-American interests in Iran was a crucial factor in the CIA-sponsored coup of August 1953 against Mossadegh.

THE STRUGGLE FOR THE CREATION OF A DEMOCRATIC ORDER

One of the aims of the popular movement was to end the authoritarian rule of the Shah and confine him to the position of a figurehead. Mossadegh's approach to this problem was to use economic and political measures to achieve this goal. Economically, the crown lands that had been repossessed by the Shah were given back to the state, hence depriving him of having abundant economic resources to meddle in politics. Politically, Mossadegh did two things. First, the army, which was the main base of support of the Shah, was reduced, and many powerful generals were retired. Second, noticing the constant interference of the royal family in the politics, Mossadegh forced them to leave the country. This move deprived the Shah of another base of support, and by the summer of 1953, the Shah and Queen Sorraya were the only members of the royal family left in Iran.

THE STRUGGLE FOR REORGANIZATION OF THE POLITICAL ECONOMY

When Mossadegh became prime minister, Iran was suffering from economic stagnation, and the majority of people were poverty-stricken. About 70 percent of the population was living in villages and more than 80 percent of the people were suffering from malnutrition (Nirumand 1969:234). Except for a privileged few, the majority of people were suffering from the unequal distribution of wealth. The aim of Mossadegh was to reorganize the political economy for the benefit of the majority of people. Creating a self-sufficient economy and land reform and increasing domestic production and property tax were the major tenets of such policy. Nationalization of the oil industry was to be the first step toward sweeping social reforms.

When the vested interest of Britain and the United States resulted in the boycott of Iranian oil, Mossadegh formulated the "economy without oil." This policy required depending on increasing domestic production (except oil), substantially cutting down imports, and resorting to import substitution policies (Parsa Benab 1982:134–48; Mazdak 1982:320–50; Zabih 1982:288–340). The economy without oil was successful to a great extent and increased domestic production. According to an American scholar, "The output of sugar refineries, textile factories and minerals rose" (Keddie 1981:136). During this period, although the Abadan oil refinery was not operating, the government kept the workers on the payroll. The government also issued special bonds called National Debts to provide more funds for economic development. Those who bought these bonds were assured by Mossadegh that they would get their money plus some interest back after the economic recovery. These bonds were boycotted by the power bloc and the Tudeh Party and therefore did not bring the expected satisfactory results. The main obstacles to social reform were the unconstitutional power of the Shah and the danger of a military coup. In order to remove these barriers, Mossadegh asked the Shah to give up the title of commander-in-chief of the armed forces and let him take the position of minister of war. The Shah refused to accept both demands and Mossadegh resigned in protest on July 18, 1952. The Shah immediately appointed Qavam-os Saltaneh as prime minister. Taking Qavam's background into consideration, a majority of the people felt that the Shah was planning to divide the movement. In response to popular sentiments regarding this new development, the National Front called for a demonstration against the court. Realizing the seriousness of the situation, the Tudeh Party relaxed its vicious propaganda against Mossadegh and joined the demonstrations (Nejati 1986:221). The army was sent to disperse the demonstrators, but the junior officers and soldiers disregarded the order of their commanders to create a blood bath. Qavam's government, faced with this crisis, resigned two days later, and Mossadegh victoriously came back and resumed his duties as prime minister and the acting minister of war. Interestingly enough, the ICJ voted in favor of Iran the same day. This incident enhanced Mossadegh's popularity. A few years later, a furious Shah wrote about this event:

Again it was clear that no one could stand against Mossadegh. On 22 July 1952 the danger of a civil war forced me to agree with his conditions and re-appoint him. By an irony of history it was on the same day that the International Court handed down its decision that it had no jurisdiction in the dispute. (Pahlavi 1961:94)

The July 22 (30 of Teer, Iranian calendar) demonstration which brought Mossadegh to power again was a turning point for the movement. The power bloc was weakened and Mossadegh emerged stronger than ever before. The Tudeh Party also reduced its anti-Mossadegh propaganda and started giving its critical support to the popular movement. Having achieved this victory, Mossadegh was ready to start land reform and reorganizing the political economy. The National Front and the Tudeh Party gradually started cooperating with each other. This new development agitated the power bloc and some conservative elements within the National Front such as Mozaffar Baghaii (leader of the Toilers Party), Hossein Makki (a historian), and Ayatollah Kashani; and Fedayan-e Islam withdrew from the National Front and accused Mossadegh of dictatorship and violation of the constitution and principles of Islam (Rahaii 1982:118–40). Following this development the Khalil Malelki group split from the Toilers Party and founded the Toilers Party of Iran, popularly known as the Third Force. The Third Force was the most radical supporter of the National Front and had a major effect on the radicalization of the movement.

By early 1953 Iran was a crisis-ridden country. Principally, the government had not succeeded in fulfilling the promises of sweeping reforms. This was mainly due to the fact that the government had failed to settle the oil problem (Katouzian 1981:179–82). The power bloc, the splinter group of the National Front, and Britain and the United States organized all their resources to overthrow Mossadegh. When the crisis became prolonged and the government proved incapable of dealing effectively with the social problems, many supporters of the movement became disillusioned and took an ambivalent position toward it. This new development allowed the CIA and the power bloc to stage a coup against the popular movement without facing serious resistance from the people.

By mid-July there were rumors about the Shah's intention to stage a coup against the movement. Mossadegh warned the people against the plot and asked them to remain united against the counterrevolution. Despite this, the United States had decided to save the "free world" by overthrowing the democratically elected government of Mossadegh. General Norman Shwartskopf (former New Jersey Police Chief and now a CIA agent), Loy Henderson (the American ambassador to Iran), and Allen Dulles (the head of the CIA) played the crucial roles in planning the 1953 coup against Mossadegh (Saikal 1980:44).

The first stage of the coup, which was executed by Colonel Nematollah Nassiri on August 16, 1953, failed (Roosevelt 1979:174–80). Fearful of the consequences of the coup, the Shah and Queen Sorraya fled first to Iraq and then to Italy. Three days later, General Fazllolah Zahedy, former collaborator with Nazi Germany, carried out the second stage of the coup. The United States spent $18 million on organizing some pro-Shah demonstrations to cover up the coup (Keshavarz 1982:143). These paid demonstrators, led by Shaban the Brainless (Beemokh) and Tayyeb Hadj Rezaii (two gang leaders from Tehran), were common criminals, goons, prostitutes, and pickpockets. They surrounded Mossadegh's residence, chanting "Down with Mossadegh" and "Long Live the Shah." Simultaneously, General Zahedy was occupying the strategic positions in Tehran (Parsa Benab 1982:142–43; Katouzian 1981:155–56; Nirumand 1969:83–90). By late afternoon Mossadegh was overthrown and the Shah and the United States were ready to celebrate this "national uprising." The Fourth Period started with the overthrow of Mossadegh and ended in the early 1960s. The 1953 coup was a result of cooperation between the power bloc, on one hand, and the United States and Britain, on the other. The power bloc had lost dearly under Mossadegh. The nationalization of oil and the economic blockade had a negative effect on the prosperity of the privileged classes, whose well-being was contingent upon the flow of oil. With the overthrow of Mossadegh the Iranian state was transformed into a royal dictatorship, which lasted until 1960. The coup was a major setback for the national bourgeoisie and a great victory for the power bloc and its Western supporters. The land reform measures adopted by Mossadegh were stopped. The comprador-bourgeoisie was strengthened by the growth of the banks, the import sector, oil revenues, and foreign loans. The position of the comprador-bourgeoisie improved to such an extent that within a decade it was able to become the champion of capitalist development and destroy the precapitalist social formation of Iran.

General Zahedy, who had executed the 1953 coup, became prime minister. The tasks of the Zahedy government were the suppression of opposition and reaching an agreement with the oil companies (Jazani 1978:125). Mossadegh and his close associates were arrested and the activities of the National Front were banned. The Tudeh Party and the CCFTU were also dissolved. Mossadegh was sentenced to three years imprisonment and was later banished to his estate at Ahmad Abad (near Tehran), where he was kept under house arrest until his death in 1968. Hossein Fatemi, minister of foreign affairs, was executed, and several other associates of Mossadegh were imprisoned.

The treatment of the Tudeh Party was much harsher. The party, which despite its strength had failed to mount resistance against the coup, paid a heavy price. The military governor of Tehran, General Teimour Bakhtiar, started a manhunt for the arrest of Tudeh Party members. Several thousands of party members were arrested and tortured, and some were executed. The party leaders either fled to the Soviet Union or were coopted. Many of the rank and file, however, remained steadfast and withstood the barbarian tortures and inhumane treatment applied against them. In mid–1955, the military branch of the party, composed of six hundred officers, was discovered and smashed, hence putting an end to the Tudeh Party as a viable political organization. Members of the military branch and especially its leader, Khosrow Rouzbeh, showed astonishing steadfastness and courage. Many of them, as a result, were executed or received heavy sentences.

Within a few months after the coup, the opposition was effectively broken down and the Zahedy government was ready to negotiate with Western oil companies about resuming oil production. A consortium of Western oil companies was founded in April 1954 to negotiate with Iran regarding the production and sale of Iranian oil. This consortium was composed of American and British companies with 40 percent of shares each, and French and Dutch companies, which received the remaining 20 percent. By August 1954, the consortium reached an agreement with Iran according to which it was to produce Iranian oil for 40 years on a fifty-fifty profit-sharing basis.

This contract, which was signed by Iranian chief negotiator Ali Amini (minister of finance) and Howard Page (vice-president of Standard Oil of New Jersey) left most of the decision making in the hands of the consortium (Engler 1961:208). This agreement was so contradictory to the interests of Iran and the goals of the Nationalization Movement that Secretary of State John Foster Dulles refused to let the public know about it in detail by arguing, "There is a danger that the exposure of these issues could again be used by irresponsible elements contrary to the interests of the United States and its allies" (Engler 1961:209).

The overthrow of Mossadegh was a major victory for Britain and the United States and a setback for the Soviet Union. U.S. influence was enhanced in Iran to a great extent and eventually shadowed that of Britain. Immediately after the coup, the United States granted a $45 million emergency loan to Iran. Between 1954 and 1962, the United States gave $681 million in economic aid and another $500 million in military aid to Iran.

In 1955, with the encouragement of the United States, Iran joined Turkey, Pakistan, and Iraq in the Baghdad Pact. The United States was not a full member, but participated in some of its committees (Singh 1980:62–68). The purpose of the Baghdad Pact, like NATO and SEATO (Southeast Asia Treaty Organization), was the encirclement of the socialist countries and the defense of its members against any "communist takeover" (Stookey 1975:137–38). The Iraqi coup of July 1958, in which the pro-British regime of King Faisal-Noori Saiid was overthrown, resulted in withdrawal of Iraq from the pact. Consequently, the Baghdad Pact was renamed the Central Treaty Organization (CENTO). The Iraqi coup frightened the Shah to such an extent that he appealed to the United States for extensive military and economic aid. The United States agreed to grant these requests only after the Shah signed the Mutual Defense Pact in 1959.

The Soviet Union was the major loser of the 1953 coup. First, the nonaligned government of Mossadegh was replaced by the pro-Western and anti-Communist government of General Zahedy. Second, suppression of the Tudeh Party deprived the Soviet Union of its instrument for forging foreign policy in Iran. Facing these realities, the Soviet Union decided to establish cordial relations with the Shah's regime. In 1955, the Shah and Queen Sorraya were invited for a state visit to the Soviet Union, where they were received warmly. In the same year, the Soviet government paid its wartime debts to Iran. Relations between the two countries were cordial until 1959 when Iran signed the Mutual Defense Pact with the United States. Following this development, the two countries started propaganda warfare against each other, which lasted until 1963.

REPRESSION AND ECONOMIC GROWTH

After the coup, martial law was put into effect until 1957. All political parties and the trade unions were pronounced illegal and tight censorship was imposed on the press. The aim of the Zahedy government, the destruction of the opposition and the resumption of oil production, was achieved by late 1954. By 1955, the Shah was in total control of the government, the opposition was totally uprooted, the flow of oil had resumed, and relations with Britain, the United States, and the Soviet Union were cordial. At that point, the Shah saw no reason to keep General Zahedy in power. Zahedy was dismissed in 1955 and sent to a permanent vacation in Switzerland. By removing Zahedy, the Shah intended to let the military know that he was in charge and would not tolerate any power base in the army.

Suppression of the opposition allowed the Shah to consolidate his power without facing a serious challenge. The military governor of Tehran, General Teimour Bakhtiar, was in charge of unifying intelligence services, intercepting the opposition, and infiltrating the factories, universities, and cultural institutions. In 1957, a new security and intelligence unit was created by Bakhtiar to increase the effectiveness of the existing systems. This new unit was the dreaded Sazman-e Ettella 'at Va Amniat-e Keshvar-e Iran or the Organization of Information and Security of Iran, known by its Farsi acronym, SAVAK. The former CIA agent, Kermit Roosevelt, reports that SAVAK was created with direct assistance and guidance from the CIA and the Israeli intelligence service, Mossad (Roosevelt 1979:9). The SAVAK was in charge of spying, anti-Communist propaganda, infiltrating the opposition groups, arresting, torturing, and maiming those accused of opposing the Shah (Klare 1980:46–49).

The Shah was aware that repression alone could not keep him in power. In order to generate popular support and legitimacy for his regime, he decided to establish a bipartisan system. Two of his close friends, premier Manouchehr Eqbal and the big landlord Assadollah Alam were put in charge of this task. Eqbal and Alam created the Mellioun (Nationalists) Party and the Mardom (People) Party respectively (Wilber 1963:116–17). There was no difference, however, between the program of the majority party (Mellioun) and that of the minority party (Mardom). Consequently, neither of these parties was able to generate public support for the Shah, and he remained as isolated from the people as before.

The flow of oil and foreign loans allowed the Shah to start reorganization of the economy. Economic growth took place under the direct supervision of Americans. The Plan Organization that had been discontinued under Mossadegh was revitalized. It became a permanent body in 1954 and was renamed the Plan and Budget Organization (PBO). The first director of the PBO, Abolhassan Ebtehadj, was the former governor of the National Bank (Bank-e Melli) of Iran, and had proven to be a tough-minded manager and a shrewd economist (Zonis 1971:67–69). The PBO was run by American-educated economists and was assisted by the World Bank, the Harvard University school of management, and the Ford Foundation (Baldwin 1967:40). Under Ebtehadj, the PBO executed the Second Seven-Year Plan in 1955. The total budget was $1.6 billion. Of the proposed expenditure, 33 percent went to infrastructure, 26 percent to the agriculture, 26 percent to the service sector, and 15 percent to industry.

The Ebtehadj policy was to fight mismanagement, lavish spending, corruption, and inefficiency of the bureaucracy. He also wanted to make the PBO the main planner and organizer of development projects. This meant that the PBO would formulate economic planning and the ministries would execute them. This was something that neither the Shah nor the government ministers could accept. Ebtehadj struggled for five years to achieve these goals. When he realized that the Shah and his entourage would not allow the PBO to organize the economic planning, Ebtehadj resigned in 1959. Because of the inefficiency of the bureaucracy, rivalries between different ministries, and corruption, most of the projects were not completed by 1962.

Dr. Manouchehr Eqbal, a close friend of the Shah, became prime minister in 1957. During Eqbal's premiership (1957–1960), the comprador-bourgeoisie grew rapidly at the expense of the national bourgeoisie. A very significant factor that led to this development was his so-called open door policy, according to which foreign investment, the import of luxury items, and domestic consumption were encouraged. Another aspect of Eqbal's economic planning was building high dams without calculating their desirability and profitability. Several dams built during Eqbal's premiership which, although eye-catching to foreign visitors, did not help increase agricultural production (Keddie 1981:148). Eqbal's open door policy and wasteful spending on showy projects eventually depleted the treasury, and many development projects were put aside.

The Iranian economy was out of control by the late 1950s. The banks had used all their credit, the Iranian market was saturated with foreign goods, many merchants were bankrupt, and more than 20 percent of the labor force was unemployed. The economic crisis resulted in political crisis and social unrest. The number of strikes, which had gone down from seventy-nine in 1953 to four in 1957, went up again. The year 1960 witnessed more than one hundred strikes and demonstrations by students, workers, government employees, and the National Front. In order to overcome the economic and social crises, the Shah turned to the United States and the International Monetary Fund (IMF) for loans. The United States agreed to grant Iran an $845 million loan in return for social reform. The IMF also promised to give Iran the necessary loan if the government agreed to freeze wages and employment. The consequence was more demonstrations against the regime. The crisis of authority manifested in strikes and popular demonstrations against the regime. Failure of the Shah to defuse the crisis resulted in the decomposition of the power bloc. It was the end of the military dictatorship. A new era was starting.

5 Crisis of the State (1960–1963)

The 1960–1963 period witnessed a major crisis of the state which resulted in serious challenges against the dictatorship of the Shah. The opposition, however, was not united and lacked effective leadership. As a result, the Shah was able to stabilize his position by 1963 and emerge stronger than ever before. The main factors that allowed the Shah to overcome the crisis of the state were the promulgation of a series of social reforms and gaining trust and strong support from the United States. That is, a series of domestic and external factors helped the Shah to strengthen his position and save this throne. By the end of this period, the traditional opposition was totally disseminated and the Shah emerged as the omnipotent dictator of Iran.

THE STATE

The economic boom of the post-Mossadegh period was over by the late 1950s. Wasteful spending, corruption, mismanagement, and the vast import of unnecessary goods were the major factors contributing to this crisis. The open door policy of Eqbal had filled the Iranian market with foreign goods, while the buying power of the ordinary citizen had shrunk (Momeni 1978:132). The foreign trade sector expanded at the expense of the bazaaris and the national bourgeoisie. The economic crisis and the Shah's lack of popular support resulted in a paralyzing crisis of the state. These developments allowed the opposition to grow stronger and pose a major threat to the regime. The Shah, however, was able to diffuse the crisis through promulgating social reforms and gaining external support.

As Gramsci notes, crisis of the state is the crisis of authority that emerges when the power bloc fails to secure the spontaneous support of the "broad masses."

And the content is the crisis of the ruling classes' hegemony, which occurs either because the ruling class has failed in some major political undertaking for which it has requested, or forcibly extracted, the consent of the broad masses..., or because the huge masses... have passed from a state of political passivity to a certain activity, and put forward demands which taken together, albeit not organically formulated, add up to a revolution. (Gramsci 1971:210)

The crisis of state was the result of the economic decline of the late 1950s. The growth of the capitalist relations of production in the late 1950s had strengthened the position of the comprador-bourgeoisie. This class struggled to dominate the power bloc but was faced with the resistance of some factions of the landowning class, its military allies, and a fraction of the hierarchy of mollahs. The crisis of the power bloc weakened its position vis-à-vis the opposition, and it was able to challenge the state. The economic and political crises had crippled the regime to such an extent that by early 1960, it was on the verge of collapse. The Shah's solution at this point was to temporarily relax repression in order to appease the opposition and generate popular support for his regime. Following this policy, he announced that the election for the Twentieth Majlis would be free for all (Jazani 1978:130). Contrary to the Shah's anticipation, the liberalization policy did not result in popular support for him. On the contrary, the opposition became more vocal and demanded social reforms and a return to democracy.

The concept of the relative autonomy of the state helps us understand relations between the state and the dominant class(es). Contrary to what instrumentalists argue, in capitalist societies the state is not merely an instrument of the ruling class. It rather functions as the organizer and the protector of the interests of the dominant class(es) in the long run. It also harmonizes the relations between the dominant class and the ruled masses. In the case of Iran, the Shah was the arbitrator of differences between the various factions of the power bloc. The Shah, therefore, could keep the state power in his hand, so far as he was able to adjust the machinery of the state with the socioeconomic development of the society. The precapitalist social formation of Iran during the time under consideration was too old to meet the challenges created by the increasing penetration of foreign capital, commodity production, the development of a banking system, and rising inflation. As the arbitrator of the differences between the various factions of the power bloc, the Shah had to resolve the problems that plagued the state if he wanted to keep it from falling apart.

Land reform was the first step toward full-fledged capitalist development. The Shah's task in relation to this problem was very complicated. On one hand, he was faced with the opposition of the conservative landlords, a faction of the mollahs, and the conservative army generals. On the other hand, he had to deal with pressures from the bourgeoisie and the United States for land reform and rapid capitalist development. Regarding the seriousness of the situation and the need for the transformation of the economy, the Shah opted for land reform. The land reform bill of 1960 was rejected by some factions of religious hierarchy and the conservative landlords. Ayatollah Hossein Borujerdi, the powerful Marj'a-e Taghlid, declared that the law was contrary to the principles of Islam (i.e., sanctity of private property) and must be abandoned (Akhavi 1980:91; Lambton 1961:82). The land reform program, as a result, was shelved until Borujerdi's death the next year.

The Shah's next step was to resort to liberalization policies to legitimize his regime and create popular support. The opposition welcomed the liberalization policies and organized all of its resources to gain a parliamentary victory. Despite the Shah's promise, the election for the Twentieth Majlis was as fraudulent and dishonest as the previous ones. This resulted in widespread protests and demonstrations by the opposition. In order to blame the rigged election on Prime Minister Eqbal, the Shah publicly announced his dissatisfaction with the conduct of the election and "advised" the new Majlis deputies to resign (Wilber 1963:129). As another conciliatory gesture toward the opposition, the Shah decided to disassociate himself from unpopular Eqbal completely. In September 1960, Eqbal was dismissed and was replaced by Ja'afar Shahiff Emami, the minister of mines and industry. The new prime minister promised to renew the elections in January 1961. He also reported the dire economic condition of the country and the need for stabilizing policies to solve these problems.

THE LANDLORDS

During the process of capitalist development in last one hundred years, many landlords invested the surplus generated from agriculture in industry and commerce. The growth of foreign investment and banking systems in the 1950s also accelerated this trend. By the late 1950s, the majority of the landlords were willing to sell their lands and invest in the industrial sector. Big landlords such as Alam, Zulfaqary, Salem-od-Dowleh, and the Shah were among the pioneers of this new development (Momeni 1978:90–101). In his autobiography, *The Mission for My Country*, the Shah explained this trend as follows:

Only a few years ago . . . landlords became very bitter when anybody broached the idea that their vast holdings should be divided, but many have now come to realize that in terms of social justice their position is untenable. Moreover, with the expansion of alternative investment opportunities, land-owning as such no longer commands quite so much profit returns from investment in Persia's expanding industry and commerce. (Pahlavi 1961:204)

Although the majority of the landlords had realized the profitability of investment in the industrial sector, their approach to the question of land reform and its consequences was different. The Shah and his close associates such as Alam and Eqbal believed that a gradual and slow-paced land reform and the creation of modern agricultural corporations would be more suitable for Iran. Some other landlords, such as the former minister of finance, Ali Amini, favored a systematic land reform followed by sweeping social reforms as the only solution to the economic problems. Only a few landlords, such as General Teimour Bakhtiar (a big landlord and chief of SAVAK), were against land reform. Land reform in general did not have serious opponents during the time under consideration. Removal of Bakhtiar and some other conservative generals in 1960 and 1961 and also the death of Ayatollah Borujerdi in 1961 opened the way for systematic land reform and a smooth transition to capitalism.

THE OPPOSITION

The opposition consisted of the National Front, the bazaaris, and a group of middle-class bureaucrats and technocrats organized by Amini. The post-Mossadegh repression and the disintegration of the labor unions prevented the working class from emerging as a major political force. The Tudeh Party was weakened to a great extent and discredited for the cooptation of its leadership and its subservience to the Soviet Union. The opposition, therefore, was limited to the bourgeoisie and petty bourgeois forces. The Marxist elements that participated in anti-regime activities associated themselves with the National Front.

From late 1959, supporters of the National Front, and especially its student organizations, pressured the leadership for active participation in the political process. With the blessing of Mossadegh (who was under house arrest in Ahmad Abad, near Tehran), the Second National Front came into being in August 1961. The leadership of the National Front, however, failed to understand the crisis of the state and mobilize the masses against the regime. The Student Organizations of the National Front, on the other hand, were pushing the leadership for a comprehensive socioeconomic program to rally people behind the National Front.

The National Front was not united and in the absence of Mossadegh, a conservative faction had taken over its leadership. Mossadegh in 1961 complained to the Student Organizations that "these leaders are solely concerned about their own political gains rather than struggling for the interests of the people (Gorouh-e Ettehad-e Communistee 1978:12). The right wing of the National Front, led by Mohammad Ali Khonji (a former Tudeh Party member) and his disciple Shahpur Bakhtiar, was insisting on the creation of a centralized party to replace the National Front. The Bakhtiar-Khonji faction also created many obstacles to prevent the popular movement from radicalization. For example, they boycotted the acceptance of Khalil Maleki's socialist group (the Third Force) and imposed sanctions on the militant National Front activists, who were insisting on continuous strikes and demonstrations. The argument of the Khonji-Bakhtiar faction was that such tactics and coalitions would agitate the regime and might result in the revival of repression in Iran. As Katouzian notes, the Khonji-Bakhtiar faction with their erratic policies led the Front and the movement into a political catastrophe (Katouzian 1981:217).

The leftist elements and the Student Organizations of the National Front, contrary to the conservative faction, insisted on the necessity of taking a militant stance against the regime. Mossadegh supported their cause but was not in a position to influence the policies of the National Front (Gorouh-e Ettehade Communistee 1978:91). Faced with the conservatism of the leadership, the Student Organizations directly called for demonstrations against the regime. On several occasions, the leadership of the Front demanded the cancellation of the demonstrations called by the students. Some of the National Front members who had strong religious tendencies and were in favor of a more militant policy toward the regime founded the Nehzat-e Azadi-e Iran (Freedom Movement of Iran) in November 1961. The most prominent members of the Freedom Movement were Ayatollah Mahmud Taleghani, Mehdy Bazargan, and Yadollah Sahabi. The Freedom Movement was founded by pro-Mossadegh elements who believed that the combination of Iranian nationalism and Islam would create a just and democratic society (Abrahamian 1982:460). The Freedom Movement was not a splinter group and remained within the National Front. Because of the militancy of the Freedom Movement, the leftist elements and the Student Organizations supported this group against the leadership of the National Front (Jazani 1978:34).

Besides the National Front, there was another group founded by Ali Amini, former minister of finance and Iran's ambassador to the United States from 1956 to 1958. Amini's group was called the Independents. While in Washington he had made friends with many American Democrats, including Senator John F. Kennedy (*Keyhan*, March 27, 1962). Amini was recalled from Washington in 1958 when he was implicated in a pro-American coup. Many Iranians did not trust him because of his role in concluding the Consortium Agreement in 1954. Amini's opposition to both Eqbal and Shariff Emami and also his insistence on land reform, however, had made him popular among some intellectuals and technocrats. In May 1960, he and some other technocrats and liberals founded the Independents group. Amini had three associates who gave his group more weight and prestige. These men were Hassan Arsanjani (a former Tudeh Party member and a fervent supporter of sweeping land reform), Mohammad Darakhshesh (leader of Tehran's Teachers Club), and Nour od-Din Alamuti (former general secretary of the Tudeh Party and a lawyer).

THE UNITED STATES

By the late 1950s the United States was fed up with the corruption and inefficiency of the Iranian government. Consequently, U.S. policymakers decided not to give the Shah blank checks any more. Marlowe reports the dissatisfaction of the United States with the Shah this way:

The Shah was lectured in private by the U.S. Ambassador about administrative corruption and inefficiency, which dissipated the effect of American financial assistance.... This changing U.S. attitude was reflected in a progressive falling off in the rate of American financial assistance. Whereas for the years 1955–57 inclusive the total influx of loans and grants from abroad amounted to an average of about 100 million dollars per annum, for the years 1958–59 inclusive the average dropped to about a quarter of this. (1963:119)

The dissatisfaction of the United States with the Shah was so great that it tried to replace him with an effective and reform-oriented politician. In January 1958 General Valyollah Qarani (Iran's chief of staff) was arrested on charges of attempting to overthrow the regime. Qarani's light sentence (three years instead of execution) and the treatment of Amini, who was also implicated in the coup attempt (removal from his post in Washington instead of imprisonment or execution), made many see the hand of the United States in this coup (Katouzian 1981:199; Mojahedin-e Khalq 1979a:16). Regardless of the truth about this coup, one thing was clear: the United States was pushing for social reform in Iran. Relations between the Shah and the United States also changed following the American presidential election in November 1960. When President Kennedy moved into the White House in January 1961, he set up a task force to deal with the Iranian problem. The main result of this task force was "to press the Shah for socioeconomic reforms and relaxation of political repression" (Saikal 1980:75). Considering the gloomy economic condition of Iran and its dependence on the United States, the Shah had no choice but to liberalize his policies.

Having discussed some of the social actors in the Iranian politics, I now examine the concrete situation during the time under consideration. Shariff Emami replaced Eqbal in September 1960. The new government was faced with many problems, including low foreign exchange reserve, inflation, unemployment, and popular demonstrations against the regime. Emami's plan for economic recovery included restricting the import of nonessential goods, discouraging the purchase of foreign exchange, and freezing wages. He also promised to resume elections in January 1961.

Despite the promises of the Shah and Shariff Emami for a "free election," the election of January 1961 was as fraudulent as the previous ones. This resulted in further estrangement of the broad masses from the power bloc, which was manifested in nationwide demonstrations and strikes against the regime. Both the National Front and the Independents group demanded the dissolution of the new Majlis, resignation of Shariff Emami, and resumption of the elections. The Student Organizations of the National Front called for a sit-in at the University of Tehran. Bazaaris joined the students to show their solidarity with them and their support for the National Front. Following this sit-in all of the National Front leaders except Allah Yar Saleh, who had been elected for the Majlis and hence had immunity, were arrested. Following this incident, popular struggle against the regime was intensified. In early April, the School Teacher Club of Tehran (led by Darakhshesh) staged a series of protests and demonstrations against their low salaries. Police fired on the demonstrators, resulting in the death of a Tehran schoolteacher named Khan Ali. This incident brought more protests and demonstrations against the regime by the supporters of the National Front and the Independents group.

This new development put the Shah in a precarious situation. To overcome the crisis, he had two options: either to launch a military coup against the opposition and restore the dictatorship, or to make a major concession to the opposition (Marlowe 1963:115). Because of President Kennedy's insistence on liberalization policies, the Shah found it more prudent to make a deal with the opposition for overcoming the socio-economic dilemmas. The Shah at that point had to choose between the popular National Front—which was identified with Mossadegh (a man the Shah hated, feared, and envied) but had no clear program for social reform—and Amini's group, who did not have a popular base but had a clear reform program and full U.S. support. With some pressure from the Kennedy administration, the Shah opted for Amini (Saikal 1980:76).

Amini accepted the premiership on three conditions, which were granted: first, dissolution of the Majlis; second, strong public support from the Shah; third, the temporary absence of the Shah from the country while Amini started his reform policies. Amini's reasons for imposing these demands were that he wanted to show his independence from the Shah and stop his meddling in politics. Also, by closing both the Majlis and the Senate, he wanted to make sure that neither landlords nor National Front deputies would obstruct the reforms. The National Front leaders, however, did not read Amini's intentions correctly. They thought that a general election would soon follow. Within a month it became clear that Amini had no intention of renewing elections. Consequently, the National Front called Amini's government illegitimate and demanded his resignation.

Amini's program was to promulgate land reform, fight corruption, stabilize the economy, limit the power of the Shah, and reduce the size and influence of the military (Laing 1977:162–66). By doing so he wanted to replace the old power bloc with a bourgeois power bloc headed by a constitutional monarch. He also tried to create popular support for this government in order to execute his reforms smoothly. In order to achieve these goals, Amini appointed his respected lieutenants in positions directly related to his reforms. These men, Hassan Arsanjani, Mohammad Darakhshish, and Nour od-Din Alamuti, became ministers of agriculture, education, and justice respectively. Arsanjani's mission was to draft the land reform program (Najmabadi 1987:79). Darakhshish's first move was to accept all of the demands of the striking teachers and ask them in return to support the government. Alamuti was put in charge of fighting corrupt military and civilian officials.

Amini's reforms started with the arrest of corrupt officials and military supporters of the landlords. Among those arrested were General Hossein Azmoudeh (a man who as former chief of military tribunals had put Mossadegh on trial), General Moghaddam (former minister of the interior), General Zargham, General Ajoudani, and General Vosough. General Bakhtiar, who was planning to overthrow Amini, was also asked to leave the country for a "vacation." The main reason behind the removal of these powerful generals was to separate the conservative landlords from their military allies (Jazani 1978:139–41). Some civilian officials such as Ahmad Aramesh (former director of the PBO) and Maham (former mayor of Tehran) were also arrested on charges of corruption. Having ousted powerful generals and some of the corrupt top civilian officials, Amini started stabilization of the economy and promulgation of land reform. His stabilization policy included restriction of nonessential imports such as foreign cars, luxury items, and televisions, cutting government spending, and restricting credit and travel abroad. Initiating land reform, however, was Amini's most spectacular achievement. Amini's land reform program was to be executed in several stages, starting with limiting landownership to one entire village (Deh-e-shesh dang). The landlords who were aware of the benefits of selling their lands to the peasants welcomed this new development. Conservative landlords, however, were agitated and started a campaign against the land reform program (Laing 1977:163–65).

THE FALL OF AMINI

Amini came to power in the midst of economic and political disarray. His plan was to stabilize the economy, initiate land reform, reduce power of the Shah, and in general create favorable conditions for rapid capitalist development. Despite his good intentions, Amini did not have popular support. A majority of the people did not trust him because of his role in concluding the infamous Consortium Agreement. He lost the support of the National Front because of his failure to schedule the election. Amini also struggled with some fractions of the power bloc, such as the court, the army, and the conservative landlords. The above-mentioned group hated Amini because he had planned to strip them of their socioeconomic power. Lastly, there was the Soviet Union and the Tudeh Party. This latter group accused him of being anti-Soviet and an agent of the United States. The Tudeh Party, which had failed to organize its force against the 1953 coup, was now proposing the creation of a united front against Amini (Momeni 1978:151).

Amini's mistake was that he did not try to create a united front with bourgois opposition (i.e., the National Front) against the court and the landlords. As a result, he had to fight different fronts at the same time. His uncompromising attitude toward his critics and opponents created hostility among every segment of the society. The animosity of different social groups against Amini was so great that only one month after his premiership, *Newsweek* commented, "No one loves Amini" (June 12, 1961). Observing Amini's erratic policy of inciting hostility instead of forging an alliance with other factions of the bourgeoisie, the London *Economist* concluded, "Caught between... crossfire from conservatives on the one hand and the National Front on the other, Dr. Amini has perhaps been over-bold in provoking hostility from other quarters as well" (*Economist*, June 3, 1961).

Amini's government fell after fifteen months of fierce struggle with economic problems, popular distrust, and the Shah's rivalry. April 1962 was a crucial month for Amini. During that month Amini was trying to reduce the budget of all ministries in order to balance the budget. At the same time the Shah was visiting the United States in an attempt to convince the Kennedy administration that he would be able to execute social reforms without the disturbances Amini was facing (Mojahedin-e Khalq 1979b:20–21). The Shah must have struck a deal with the Kennedy administration that he would push rigorously for social reforms should the United States shift its support from Amini to him (Katouzian 1981:223; Momeni 1978:148).

Having secured full U.S. support, the Shah decided to force Amini out and personally take charge of social reforms. Following this policy, the Shah rejected Amini's proposal to cut the budget of the ministry of war. Failing to achieve the Shah's approval for this measure, Amini tried to get a loan from the United States to solve the economic problems. When his proposal was rejected, Amini realized that he had lost U.S. support. On July 17, 1962, he resigned, giving as his reason inadequacy of American financial aid (Marlowe 1963:121; Saikal 1980:77). The next day, Assadollah Alam, leader of the Mardom party, a big landlord and a faithful friend of the Shah, became prime minister.

Contrary to Amini, Alam had no interest in liberalization policy or ambition to challenge the Shah's authority. His main aim was, rather, serving his master and helping him reorganize his embattled monarchy. Between July 1962 and February 1963 (when the Shah announced his White Revolution), Alam tried to co-opt the National Front, reorganize SAVAK and the military, and reassure the landlords that land reform would not jeopardize their interests (Cottam 1979:305–7). Although Alam failed to co-opt the National Front, he succeeded in his other goals. By January 1963, the ground was laid for the Shah to emerge as the sole leader of Iran.

THE WHITE REVOLUTION

During the 1961–1963 period, the Shah was forced (by different socioeconomic factors) to resort to liberalization policies to run the state. During that period, he had to deal with economic problems, face U.S. reluctance to grant him financial assistance, and face challenges from the opposition. Between 1960 and 1963, the Shah chose to keep a low profile and play off his opponents against one another. Through Amini, he rid himself of powerful generals such as Bakhtiar and Azmoudeh and weakened the National Front. The National Front was also used to weaken and discredit Amini. While the opposition forces were exhausting all of their energies to fight one another, the Shah was preparing himself to do away with all of them. By early 1963, he was ready to strike back at all of his opponents and competitors and reorganize the machinery of the state for the restoration of dictatorship.

Having ousted Amini, demoralized the National Front, strengthened his position, and secured American support, the Shah was now ready to become the champion of social reform. In mid-January 1973, leaders of the National Front and all of the politically active students were arrested en masse on no charges. A week later (January 23), the Shah announced that he had started a "White Revolution." This White Revolution (later known as the Revolution of the Shah and the People) was a six-point reform program including: (1) land reform, (2) sale of state-owned factories to finance land reform, (3) voting rights for women, (4) profit-sharing for industrial workers, (5) the creation of a literary corps, and (6) nationalization of forests. In order to show his popularity to the whole world and especially to the United States, the Shah submitted his six-point reform program to a plebiscite. The referendum was boycotted by the opposition and by mollahs. Despite this, the government announced that 99 percent of the voters had approved the program (Abrahamian 1982:424). Over time, the Shah added more points to his reform program (by 1978 they had amassed to nineteen) to show that he had started a permanent royal revolution!

The aims of the White Revolution were to destroy the precapitalist social formation of Iran and start full-fledged capitalist development in both the country and the city (Halliday 1979:104–23; McLachlan 1977:135–40). With the implementation of land reform, the power of the landlords was eradicated in the country. The state-owned factories were also sold to such landlords, hence incorporating them into the growing bourgeoisie of the city. During the process of the land reform, capitalist relations of production dominated the country, capital penetrated into the rural areas (through the state-owned banks and rural cooperatives), and the land itself became a commodity (Halliday 1979:134–35). A major consequence of the White Revolution was the transformation of the rich peasants into a rural bourgeoisie and formal landlords into the entrepreneurial class of the city (Fischer 1977:184–85).

6 Socioeconomic Development of Iran (1963–1977)

This chapter analyzes the socioeconomic development of Iran from 1963 to 1977, a period characterized by rapid industrial development, failure of agriculture, rural migration, the ever-increasing power of the Shah, and popular discontent. The significance of this period is that the precapitalist social formation of Iran was transformed into a capitalist social formation and capitalist relations of production predominated in both rural and urban areas. The chapter consists of three parts: agricultural development, industrial development, and political underdevelopment.

AGRICULTURAL DEVELOPMENT

The agricultural development of Iran must be studied in light of a careful analysis of the land reform. The land reform program (1962–1971) broke the precapitalist social formation of the countryside. It was a revolution from above, which aimed to create a new propertied class as the support base of the regime (Fischer 1977:184–85). The program did not have an egalitarian purpose and as a result widened the gap between the poor and the rich peasants. The rich peasants became richer and were transformed into the rural bourgeoisie. The poor peasants became poorer and either became wage-laborers in villages or left the country to find a job in the city. Besides that, only those peasants who had cultivation rights (Nasagh-holders) were affected by the land reform. The landless agricultural workers (khoshneshins) were deprived of landownership (Abrahamian and Kazemi 1978:169–270).

Land reform was executed in four phases. During the first stage (1962–1964), landownership was limited to one entire village (Deh-e-shesh

Dng) or to the equivalent of one village in different estates owned by the landowners. Mechanized lands, groves, plantations, orchards, and homesteads were exempted from divisions regardless of their size. The peasants who received lands were required to become members of the state-run rural cooperatives. The law required the landowners to sell their lands to the peasants based on the previous year's tax paid to the government (Amouzgar and Fekrat 1971:116). The government would compensate the landowners over a fifteen-year period. The peasants were to pay the government within fifteen years with 10 percent interest. By the end of this stage, the power of the landlords in the villages was effectively broken and replaced with the ever-increasing power of the state (Katouzian 1974:236; Mahdavy 1965:142).

The land reform, however, had loopholes which allowed many landlords to evade the division of their lands. Many landlords divided their estates among family members or registered them as mechanized lands (Fischer 1977:184). A report from the Department of Economics and Social Affairs of the United Nations also indicates that the land reform mainly benefitted the landlords as well as those peasants who had connections with them. This resulted in the creation of a new landowning class.

These land reform measures, have, however, by no means solved the problems of Iranian agriculture.... There was nothing to prevent landlords from reordering the cultivation pattern in their villages before the land reform reached them in such a way as to ensure that the best land—or indeed any land at all— went to their friends, relatives and their loyal dependents.... Again, in those districts where there was a tenancy hierarchy, the land has sometimes gone to the entrepreneurial gavbands who did not cultivate directly, rather than to the crop-sharing labourers who have derived no benefits from the reform. Thus a new class of landlords may have been created. (United Nations [UN] 1966:24)

The number of Iranian villages is estimated to be about 50,000. Although 13,904 villages were affected by the first phase, only 5,000 entire villages were sold to the peasants (Mahdavy 1965:136). About 20 percent of the rural population (i.e., 690,000 families) were affected during this period (Nima 1983:39). The khoshneshins, constituting about 600,000 families, were excluded from the land distribution. The Second Phase (1964–1968) affected most of the lands that were not touched in the previous stage. This phase was more conservative and according to an Iranian scholar was mainly a tenancy reform to prevent the peasantry from emerging as a strong political entity (Katouzian 1974:228). During the second phase, the lands were mainly rented to the peasants, and the crop-sharing system was reinstituted. The second phase affected about 40,000 villages and a total of 1,556,480 families. Altogether, 57,226 peasant families were able to purchase land, 156,279 families acquired land through division, and 110,126 peasant families received land through shares in agricultural cooperatives. The remaining 1,232,849 were given leases on the land (Katouzian 1974:230; Mahdavy 1965:137–39). Although about two-thirds of the villages were affected during the second stage, only a small portion of peasants (57,226 as compared with 700,000 peasant households in the first phase) were actually able to purchase land. The second phase of the land reform shows how the "radicalism" of the first phase was replaced by conservatism and the reinstitution of the sharecropping system.

During the third and fourth phases (1968–1971) the land was not distributed among the peasants. The aim of these two stages was the creation of large-scale farming and agribusiness (Pahlavi 1966:48). To achieve this goal, the boundaries of the Iranian villages were broken down and the small and scattered lands were consolidated into large holdings. At the beginning joint ventures by the peasants and the landlords were established. Later, however, the high cost of operating these ventures forced the small holders to sell their lands and become agricultural workers on their own lands. In many cases the peasants were forcibly evicted from their lands in order to allow the agribusinesses to operate (Katouzian 1981:302–10).

The agribusiness and agricultural corporations were created in order to transform traditional Iranian agriculture into a modern, capitalist sector. Both Iranian and foreign capital soon penetrated the countryside to establish large-scale mechanized farming and agribusinesses. Multinational corporations such as Hashem Naraghi AgroIndustries of Iran and America; First National City Bank, New York; Trans-World Agricultural Development Corporation; John Deere Corporation; Shell International Ltd.; Chase Manhattan Bank; and Mitsui (of Japan) poured capital and technology into some targeted areas. The poor performance of these ventures, however, led many of these corporations to sell their businesses to the government (Katouzian 1974:234–36). Poor planning and forced eviction of the peasants from their lands (to allow the operation of agribusinesses) resulted in the decline of agriculture and the mass exodus of the peasants to the cities.

FAILURE OF LAND REFORM

Agrarian reforms in general are launched to liberate peasants, break up the power of landlords, increase agricultural productivity, and invest the extracted surplus of the country in the industrial sector. Land reforms, therefore, have both political and economic objectives. The Iranian land reform, however, became mainly political and served the Shah's increasing political power (Halliday 1979:140–75). The main goals of the Shah in pushing for land reform were the rapid industrialization of Iran and the mechanization of agriculture. The mechanization of agriculture without proper planning and the miscalculation of the potential of the country for this development eventually resulted in the decline of agriculture (Katouzian 1974:300–310). To the Shah, traditional agriculture and a large number of peasants dwelling in the countryside was equivalent to backwardness. His main aim in promulgating land reform was the reorganization of the political economy of the rural areas. This development was to occur in two steps: first, through the creation of a propertied class in the country, and second, through the development of large-scale farming, agribusinesses, and agricultural corporations. While the first stage of land reform provided lands for some peasants, during the second and throughout the third stage the small holders lost their lands and became landless again. These newly dispossessed peasants and khoshneshins eventually migrated to the cities to search for jobs. This resulted in the depopulation of the villages and contributed to the decline of agriculture.

Originally, the peasants were to be the main beneficiaries of the land reform. In reality, however, only a small segment of peasants benefitted from the land distribution, and the majority of them remained poor and destitute. Government documents show that about two-thirds of the peasants either did not acquire land or received less than five hectares (Plan and Budget Organization [PBO], 1975). The majority of the peasants during the second, third, and fourth phases of land reform lost their lands either because they could not get enough credit or because they simply could not keep up with the rising costs of agricultural production. Only a small group of the newly landless peasants were able to find jobs in agricultural corporations or agribusinesses. A majority of these peasants migrated to the cities in search of employment (Kazemy 1980:33–36).

Contrary to the peasants, a majority of the landlords benefitted from the land reform (although they ceased to exist as a landowning class). First, loopholes in the land reform bill allowed many landlords to transfer the ownership of their lands to their families, relatives, and friends. Second, mechanized lands, groves, and plantations were exempted from the distribution. Those lands which either fell in such categories or were registered as such (by bribing corrupt officials) remained in the hands of their owners. Third, during the second and the third phases of land reform many landlords were able to reclaim their former lands and turn them into agricultural corporations and agribusinesses. Fourth, the landlords who sold their lands were allowed to buy shares in the state-owned factories and become entrepreneurs. In fact, long before the land reform was launched, many landlords had started selling their lands and investing their money in industry and commerce.

After the land reform the last barriers to state control of the countryside was removed, and the rural areas were totally dominated by the state. Looking at the increasing role of the state in the rural areas, an Iranian scholar notes that "the shift from big landlordism to small landlordism ... has extended the power and influence of government and petty officials in the rural areas" (Mahdavy 1965:141–42).

The means through which the state executed its policy of controlling peasant life were rural cooperatives and the agricultural bank. The rural cooperatives were in charge of providing seeds, fertilizers, agricultural machinery, and short-term loans to the peasants. The agricultural bank, on the other hand, was responsible for providing long-term loans to the peasants. Membership in the rural cooperatives was required for receiving land and loans. As a result, only those peasants who were members of rural cooperatives received lands. Besides that, only those peasants who were affected by land reform received assistance from state institutions.

Interestingly enough, the directors of rural cooperatives were chosen by the government. Rich peasants were selected for these jobs. The reason that poor peasants were deprived of decision making in rural cooperatives was that the government wanted to create a rural bourgeoisie in place of the landlords in the countryside. Rich peasants were the natural choice of the government for running the cooperatives. Moreover, the richer peasants had a way with corrupt government officials both for the selection of the board of directors of rural cooperatives and for obtaining sufficient loans from the agricultural bank.

During the First Stage of the land reform two different views regarding the role of peasants in the land reform process prevailed. The minister of agriculture, Hassan Arsanjani, argued that an independent peasantry should be created as the regime's base of support (Cottam 1979:316–17). The Shah, on the other hand, did not want to see the power of his former allies (landlords) replaced by a large and volatile peasantry (Katouzian 1974:225–31). In order to impress his master, Arsanjani organized the first congress of Iranian peasants in January 1963. This congress, in which 4,700 representatives of the peasants participated, reflected the strength of a unified and strong peasantry as well as the popularity of Arsanjani. This congress made the Shah more determined to create a propertied class in the country as his base of support. Within a few weeks, Arsanjani was dismissed and his plan for the creation of a strong and independent peasantry was shelved. This development was followed by the second and third phases of land reform, which made many small holders landless again and turned them into agricultural workers.

To conclude, the major impact of land reform was the total domination of the rural areas by the state and the breaking down of the precapitalist social formation of the villages. The land reform, however, did not improve the conditions of the lives of millions of peasants (Fischer 1977:84–85). Moreover, agricultural production did not increase as a result of this reform. In fact, agricultural growth since the mid–1960s was less than 3 percent, while population growth was over 3 percent. A student of the Iranian economy, Professor James Baldwin indicates that "the overall goal of the Third Plan was to maintain the 6% annual increase in national output achieved during the late fifties" (Baldwin 1967:76). This shows that the achieved goal of the post–land reform era was 50 percent less than intended. An Iranian scholar further argues that the comparison of the population growth (3 percent) and agricultural output (less than 3 percent) shows that agricultural productivity was zero or even negative (Katouzian 1981:305).

THE INDUSTRIAL DEVELOPMENT

Land reform provided the conditions for rapid capitalist development in Iran. Breaking up the old tenure system, the penetration of capital in the countryside, the circulation of money in rural areas, the creation of a rural bourgeoisie, and the establishment of agricultural banks and mechanized agriculture and agribusinesses in the rural areas were determinant factors that broke the structure of the economy and changed the social relations of production in the village. These developments resulted in a new division of labor that was more compatible with capitalist relations of production. Capitalist development everywhere has been financed through the extraction of surplus from the rural areas. The oil revenues, however, relieved the Iranian state (as well as the other oil-producing countries) from resorting to such measures.

The industrial development was, therefore, conditioned by the export of oil. The oil factor, as a result, was both a liability and an asset: an asset because the country was not squeezed hard, and a liability because industrial development was conditioned by the fluctuation of oil prices in the international market and the demand for Iranian oil. This phenomenon allowed rapid industrial development following the quadrupling of oil revenues from 1973 to 1975 and resulted in recession after 1976, when the demand for Iranian oil had declined. The Iranian state's industrial policy was concentrated on three sectors: oil and petrochemicals, heavy industry, and consumer durables.

In the last forty years, Iranian industry has been totally dependent on oil revenues, the only exception since 1941 being the Mossadegh years (1951–1953) when the "economy without oil" was put into practice. During that period, agriculture and other domestic products replaced oil revenues. After the overthrow of Mossadegh, the trend that he had started was reversed. Since 1953, the Iranian economy has been increasingly dependent on oil revenues. This was even more true following the White Revolution, when the need for more capital (for rapid industrialization) resulted in increasing the production of oil. Oil revenues rose from $817 million in 1968 to $2.5 billion in 1972 and $5.6 billion in 1973. These revenues jumped to $20 billion in 1974 following the OPEC (Organization of Petroleum Exporting Countries) conference held in Tehran in December 1974. The significance of the oil revenues in the industrial development of Iran was so great that an Iranian economist once called these revenues "the lifeblood of the whole development efforts" (Fekrat 1976:77).

In order to diversify the oil industry, increase exports and provide more foreign exchange, and reduce the reliance on the export of crude oil alone, plans for creating a petrochemical industry were set into motion. The National Iranian Oil Company signed three joint ventures with American firms between 1963 and 1968. A fourth contract was signed with Japanese companies in 1971. The petrochemicals industry manufactured such products as ammonia, urea, sulphur, polyvinyl chloride (PVC), detergents, and caustic soda for both domestic consumption and export (Amouzgar and Fekrat 1971:48). Given the high cost of erecting such complexes in Iran and international competition, the petrochemical industry did not reduce Iran's dependence on oil revenues (Halliday 1979:145-46).

The establishment of heavy industry was left to cooperation with the Soviet Union and other East European countries. In 1963, Iran and the Soviet Union signed an agreement, and the Soviet Union began building a steel mill in Isfahan and machine tool factories in Arak and Tabriz in return for Iranian natural gas. This agreement was beneficial for both parties. The Soviet Union could exploit this new development as helping a Third World country to build its infrastructure while benefiting from cheap Iranian natural gas. The Shah, on the other hand, could boast about his independence from the East and the West. Following this new development, both the Soviet Union and the Tudeh Party lavishly praised the Shah for his "independent and progressive" policies. Iran also signed an agreement with Czechoslovakia for building a machine tool factory in Tabriz. Romania had already signed a contract with Iran to install a tractor assembly plant in Tabriz in 1967 (McLachlan 1977:145). All of these plants were operating by 1972.

An import substitution sector was also established to provide the Iranian market with consumer goods such as cars and home appliances. These goods were manufactured abroad and assembled in Iran. Contrary to the oil and heavy industries, this sector was left to the "private sector," which was directly subsidized by the government. That is to say, the oil money was injected into the private sector to enable it to compete with foreign goods. The modern bourgeoisie of Iran, therefore, was the creation of the state and made its fortune through connections with the

Court and top government officials (Rah-e-Kargar 1983). In other words, the Iranian entrepreneurs had access to oil revenues and transferred these monies to make millions by investing in consumer goods. Entrepreneurs such as the Khayami brothers, Vahab Zadeh, and Elghanian all had meager backgrounds and made it to the top through their connections with the royal family and through taking advantage of the low interest rate.

GOVERNMENT POLICIES AND RAPID INDUSTRIAL DEVELOPMENT

The government in general favored large, capital-intensive industry. Private investors were given tax exemptions and were allowed to repatriate their profits whenever they wished. The return of profit was estimated to be as high as 30 to 40 percent. Large Iranian and foreign entrepreneurs were eligible for a subsidized rate that was below 12 percent. The small businesses (and bazaaris), on the other hand, had to borrow at much higher rates, between 25 and 100 percent (Keddie 1981:171). This policy allowed the large and capital-intensive factories to grow at the expense of small and labor-intensive factories.

The Fourth and Fifth Development Plan (1968–1972 and 1973–1978 respectively) were designed to materialize the rapid industrial development of Iran. Between 1964 and 1975 industrial development grew 15 percent annually. By 1977 there were 250,000 industrial units, of which 6,000 were categorized as large industrial establishments. Among these large industrial establishments 34 employed 7,000 or more workers and at least 95 factories employed more than 500 workers (Fekrat 1976:77). Fred Halliday notes that the automobile industry grew very rapidly between 1964 and 1975. "Automobile output rose from 2,300 in 1964 to 73,000 cars, 1,911 buses and 29,365 trucks and vans in 1974–75" (Halliday 1979:148). The labor force including the construction sector also rose to 2.5 million by 1975.

Despite all of the efforts made towards the industrialization of Iran, by 1977 the total value of nonoil exports constituted only 2 percent of the export (Katouzian 1981:279). Ironically, industrialization had increased Iran's dependence on imports (Tarzi 1982:264). The imports mainly consisted of foodstuffs, industrial products, and luxury consumer goods. This imbalance between the volume of exports and imports shows that despite rapid industrial growth, the aims of industrialization, which were self-sufficiency and the growth of the export sector, had failed. Several factors led to this failure, particularly the absence of a strong bourgeoisie, the overgrowth of the service sector, mismanagement, an insufficient infrastructure, neglect of the agricultural sector, and low productivity.

The Absence of a Strong Bourgeoisie

The absence of a strong bourgeoisie and the state control of the economy allowed the state to invest directly in industry. With the increasing oil revenues, the state was more capable of investing in industrial projects. During the oil crisis (1951–1953), bazaaris and the national bourgeoisie supported Mossadegh. They benefited from the economic embargo because the relative weakness of the state allowed them to invest in small manufactures, grow stronger, and have more impact on the political process. With the fall of Mossadegh, the state once again became both commercially and politically powerful. Relations between the bazaaris and the state, however, were ambivalent. Despite its dislike of the bazaaris, the state did not intervene in the social and economic affairs of the bazaar. It was only in the mid–1970s that the state tried to control the bazaar, a policy that forced the bazaaris to start a life-and-death struggle against the regime.

The White Revolution created favorable conditions for capitalist development, but the national bourgeoisie was weakened to such an extent that it could not play a crucial role in industrial planning. The state therefore enhanced its efforts toward industrial planning and also created a bourgeoisie that was dependent on it for subsidization and protection. Moreover, the constant increase in the oil revenues allowed the state to invest in heavy industry, hence creating a bureaucratic bourgeois class. At the same time, the former landlords were allowed to invest in industrial planning. The modern bourgeoisie of Iran also included those who had access to government funds and were able to use the oil revenues for their own good.

The White Revolution provided for the sale of the state-owned factories to the landlords whose land was distributed among the peasants. This policy resulted in the creation of a conservative bourgeoisie that was dependent on the state for protection, loans, and subsidization. Additionally, the state mainly invested in heavy industry and left the small factories to the private sector. Under the fifth plan direct investment of the state in industrial development amounted to 40 percent of total industrial investments. This amount was increased to 60 percent following the quadrupling of oil revenues in 1974.

Domination of the capitalist relations of production was made possible by direct investment by the state and state subsidization of the private sector. As a result, the modern capitalist class of Iran was composed of a bureaucratic capitalist class and also a private sector that was totally dependent on the state for subsidies and loans. This situation enhanced the dependence the modern bourgeoisie on the state.

A significant aspect of the Iranian state is that it dominates social classes. During the precapitalist social formation of Iran, the landlords were totally weak and dependent on the state. With the domination of the capitalist relations of production, the modern bourgeoisie was created by the state and hence dependent on it. This allowed the state to impose its policies on the modern bourgeoisie without facing serious challenges from this class. In its relations with the working class, the state resorted to the policy of punishment and enticement. On the one hand, it was against the formation of workers' unions or syndicates. On the other hand, it sided with the workers in their disputes with entrepreneurs. In order to execute this policy, SAVAK agents were stationed in the factories to regulate relations between the workers and their employers. SAVAK agents kept a close eye on the "disturbances" and "subversive" activities of the workers, while putting pressure on the management to agree with the workers' demands for higher wages (Halliday 1979:202–9). These measures were taken not to defend workers' rights, but rather to keep the workers quiet and to avoid politicization of their demands. Another aspect of the state's intervention between the workers and the industrialists was the program of profit sharing between the workers and entrepreneurs. This policy was intended to bring workers over to the side of the state. This program, however, was not successful and caused more animosity among the workers toward the state. The private sector was also against the profit-sharing program, but because of its dependence on the state could not openly oppose this program. This class was demoralized and alienated from the state. As a result, when the paralyzing crisis of the state started in 1976, the modern bourgeoisie did not support the regime and allowed it to collapse.

The Overgrowth of the Service Sector

The growth of the service sector in industrialized countries took place only after economic maturity. In the Third World, however, this happened in the early stage of industrial growth. In 1960 the service sector constituted 30 percent of the labor force in Mexico. In the same year, the service sector in Peru and Brazil constituted 31 percent and 35 percent of the total labor force of these countries respectively. Halliday reports the growth of the service sector at the expense of the productive sector in Iran this way: "Whereas in 1959–60 the service sector accounted for 31.5% of GDP, in 1974–75 it accounted for 39.4% with industry making up only 16.1%" (1979:157). A report from the Plan and Budget Organization (PBO) also indicates the growth of the service sector in urban areas of Iran: "While the service sector constituted 51.3% of the total labor force in urban areas, this was increased to 54.2 in 1966 and 58% in 1976" (Danesh 1984:15).

The continuing growth of the service sector was an indication of the enlargement of state bureaucracy at the expense of the productive sector. It also showed that most of the economic resources were allocated to the urban areas. This trend had two negative effects: first, it diverted economic resources from industry and agriculture and invested them in a nonproductive sector; second, it resulted in the growth of urban areas at the expense of rural areas (Afshar 1985:68). In fact, most of the development projects were concentrated in big cities and especially in Tehran. This policy had another negative effect. It benefited the well-to-do at the expense of the poor. Banking services and the import sector for luxury items grew very fast. As Katouzian notes, the growth of the service sector had another effect: it camouflaged expenditures for military purposes and security forces (Katouzian 1981:258). The service sector widened the gap between rural and urban areas. In 1978 the service sector constituted 34.6 percent of the gross national product (GNP), 55.6 percent of nonoil output, and 34 percent of the labor force.

Mismanagement

Mismanagement has been the trademark of the Iranian economy. This problem became even more acute following the quadrupling of oil prices. The new wealth made the Shah dream of transforming Iran into the fifth economic and military power of the world by the late 1980s. More capital-intensive factories and modern weaponry were purchased to achieve this goal, which the Shah called "the Great Civilization." These capital-intensive factories and sophisticated weapons required skilled managers and workers. While Iran had enough capital to buy factories, it lacked skilled personnel to run them. The motto of the economic decision makers was that Iran could solve all its problems with its recent wealth (Homayoun 1982:22–59). Skilled workers and managers were brought in at high salaries to run the Iranian industries. But in spite of this, no provision was made for training the Iranian workers for the future. The social consequences of hiring a large number of Western technicians (about 65,000 by 1977) was even more damaging than its economic aspect. Regarding this problem, Keddie notes that the extremely high salaries of foreign personnel and their behavior resulted in the indignation of many Iranians (1981:173).

In fact, lack of skilled personnel was a major obstacle impeding industrial development. This problem was mainly due to the inefficient educational system and economic mismanagement. In 1948 only 10 percent of the population over ten years of age was able to read and write. The number of vocational and training schools was also limited. By 1966, the number of vocational schools was 181 in comparison to the number of high schools, which was 1,862. In the same year, the number of colleges and universities was only 48. But by the 1970s, the number of educational institutions and student enrollments increased rapidly. High-school enrollment had increased to 1.4 million by 1972 and to 2.3 million by 1978. The number of university students had increased from 59,000 in 1968 to 154,000 in 1978 (Katouzian 1981:287).

Though the number of students increased, the educational system did not train them to join the labor force in the industrial sector. The majority of students, therefore, were absorbed by the service sector, where very little formal training was required. Even those high-school graduates who were absorbed by industry did not have proper training for working in the factories. Surprisingly enough, neither the managers of the factories nor the industrial planners were concerned about training workers efficiently. This factor plus the mismanagement of the planners resulted in the low productivity of Iranian industry, a problem which was exacerbated after 1973 when industrialization assumed a speedy pace. Consequently, thousands of foreign technicians and engineers were employed to run Iranian industry. Despite the high wages paid to the foreign employees, Iranian planners did not train Iranian workers to replace their foreign counterparts in the future.

The economic mismanagement was not limited to the lack of skilled personnel. Those involved in key economic decision making like the Shah and Premier Hoveyda did not heed the suggestions of the economic advisers. Dariush Homayoun, former minister of information, quotes the then Premier Hoveyda as boasting of doing exactly the opposite of what the economic advisers of the state had recommended (Homayoun 1982:32). Besides that, the recommendations of the PBO for sound economic growth were neglected. Instead, there was a frenzy for spending as many petrodollars as possible on capital-intensive factories, armaments, and the service sector. This sort of economic (mis)planning was the direct result of the Shah's dreams of transforming Iran into a second Japan by the late 1980s.

The economic mismanagement was so overwhelming that by 1975 the economy was out of control (Graham 1980:86). The banks had exhausted all their credit, imports had risen to $1.2 billion a month, cement was scarce in the market (this factor paralyzed the construction sector by 1976), and the ports were jammed with ships that had to wait up to six months to unload their cargoes. The economic mismanagement and overspending paralyzed the whole economy by 1977. This new development forced Iran to seek international loans, a sharp contrast with the 1973–1976 period, in which Iran was a creditor. This was definitely the end of the boom period and the beginning of new problems for the state. The economic boom had created new hopes among people and raised their expectations. The end of the boom, however, dashed the hopes of those who had expected that their standard of living would rise. Alarmed by the uncontrollable economy and the crisis of the state, the Shah announced in a speech in 1977 that the time for spending was over and should be replaced by hard work and saving (*Kayhan International*, October 26, 1976).

Insufficient Infrastructure

Historically, the Iranian state has been in charge of building and maintaining the infrastructure. Despite this, during the time under consideration, roads, railroads, port facilities, and water and power supplies were so insufficient and poorly maintained that they became one of the major obstacles toward industrial development. By the early 1970s Iran had only 5,000 miles of asphalt roads and 14,000 miles of gravel roads. These roads were poorly constructed and were not maintained properly, and as a result could not cope with the rapid industrial development. The railways were also in a miserable condition and, worse than that, were far from all the industrial centers except for Tehran. A student of Iranian economic development notes, "Apart from Tehran and Ahwaz the routes touched no major cities" (Bharier 1971:206). Water transportation was almost confined to the Persian Gulf ports, which were not prepared for the massive import of goods.

The Iranian ports were poorly maintained and concentrated in the Persian Gulf area. Between 1947 and 1957 about 72 percent of the imports entered Iran through the Persian Gulf ports. This percentage, however, went up to about 100 percent by the mid–1950s (Bharier 1971:212). Because of the lack of skilled manpower and an inefficient bureaucracy, ships had to wait in the port for about six months to unload their cargoes. After unloading, the goods would have to remain unwarehoused before being removed. As Graham notes, in Khorramshahr port, out of twelve thousand tons unloaded, only nine thousand tons could be removed per day (1980:87). As a result of the shortage of port facilities and the lack of skilled manpower and technical know-how, Iran was paying $1.5 billion in demurrage charges annually. This amount was over 7 percent of the annual oil revenues (Halliday 1979:163).

Road transportation was in an equally abysmal condition. First, the roads were insufficient and poorly maintained. Second, there were not enough trucks and drivers to transport goods. In order to boost its ground transportation of goods, the government purchased eight thousand trucks and trailers in 1975. The economic planners, however, failed to train Iranian personnel to drive these trucks. About one thousand South Korean, Pakistani, and Indian drivers were employed to drive these trucks. Because of the lack of personnel and the failure of the government to train Iranian drivers, thousands of trucks corroded in the Iranian deserts while waiting to be operated (Graham 1980:88; Homayoun 1982:28–29).

Neglect of Agricultural Sector

During the time under investigation, the government's main aim was to push for rapid industrial growth. The economic advisers of the Shah suggested that industrialization should be given priority over agriculture. Their solution for agriculture was the mechanization of agriculture, without even considering the scarcity of technicians or the inability of the state to provide proper and adequate technical assistance for this purpose. The logic of the planners was that since in most Third World countries agricultural production does not constitute more than 2.5 percent of the total economic output, Iran should become industrialized first and then mechanize its agriculture to increase production (Motamedi 1971:90–96). Despite the hues and cries about mechanized agriculture and spending millions of dollars, large-scale farming and mechanized agriculture had a negligible impact on improving production or revolutionizing Iranian agriculture. A serious student of Iranian land reform, Eric Hooglund, comments that "at most only 2.7% acres, 5% of the country's arable lands, were affected.... Their [mechanized agriculture and large-scale farming] contribution to agricultural production was not any greater than those when the lands had been cultivated by peasant proprietors" (Hooglund 1981:18).

The emphasis on rapid industrialization and mechanization of agriculture was the consequence of the Shah's negative attitude toward traditional agriculture and the existence of a large rural population. He regarded the Iranian villages and the traditional agricultural sector as signs of backwardness and wanted to minimize their role and significance in the political economy. The Shah had emphasized that the growth of Iranian industry required reduction of the village population from 65 percent to 25 percent (Pahlavi 1966:19). The overemphasis on mechanized agriculture, the failure of the government to provide sufficient credits to the peasants, and the lack of egalitarian land reform resulted in the failure of agriculture. Consequently, the goverment had to import foodstuffs from countries such as the United States, Australia, and Turkey.

The government also had to spend large amounts of money for subsidizing food. This amount reached a total of $3 billion by 1978 (Halliday 1979:165; Hooglund 1981:19). The government also placed too much emphasis on the development of urban areas, while deliberately depopulating the villages. This policy resulted in the migration of more than two million peasants to the cities. As a result, the peasant population declined from 65 percent in 1963 to 53 percent in 1978. The disinherited peasants migrated to the cities in search of a better life, prosperity, and greater opportunities for growth. Their hopes were dashed, however, in the cities. They did not have the means to live "in" the cities and as a result, resided on the outskirts of the cities or in the shantytowns called Halabi-abad, or Kapar-abad in Farsi. Most of these rural migrants could not find steady jobs and earned their living by selling lottery tickets, polishing shoes, or other types of menial work. Those who were fortunate enough found jobs in the construction sector. Rural migrants in general were not integrated into the social life of the cities, and witnessed the prosperity of the city dwellers without benefiting from the economic boom themselves. This contradiction made them eager to destroy the system which had resulted in their misfortune.

Low Productivity

Iranian industrialization efforts were badly hurt by low productivity during the time under consideration. Lack of skilled workers was the main cause of low productivity. Graham illustrates this obstacle as follows: "General Motors calculated in late 1975 that it took more than 45 man-hours to assemble their Chevrolet Iran in Tehran against 25 man-hours in West Germany for the same car, the Opel Commodore" (Graham 1980:121). Government subsidies and high protective tariffs and tax exemptions were the methods used by the state to help the factories combat low productivity. Despite this, Iranian manufactured goods were so expensive that they could not compete internationally. In fact, Iranian manufactured goods were 25 to 33 percent higher than the average world prices in 1972. This percentage must have grown even higher following the quadrupling of oil prices in 1973 (Halliday 1979:159; Looney 1973:158).

POLITICAL UNDERDEVELOPMENT

Despite the economic development, the Iranian political machinery remained underdeveloped and did not correspond to the needs of a rapidly industrializing nation. That is, the Shah obstructed the formation of political organizations through which different social classes could express their grievances against one another on the one hand, and toward the state on the other. As a result, both the old and the new classes were estranged from the state. The Shah's pillars of support were limited to the military, security forces, and the state bureaucracy. The task of the army and security forces was to protect the Shah from any political challenge and from domestic opponents. The Shah identified himself with the armed forces and devoted a great deal of his time to reorganizing the armed forces (Hoveyda 1979:80–90). Retired army officers were employed in the factories to control the workers and intimidate the employees. The bureaucracy also grew very fast in the post–1963 period to ensure the supremacy of the state in both urban and rural areas.

In the absence of popular support, the armed forces and SAVAK were used as the source of legitimacy. This kind of legitimacy might be called legitimacy through repression and intimidation. The size of the military increased from 80,000 in 1941 to 200,000 in 1963 and 410,000 in 1977. SAVAK was responsible for collecting information, penetrating the political opposition, and arresting and torturing political opponents of the regime. By the late 1970s SAVAK was composed of 5,300 full-time employees and a large but unknown number of part-time informers (*Iran Times*, August 31, 1979). The first chief of SAVAK, General Teimour Bakhtiar, was dismissed because he had created his own power base in both the army and SAVAK (he was later assassinated in Iraq by a SAVAK agent in 1969). General Hasan Pakravan replaced Bakhtiar in 1961. Pakravan was a liberal general who fitted the liberal period of the early 1960s. In 1963, General Nematollah Nassiri, a close and highly loyal friend of the Shah, became chief of SAVAK. Nassiri was a tough and ruthless general who increased the efficiency of SAVAK in repressing the opposition and intimidating civilians. Nassiri was dismissed in 1978 because of "mishandling" the popular uprisings of Qom and Tabriz.

The military was directly controlled by the Shah. He was commander-in-chief of the armed forces and kept a very close eye on the well-being of the military personnel. The members of the armed forces were getting handsome salaries, pensions, free health care, fringe benefits, and cheap housing. The military budget was constantly increasing. It went up from $293 million in 1969 to $7.3 billion in 1978 (Halliday 1979:394). By the late 1960s Iran began buying the most sophisticated weapons from the West. The Nixon Doctrine, according to which the United States had decided to promote its clients in the strategically important areas of the world with massive military aid and training to protect these regions, made the Shah the policeman of the Persian Gulf. Following Nixon's visit to Iran in 1973, the United States agreed to give the Shah any non-nuclear weapons he wanted. Britain also became a major supplier of weapons to Iran in order to fill the vacuum created by its departure from the Persian Gulf and to use Iran's petrodollars to remedy its staggering recession.

The creation of a large and modern army became a great obsession of the Shah following the quadrupling of oil prices (in the 1973–1974 period). Iran's former ambassador to the United Nations, Fereidoun Hoveyda, notes that between 1971 and 1978 Iran purchased $19 billion worth of arms from the United States alone (Hoveyda 1979:98). The Iranian arms included 166 F5 fighters, 20 F140 Thomac fighter planes, 760 Chieftain tanks, 250 Scorpio tanks, 80 helicopters, and 28 hovercrafts (Abrahamian 1982:435). Nikki Keddie comments on the sophisticated weapons the Shah was acquiring from the West: "The British provided

Iran with more Chieftain tanks than they had in their own armed forces, and the United States let the Shah be the first to buy a series of sophisticated fighter planes, often before they were in production or their reliability had been proved" (1981:176).

Bureaucracy constituted another pillar of the Shah's regime. While in the mid–1950s Iran had twelve ministries with some 150,000 employees, the number of these instituions had increased to nineteen with 560,000 civil servants by the mid–1970s. The actual effect of the enlargement of the bureaucracy was the total domination of the state over every aspect of the life of ordinary citizens. The state owned and controlled the total heavy industry, the oil industry, and the infrastructure. It distributed water, power, gas, kerosene, gasoline, and electricity. Health services, social welfare, the educational system, and the rural cooperatives were also administered by the state. The growth of bureaucracy allowed the Shah to tighten his control over state power. Marvin Zonis explains this trend as the domination of the everyday life of the people by the state and the domination of the state by the Shah (1971:18).

An Iranian scholar also notes that the bureaucracy had grown so much that between one-third to one-half of the urban employees were working for the government (Nima 1983:44). The state not only paid salaries to its employees, but also provided health care, social welfare, pensions, and unemployment insurance. According to Abrahamian, "The dramatic growth of the bureaucracy enabled the state to penetrate more deeply into the everyday lives of ordinary citizens" (Abrahamian 1982:438). The bureaucratization of society had two functions: Through its civilian branch it provided services to the citizens. The military branch of the bureaucracy, on the other hand, harassed the people and repressed the opposition.

The bureaucratization of the society was not confined to the cities. The White Revolution brought the countryside under the domination of the state as well. The landlords, kadkhodas, and mobashers were now replaced by the state employees, rural banks, rural cooperatives, literacy and health corps, and gendarmes. This new development made the state responsible for the everyday lives of the rural population. The peasants now were dependent on the state for loans, credits, fertilizers, water distribution, education, and security. More specifically, the state was directly in charge of distributing land and water, pricing agricultural production, law enforcement, the administration of justice, the running of 8,500 rural cooperatives, and providing health care for the rural population. Bureaucratization of the rural areas, however, was a double-edged sword. On the one hand, it effectively destroyed the power base of the landlords in the rural areas and replaced it by the state power. On the other hand, the failure of agriculture, mismanagement of rural cooperatives and poor planning were directly blamed on the state and more specifically on the Shah.

Following the quadrupling of the oil revenues, the bureaucratization of the rural areas took yet another turn. The state rapidly increased agricultural corporations and agribusinesses. Moreover, the state deliberately decided to depopulate villages and urbanize the whole country. In 1974, the government drew up a plan for the reorganization of rural areas. According to this plan, the Iranian villages would be divided into "development and nondevelopment zones." The development zones would consist of twenty "poles of development" covering 4.5 million acres. The zones of development would receive credits, subsidized fuel, and technical assistance from the state. They would also receive services such as schools, roads, irrigation systems, and health care. The rest of the rural areas were regarded as "outside the poles" and "marginal zones" and subsequently would not receive anything (Brun and Dumont 1978:18). This policy of depopulating the villages and confining the entire village system in "poles of development," however, failed. The bureaucratization of the rural areas had only one result: the destruction of the agricultural sector and the increase in the import of foodstuffs.

THE RASTAKHIZ PARTY

By the early 1970s lack of popular support and political participation by the people made the Shah deeply concerned about the future of the monarchy. The Mardom and Iran Novin parties had failed to mobilize the masses for political participation. The Shah's solution was to create a strong single-party system that had elements of capitalism and socialism (i.e., like Ba'ath Party) to generate political participation and popular support (Abrahamian 1982:440–41; Fischer 1977:173). In March 1975, he dissolved the Mardom and Iran Novin parties and announced the establishment of Rastakhiz (Resurgence) Party. Membership in the party was semicompulsory. The Shah announced that all Iranians should join the party. The opponents of the party were labeled "traitors" and "communists" who had only two choices: either leave the country or go to jail (*Kayhan International*, March 8, 1975). Joining the party required accepting the principles of the White Revolution, the monarchy, and the constitution.

The creation of the Rastakhiz Party put an end to the Shah's previous claims that he supported pluralism. Interestingly enough, the Shah had repeatedly equated multiparty systems with democracy and single-party systems with fascism and communism. In his autobiography, *Mission for My Country*, published in 1961, he had argued:

If I were a dictator rather than a constitutional monarch, then I might be tempted to sponsor a single dominant party such as Hitler organized or such as you find today in Communist countries. But as a constitutional monarch I can afford to encourage large-scale party activity free from the straightjacket of one-party state. As a symbol of the unity of my people, I can promote two or more parties without directly associating myself with any. (Pahlavi 1961:173)

A very important factor that made the Shah decide to create a one-party system was the suggestion of some of his Western-educated advisers that prosperity and rapid economic growth depended on popular participation. This would be possible only through the creation of a disciplined single-party system (Stemple 1981:32–35). The advisers who were so enthusiastic about the creation of an authoritarian single-party system were influenced by the proponents of modernization theories such as David Apter and Samuel Huntington. Both Huntington and Apter had argued that the lack of political participation would result in instability of the government. They suggested that in developing countries, a disciplined single party can link the government to the people and mobilize the masses (Apter 1965:13–15, 179–200; Huntington 1970:397–403).

Organizationally, the Rastakhiz Party grew very rapidly. By June 1975, it had created women's and youth organizations and convened a labor congress. It also established five newspapers, the *Daily Rastakhiz* (the party's official organ), *Youths' Rastakhiz, Workers' Rastakhiz, Peasants' Rastakhiz*, and also the party's theoretical journal called *Andisheh Rastakhiz*. By June 1975, the party consisted of five million members, had chosen a central committee, and had enrolled all of the Majlis deputies, cabinet members, and other high-ranking officials as members. Prime Minister Hoveyda was selected as the first general secretary of the party by the Shah (Abrahamian 1982:442).

With the creation of Rastakhiz Party, dictatorship was in full swing. With active assistance from SAVAK, the party purged all of those who were suspected of disloyalty to the Shah from the ministries, mass media, and the PBO. It also tightened government control over artists, filmmakers, writers and poets. More than 70 percent of the journals and newspapers were closed, and by 1976 twenty-five poets, playwrights, and writers were imprisoned.

One of the main goals of Rastakhiz was the modernization of the country and the destruction of the power of the bazaar and the hierarchy of mollahs (Nima 1983:44–45). Branches of the party were established in the bazaar and started squeezing bazaaris for membership and donations for the party. The party also gradually took over the administration of religious endowments (Sazman-e-Oughaf), thus depriving the mollahs of one of their sources of economic support. By putting pressure on the bazaaris and mollahs, the regime created favorable conditions for a formidable alliance between these two groups. This alliance became stronger during the popular uprising of 1977–1979 and allowed these two traditional social forces to take over the leadership of the revolution.

By June 1975, the party was getting ready to put its strength into practice. The target was the Iranian bazaar. In order to do this, the party did two things. First, it dissolved the old guilds and replaced them with government-sponsored guilds under the supervision of SAVAK. Second, the party started an antiprofiteering campaign. The real aim of this plan was to scapegoat the bazaaris for the inflation. Some 20,000 party members were mobilized to carry out this campaign. Between 1975 and 1977, more than 250,000 shops were closed down, and 31,000 bazaaris were imprisoned or exiled.

To make the situation worse, the government changed the Iranian calendar from the 1355 Hejira to the 2535 Royalist calendar. This, along with economic pressure on the mollahs, made them conclude that the government wanted to deprive them of their social and economic privileges and to control the administration of religious affairs. Ayatollah Khomeini and several other ayatollahs denounced the party as non-Islamic and contrary to the principles of the constitution. The creation of the party made the clash between the mollahs and the state inevitable. Even the nonpolitical mollahs such as Ayatollah Shariatmadary and Qomi found themselves trapped between joining the party or opposing it. By 1976, many high-ranking mollahs, such as Ali Akbar Hashemi Rafsanjani, Hossein Ali Montazeri, Azari Qomi, Ali Khamenei, and Mahmud Taleghany, were serving time in jail.

The main goals of the Shah in creating the Rastakhiz Party were mobilizing the masses for political participation, tightening his grip on political power, weakening the power of the bazaaris and mollahs, and intimidating the potential opposition (Laing 1977:218–22; Stemple 1981:31–38). The Shah failed in achieving any of these goals except tightening his control over the social life of every citizen (Hoveyda 1979:102–3). By openly identifying himself with the Rastakhiz Party, the Shah made himself the person responsible for economic inequality, the plight of agriculture, and the abuse of power (Homayoun 1982:10–41). The unwillingness of the people to participate in the political process, the increasing militancy of the opposition, and the dependence of the Shah upon the use of naked force signalled the total failure of the Rastakhiz Party.

The Rastakhiz Party was created as a last resort to salvage the Pahlavi state (Homayoun 1984). Ironically, it intensified popular discontent and alienated the people from the regime further (Hoveyda 1979:102). The party had made the situation virtually intolerable for all social classes. First, the antiprofiteering campaign had made the bazaaris a scapegoat for inflation. By mid–1976, 250,000 shops were closed down and 31,000 bazaaris were imprisoned. Second, in 1976, the Hejira calendar was changed to the royal calendar, hence forcing people to identify themselves more with the monarchy. Third, the antimollah campaign and the govermment's attempt to take over religious duties of the mollahs and its creation of a religious corps had agitated the religious hierarchy. Fourth, closing 70 percent of the newspapers and journals and trying to force intellectuals to cooperate with the regime turned these groups more adamantly against the Shah. In mid–1976, the renowned Iranian sociologist Ali Asghar Hadj Seyyed Javady wrote a 200-page open letter to the Shah in which he condemned the repressive measures used to run the country. All these factors as well as forcing people to join the party left no alternative for the majority of the people but to openly oppose the regime, regardless of the consequences.

TOTAL FAILURE OF THE REGIME

Following the White Revolution, the Shah was able to destroy the opposition and discredit his competitors such as Ali Amini and Teimour Bakhtiar. The National Front disappeared from the political scene. The Tudeh Party had already been dismantled by the mid-fifties. Even the close friends, advisers, and relatives of the Shah who were suspected of disloyalty or of becoming a power base were sacked (Hoveyda 1979:137–39; Zonis 1971:20–89). The former chief of SAVAK, General Bakhtiar, was first dismissed (1961) and later assassinated (1967). Ali Ameri, the secretary general of Mardom Party and General Khatemi (the Shah's brother-in-law) were also killed solely because they were not trusted as faithful allies. SAVAK hunted down leftist intellectuals and penetrated factories, universities, government agencies, clubs, cultural institutions, and mass media. The situation became worse following the quadrupling of the oil revenues. The Shah's dream of transforming Iran into the fifth industrial and military power of the world by late 1980s culminated in his plan to lead Iran to the Great Civilization. The Great Civilization for him meant a modern and industrialized country that was highly urbanized. Almost everyone except the Shah was aware that the chance of Iran's becoming a great industrialized nation was minimal. William Sullivan, former United States ambassador to Iran (1977–1979), had serious doubts about the chances of Iran's becoming a highly industrialized country in the near future. He correctly argued that because of the bottlenecks, rapid industrial growth would result in inconceivable social and economic problems (1981:64–68).

Graham reports that Iran's top economic planners such as Mohammad Yeganeh (head of the Central Bank of Iran), Abdol Majid Majidi (director of the PBO), and Houshang Ansari (minister of finance) were concerned that because of the lack of a viable infrastructure, skilled personnel and possible shortages of water and electricity, rapid industrialization would cause more damage to the economy and would hinder economic development (Graham 1980:77–78). Although the economic planners were fully aware that rapid industrial development without proper planning would lead to staggering inflation, shortages, and social problems, they did not dare to mention to the Shah that his dreams might turn into a nightmare in the future (Sullivan 1981:70). By 1976 the regime was facing political and economic challenges that it was not prepared to meet. The Rastakhiz Party had not only been unable to mobilize the masses to support the regime, but it had added to the popular discontent. Demand for oil had also dropped, hence causing more economic problems. Iran therefore had to start borrowing from the World Bank. This new reality made the Shah personally announce that prosperity was based on the steady increase of oil revenues, and since oil revenues had decreased, hard work and sacrifice would be the only solution to the economic problems (*Kayhan International*, October 26, 1976).

To conclude, several factors resulted in the failure of the regime and emergence of the popular uprisings of 1977–1979. The quadrupling of the oil revenues and the creation of the Rastakhiz Party made the Shah believe that he would be able to plan for rapid industrial development. Ironically, both of these factors combined resulted in the failure of the monarchy. First, the oil revenues raised people'e expectations and created more cleavage between the poor and the rich and between rural and urban populations. Second, the Rastakhiz Party made dictatorship more intolerable than ever before. This resulted in a paralyzing crisis of the state which had occurred once before in the late 1950s. At that time, Premier Eqbal was sacrificed as a scapegoat for corruption, mismanagement, and failure of economic planning. This time, Premier Hoveyda, who had served the Shah for thirteen years, was to be blamed for all of the economic and political problems that Iran was facing. In mid-August 1977, Hoveyda was dismissed and replaced by the arrogant Amouzgar, the former secretary general of the Rastakhiz Party and the minister of interior. Amouzgar's policy was based on fighting inflation for economic recovery. This policy, however, brought rapid unemployment and resulted in more popular discontent. Once again, as in 1960, the crisis of the state and the foreign policy of the United States, which was advocating the implementation of human rights, made the Shah resort to liberalization policies to defuse the crisis. This time, however, the situation was much more complicated and the Shah failed to handle it correctly. The crisis brought popular demonstrations which eventually resulted in the overthrow of the monarchy in 1979.

7 The Revolution

The Iranian revolution was one of the most popular and mass-based upheavals of history. Richard Falk has called it "one of the great watersheds of modern history" (Falk 1979:9). This chapter investigates the socioeconomic factors that led to the revolution. In general, there are four theories about the Iranian revolution. The monarchists and their apologists blame the revolution on the conspiracy of foreign powers and Ayatollah Khomeini and the reaction of the traditional society to the modernization efforts of the Shah. Proponents of the conspiracy theory base their arguments on two premises. They claim that the overthrow of the monarchy was a British conspiracy that aimed at destroying the Shah for his independent policy and "nationalization" of the oil industry (Sullivan 1981:176–77). They also maintain that the Iranian revolution was a fetneh (conspiracy) of Khomeini (*Nehzat*, January 20, 1982; Sharifi 1983). The proponents of the structural-functional approach to the revolution and the monarchists contend that rapid modernization resulted in the disintegration of the society and disruption of the Iranian culture. According to this view, the consequence of these developments was social upheaval and the overthrow of the monarchy (Pahlavi 1980:125–60; Zabih 1979:38).

Fundamentalist Islamic groups such as the supporters of Ayatollah Khomeini hold that the revolution was a direct result of the "anti-Islamic" nature of the Shah's regime. This view contends that the Islamic revolution was both predestined and inevitable. The proponents of this approach see the Iranian revolution as the struggle of the Moslem people of Iran against their irreligious oppressors (Taghut). This view downplays the impact of the economic and political developments in the revolution by arguing that it was a miracle and people were simply fulfilling God's will.

A third view emerges among the liberal forces, which emphasize the dictatorship of the Shah as the main cause of the Iranian revolution. The secular National Front, the religious Freedom Movement of Iran, and the liberal and constitutionalist mojtaheds such as Ayatollah Shariatmadary, Ayatollah Qomi, and Ayatollah Khoii are among the proponents of this view.

The leftist forces of Iran in general emphasize the roles of the economy and class conflict as the main causes of the revolution. They argue that the economic recession of the mid–1970s resulted in the unemployment of a large segment of the working class and their uprising against the regime. They also argue that the revolution was the result of the international economic recession and the failure of Iran's dependent capitalism.

Some of the above-mentioned theories have a certain validity, but cannot explain the complexity of the Iranian revolution. The first and second views do not touch the reality of the situation. As far as the conspiracy of foreign countries is concerned, both Britain and the United States stood by the Shah and supported him until the last moment. As the British ambassador to Iran, Anthony Parsons, reports, he and William Sullivan, the U.S. ambassador to Iran, were in daily contact with the Shah and advised him on the handling of the crisis (Parsons 1984:117). Documents that pro-Khomeini Iranian students seized from the U.S. embassy in Iran (hereafter referred to as the embassy reports) show that the American authorities in Iran were trying to convince the opposition to come to terms with the Shah (*Iran Times*, January 12, 1981).

Supporters of Ayatollah Khomeini fail to realize that destruction of all political organizations and a long period of repression had prevented the growth of political organizations. The result was the emergence of religious institutions as the only open source of opposition to the Shah (Hosseiny 1983:9; Massaly 1983:14). They also forget that throughout 1977 it was the salaried middle class and intellectuals (both secular in outlook) who organized the anti-Shah demonstrations (Mirzazadeh 1983, Nateq 1982:17–18). It was only in late 1977 that the religious groups started mobilizing their forces against the regime.

By overemphasizing the role of the struggle for freedom, the liberals undermine the economic aspect of the revolution. The leftist forces, on the other hand, underestimate the political and cultural factors as well as the role of external forces such as international pressure on the Shah for political liberalization. Consequently, both fail to see all of the factors which together resulted in the overthrow of the monarchy.

My argument is that the Iranian revolution was much more complicated than these views suggest. Its causes could be found in a variety of complex socioeconomic factors such as class conflict, the arbitrary use of power by the Shah, economic mismanagement, the decomposition of agriculture, the migration of the indigenous village population to the cities, and the sharp economic decline after a period of prosperity. Besides these domestic factors, the international pressures on the Shah since the mid-1970s to liberalize his policies provided favorable conditions for the opposition to challenge the Shah without fear of a heavy reprisal (compared to the pre-1977 period). The liberalization policies of the Shah starting in early 1977 emboldened the opposition to come out and organize itself against the regime. The combination of these factors resulted in the overthrow of the monarchy. In the following discussion, I will analyze the impact of domestic and external factors on the Iranian revolution.

UNDERGROUND POLITICAL ORGANIZATIONS

The June 1963 uprising was a turning point for the political organizations. The suppression of the June upheaval made many young supports of the Tudeh Party and the National Front conclude that neither organization could mobilize the masses against the regime. Following the June 1963 massacre, the National Front stopped all of its activities and remained silent until 1977. The Tudeh Party had already stopped operation since the mid-1950s and was reduced to mild opposition abroad. The victory of the armed struggle in Algeria and Cuba and also the experience of guerrilla warfare in Vietnam and Central America had a major impact on many young political activists. Several guerrilla organizations were created with the aim of overthrowing the regime through a protracted armed struggle. Among all of these groups only the People's Fedaii Guerrilla Organization of Iran (hereafter referred to as the Fedaii Organization) and the Mojahedin-e Khalq Organization were able to gain popularity among the people.

The Fedaii Organization was founded by former members of the Youth Organization of the Tudeh Party and leftist supporters of the National Front. It was created in 1970 from the merger of a group founded by Bijan Jazani and Hassan Zarifi (both were former members of the Youth Organization of the Tudeh Party) and Amir Parviz Pouyan and the Masoud Ahmadzadeh group (the latter group had a religious background and was formerly affiliated with the National Front). Ahmadzadeh and Pouyan denounced the reformism of the Tudeh Party and the National Front and argued that the Pahlavi state could be overthrown only through the armed struggle (Ahmadzadeh 1977:12–25). The Fedaii Organization was Marxist-Leninist but denounced the Soviet Union for establishing close ties with the Shah's regime. Despite this, it was not a Maoist organization and did not brand the Soviet Union as social imperialist. The Fedaii Organization was much influenced by Regis Debray, the French advocate of the armed struggle, who thought that the guerrilla organization was the nucleus of the revolutionary party and that through the course of the struggle, the party would be created to lead the revolution (Ahmadzadeh 1977:20–45). Jazani also argued that the armed struggle was the principal means of organizing the masses against the regime (1978:200–214). Contrary to Ahmadzadeh and Pouyan, Jazani argued that the role of the guerrillas was to provide the conditions for the creation of the hegemony of the working class (1974:21–50).

The Fedaii Organization started its activities by attacking a gendarmerie post in Siahkal, a village near the Caspian Sea, on February 8, 1971. This incident was welcomed by many young people, mainly university students and graduates. Many compared Siahkal to Moncada, where the Cuban revolution started, and expected people to join the movement to overthrow the regime. The regime, however, mobilized its forces in the Caspian Sea area, arrested most of the guerrillas, and executed them.

Despite the execution of the most of the prominent members of the organization, it grew in number and popularity. Fedaiis were able to carry out several successful attacks on the security forces of the regime including bombing police headquarters in Tehran, Tabriz, Rasht, and Abadan. They also assassinated the chief military prosecutor of Tehran (General Farsiv), several SAVAK agents, and an industrialist, and held up eight banks (Abrahamian 1982:488).

The Mojahedin-e Khalq Organization was also a proponent of the armed struggle in Iran. It was founded by Saiid Mohsen, Mohammad Hanif Nejad, and Ali Asghar Badii Zadegan in 1965. These men were former members of the Freedom Movement of Iran, but broke away from it because they believed that it was not radical enough to lead the social revolution in Iran. Mojahedin believed that Islam and Marxism were compatible. They concluded that Islam in its pure sense was in favor of the socialization of the means of production, elimination of exploitation, equality of men and women, and the creation of a classless society (Mohsen 1978:1–34). Mojahedin's interpretation of a classless society was based on the elimination of classes as well as belief in God, hence the slogan Peesh Be-sooy-e Jameh-e Bee-Tabagheh-e Touhidi (Forward to the Creation of a Classless Society Based on Monotheism).

Mojahedin, like Fedaiis, had great appeal among university students. Mojahedin, however, had a better chance of growing because of the focus on social justice and revolution in an Islamic context. Consequently, their supporters were not confined to the intellectual circles. Some bazaaris and several mojtaheds, such as Ayatollah Mahmud Taleghani, Ayatollah Hossein Ali Montazeri, and Ayatollah Morteza Mottahari, were among their supporters. Mojahedin activities against the regime included assassinating a police general and three American military advisers and holding up several banks.

Despite the heroism, sacrifices, and dedication of both of these organizations, they failed to mobilize the masses against the regime. Their failure was due to several factors. First, their brutal suppression by the regime. By 1976, more than 90 percent of the founders and the original members of both organizations were executed or in prison. Second, they were obsessed with guerrilla activities instead of working among the masses and preparing them for a popular uprising.

Third, splits in both organizations also weakened them to a great extent. In August 1975, the Mojahedin organization was split into its original Islamic group and a Maoist faction. The Maoist offshoot (later renamed Peykar) did not grow, and the original Islamic organization was virtually destroyed by SAVAK (see chapter 3). The Fedaii organization split into a group that kept its identity and continued its guerrilla activity and a group that denounced the armed struggle and joined the Tudeh Party. Both of these underground political organizations were weakened to such an extent that they ceased operating by late 1976. As a result, when the revolution started, they were not in a position to mobilize the masses against the regime.

BAZAARIS

Bazaaris were victims of industrialization and the growth of the capitalist relations of production. The increasing role of the banks and the emergence of modern supermarkets hurt bazaaris a great deal (Green 1982:41–42). Despite this, the bazaaris played a crucial role in the economic activities of Iran. Graham notes that "despite the modernization of the economy, the bazaar still controls over two-thirds of domestic wholesale trade and accounts of 30 percent of all imports" (1980:224). The Shah felt threatened by the independence of the bazaaris from the state, their economic power, and their close connection with the mollahs. Besides that, he personally despised the bazaar and regarded it as a sign of the backwardness of Iran society and had plans to replace it with supermarkets. In his *Answer to History*, the Shah comments, "The bazaaris are a fanatic lot, highly resistant to change because their locations afford a lucrative monopoly. I could not stop building supermarkets. I wanted a modern country. Moving against the bazaars was typical of the political and social risks I had to take in the drive to modernization" (Pahlavi 1980:156).

It is worth mentioning that the bazaar was a conservative entity that had its own norms, values, and social relations (Nima 1983:47). Ideologically, it was dependent on the mollahs for guidance. The mollahs, on the other hand, were economically dependent on the bazaaris. The bazaaris paid the religious taxes and the cost of the maintenance and management of shrines to the mollahs. Halliday notes that the bazaaris contributed more money to mollahs than they paid in taxes to the government (1979:19). The independence of the mollahs and bazaaris from the state, their traditional outlook, and their conservatism created a long-lasting alliance between them. The creation of the Rastakhiz Party, which aimed at weakening the position of bazaaris and mollahs, made the alliance between these two groups stronger. Eric Rouleau quotes bazaaris as saying that the Rastakhiz Party had turned the White Revolution into a red revolution (Abrahamian 1980:25). As a result of the constant pressure of the state on the bazaaris, they started a life-and-death struggle against the regime. Their alliance with the religious hierarchy and their financial support of the revolution broke the back of the Pahlavi monarchy.

THE SALARIED MIDDLE CLASS

The salaried middle class, totaling one million civil servants, teachers, doctors, engineers, lawyers, university professors, and students, became frustrated with the socioeconomic policies of the regime. Although the professional strata of this class (i.e., doctors, engineers, and lawyers) benefitted from the oil boom, it opposed the increasing interference of the state in their lives. The rest of the salaried middle class was suffering both economically and politically. The rising inflation rate (over 40 percent), the high cost of housing, and insufficient housing intensified their animosity toward the regime. By 1976, middle-class families found themselves paying 50 percent of their annual income for housing (Abrahamian 1978:4). According to government sources, during the 1975–1976 period alone, the average consumer price index rose 16.6 percent. The index for housing increased by 36 percent, for foodstuffs, it rose 13 percent, and for clothes and furniture 11 and 13 percent respectively (Bank Markazi 1977:8). The increasing cost of living made this class more and more frustrated with the state following the economic crisis of the mid–1970s.

THE SQUATTER MIGRANTS

Rural to urban migration is an inevitable concomitant of industrial development. Causes of rural migration can be conceptually divided into rural push (Castells 1979:45–50) and urban pull (Sovany 1964:118–20). In the case of Iran, the rural push factors included the decline of agriculture, the breakdown of the village system (boneh), and the government policies regarding the depopulation of villages. Pull factors were amenities of city life, permanent jobs, educational opportunities, and proper health care. These two factors combined resulted in the migration of more than two million peasants and khoshneshins to the cities between 1963 and 1977. The high cost of housing and the negative attitude of the city dwellers toward the villagers made the rural migrants live on the outskirts of the cities. As a result, the rural migrants had to live in shanty towns such as Halaby Abad, Yakhchi Abad, and Kapar Abad. Most of these houses lacked electricity, water, gas, and adequate drainage (Sarjehpeyma 1984:185; Shekooee 1975:12–25).

The majority of the rural migrant workers either were employed in the construction sector or held temporary jobs in the most unproductive segments of the service sector such as washing cars, selling lottery tickets, and other menial jobs (Danesh 1984:58). The rural migrants were the main victims of the White Revolution. The socioeconomic conditions in the rural areas after the land reform (i.e., mechanization of agriculture, insufficient lands, and lack of government support) had forced them to come to the cities. The living conditions, however, were even harsher in their new place of residence. As an Iranian scholar notes, the living conditions were very distressing for them, and they were always in danger of losing their jobs (Kazemy 1980:42–43).

Most of the rural migrants either were illiterate or had finished only elementary school. They were not incorporated into the cities and remained outsiders. There was no political party through which they could express their discontent with their social conditions. The only contact they had with the social life of the cities was through mosques, religious processions, and ceremonies (Hooglund 1980:5). While the rural migrants were alienated from the government and were not attracted by the underground political organizations or the National Front and the Tudeh Party, they found their natural allies among the mollahs. As Nima notes, "In the absence of the legal political organizations, the rural migrants found no alternatives to the religious ideology within urban society." (Nima 1983:48).

STUDENTS

Iranian students have long been politically active (Graham 1980:212). During the height of the activities of the National Front and the Tudeh Party, students closely cooperated with them. After the 1953 coup, students were the most active opponents of the regime. When on November 1, 1953, Vice-President Richard Nixon visited Iran, students organized a huge demonstration against U.S. foreign policy in Iran. Police opened fire on the crowds and killed three students. With that incident, November 1 (16 of Azar, Iranian calendar) became the day of students. From 1953 until the overthrow of the monarchy in 1979, Iranian students throughout the world commemorated this day with demonstrations against the regime.

In the early sixties, students cooperated with Mossadegh for the reorganization of the National Front. But when the common struggle of Dr. Mossadegh and the students failed and the conservative elements within the National Front got the upper hand, the students became disillusioned with this organization (Gorouh-e Ettehad-e Communistee 1977:15–90). After Mossadegh's death in 1967 the students completely broke away from the National Front and supported the underground political organizations. Students also helped the victims of several earthquakes and organized demonstrations against government policy that increased the price of bus tickets in 1969 (*Kar,* August 5, 1981; Nateq 1982:12). Founders of the major underground political organizations also came from the core of the active students.

After the White Revolution, the number of students and educational institutions grew rapidly. The total number of secondary schools rose from 260,000 in 1962 to 2.3 million in 1978. The number of the university students during the same time period rose from 50,000 to 154,000. These figures might be deceptive, because the statistics show that during the same period, the number of illiterate persons rose from 13 million to 15 million, and 60 percent of children failed to complete elementary school. The increasing number of students in higher education does not indicate the number of those who applied to these institutions. Of the 290,000 students who applied to the universities each year, only 60,000 were accepted. The standard of education was also very low and did not provide students with adequate technical and scientific knowledge for the rapid economic growth. As a result of the insufficient educational institutions and the backwardness of the educational system, many young people went abroad to study. The number of Iranian students abroad (mainly in the United States and Western Europe) during the 1970s was more than 100,000.

Faced with a backward educational system, political dictatorship, and the penetration of SAVAK on the campuses and opposed to the socioeconomic policies of the state, students constantly challenged the regime. As a result, they frequently went on strike or boycotted classes and exams (Graham 1980:214). The strikes and demonstrations were usually broken violently by the security forces. The leftist students organized secret groups to study, translate, and distribute works of Mao, Che Guevera, Marx, Lenin, and literature provided by the Iranian and Palestinian guerrilla organizations. The regime's reaction to these activities was quick and harsh. The students arrested for "subversive" activities were usually first sent to jail and then to military service.

The number of Iranian students abroad exceeded 100,000 during the 1970s (Keddie 1981:235). Most of these students opposed the regime.

The secular and leftist students were organized in the Confederation of the Iranian Students. The confederation was initially influenced by the National Front and the Tudeh Party. By the late 1960s, because of its conciliatory policies toward the Shah, the Tudeh Party was totally discredited and was ousted from the Confederation. The National Front was also rejected by the students abroad, since it had lost its effectiveness and no political platform or program for action. The leftist supporters of the National Front abroad were organized in the Sazmanhay-e Jebhey-e Melli Kharej-e Keshvar (the Organizations of the National Front Abroad). This organization played a crucial role in the radicalization of the confederation and in building a support base for the Mojahedin and the Fedaii organizations abroad (Gorouh-e Ettehad-e Communistee 1977:42–50).

The religious students founded the Moslem Student Association (MSA). The MSA supported both Ayatollah Khomeini and Bazargan's Freedom Movement of Iran and was conservative in outlook. Many leaders of the MSA, such as Ebrahim Yazdi, Sadegh Qotb Zadeh, Abol Hassan Bani-Sadr, and Mostafa Chamran, assumed high political positions following the overthrow of the monarchy. Besides opposing the regime, these students were engaged in an anticommunist campaign. Because of the conservatism of the MSA, some of its former members split and founded the Moslem Student Organization (MSO) in 1976. The MSO supported the Mojahedin Organization and was more radical than the MSA.

THE WORKING CLASS

The White Revolution resulted in the growth of the working class. The total number of the labor force was 10.6 million in 1977. Out of this number, about 2.5 million worked in the industrial sector. The growth of the working class, however, was not accompanied by its political power. The Labor Law of 1959 disbanded the existing labor unions and barred the workers from creating new unions. The workers were only allowed to enter the labor unions created by the state. These labor unions were created as a support base for the regime instead of dealing with the grievances of the workers against their employers. As a result, very few workers joined them. The state policy toward the workers was one of punishment and enticement. On the one hand, the state supported most of the workers' demands for higher wages; on the other, political demands of the workers (such as the right for creating independent unions) were suppressed. SAVAK branches were created in the factories. They had two functions: first, to harass the workers, and second, to make sure that the entrepreneurs were not pushing workers so hard as to cause strikes and violence.

The policy of the state, therefore, was to control both workers and entrepreneurs. The profit-sharing and share-participation programs were significant aspects of this state policy. According to the profit-sharing program, workers theoretically were entitled to up to 20 percent of the profit (the oil company and tobacco industry were excluded from profit sharing). In 1975, the Shah pushed for selling shares of the industries to the workers. The share-participation program included 99 percent of the state-owned factories and 49 percent of the private enterprises (Pahlavi 1980:92). These policies intended to increase the productivity and convince the workers that the Shah was on their side. This program, however, failed for several reasons: First, the entrepreneurs regarded it as a violation of the principle of private enterprise. Second, the workers were not allowed to inspect the profit made by the factories. Third, as Halliday notes, of 20,000 companies submitting their tax returns only 53 percent reported any profit (Halliday 1979:194).

In spite of tight control of the factories by SAVAK and the state's attempt to show itself as the guardian of the interests of the workers, workers struggled with both the management and the state for higher wages, unionization and limiting weekly work hours to 40 (the work week was and still is 48 hours). The bloodiest clash between workers and the security forces was in 1969, when the workers of the Jahan Cheet, (a textile factory near Tehran, went on strike for higher wages. The security forces opened fire on them, killing fifteen and wounding many others.

Despite the government's attempt to buy the support of the workers, the harsh conditions of life made confrontation between them inevitable. Rising inflation had made living conditions unbearable for the workers. A majority of workers (about 78 percent) did not own their houses and were living either in rented rooms or small houses (Nima 1983:49). While rents were increasing almost monthly, the salaries of the workers did not change much. The inflation rate (over 40 percent) did not correspond with the wage increase, which amounted to about 15 percent. The result was a constant worsening of living conditions for the workers. The economic recession starting in late 1975 shook the economy and made the situation worse. Many construction projects were stopped, resulting in the unemployment of about one million workers.

In response to their worsening economic condition, the workers challenged both the management and the state by slowdowns, strikes, and sabotage. These strikes were sometimes tolerated and sometimes crushed by the security forces. Despite the suppression of some of the strikes, the state was not following a policy of confrontation with the workers. The Shah was aware that he could not afford to alienate skilled workers by totally suppressing them. Another consideration was that by jailing the workers, the factories would be deprived of the skilled workers. Moreover, the workers in prison could be exposed to the "subversive" ideas of the political prisoners. As a result, on most occasions the leaders of the strikes were not persecuted.

THE MODERN BOURGEOISIE

The modern bourgeoisie was the creation of the state and depended on it for protection and subsidization (see chapters 2 and 6). The oil revenues were distributed among the entrepreneurs to create a strong capitalist class as the main support base of the regime. Through subsidization, protectionist policies, tax exemptions, and easy credits, the state guaranteed the constant growth of this class. The state, however, kept tight control of the economic policies and regulated the relations between the workers and the entrepreneurs. The Shah wanted to be regarded as the father of the nation and protector of the interests of all classes. The antiprofiteering campaign of 1975–1977, profit sharing, and share-participation programs of the government represent the view of the Shah.

Although the entrepreneurs owed their existence (as a class) to the Shah, they disliked his interference in economic activities. Ali Rezaii, an industrial magnate, once complained to the Shah: "Your Majesty determines the prices, the wages, the profit, and the custom duties. Wouldn't it be better if you run the industry yourself?" (Mojahedin-e Khalq 1979a:52).

Another industrialist, Kazim Khosrow Shahi, even threatened that government interference in the private sector might result in violence.

If in the past, government interference in the activities of the private sector used to take place only for the sake of the economic and social justice, now such interferences have assumed other aspects. . . . This results in more government interference in the limits and activities of the private sector. . . . If the relations between the private and public sectors are not matured, there is a possibility of a clash between them sometimes accompanied by violence. (*Iran Almanac and Book of Facts* [Iran Almanac] 1973: 206)

The antiprofiteering campaign and price control policy, although aimed at the bazaaris, affected some industrialists as well. The businesses of two leading industrialists, Habibollah Elghanian and Hossein Sabet, were closed down, and both were imprisoned on the charges of profiteering. These policies discouraged some of the industrialists, and they slowed down their economic activities and transferred their liquid assets abroad. *Business Week* reports that by 1975, industrialists had transferred about $2 billion abroad (November 17, 1975). This shows how fragile the alliance between the Shah and the industrialists was. When the crisis of the state intensified in 1977, the entrepreneurs withdrew their support from the Shah and flew abroad.

THE STATE

The Iranian state dominated the society and social classes. Since the overthrow of Mossadegh, the bureaucracy of the state controlled every aspect of the lives of all individuals. The Shah himself dominated the bureaucracy. According to former Tehran mayor Gholamreza Nikpay, who was executed in the revolutionary tribunals in March 1979, the Shah determined most political and economic decisions without responsibility to anyone (Nikpay 1977:23–56). This, however, did not mean that the Shah was acting without regard to the interests of the social classes. As Poulantzas and Gramsci argue, the state preserves the interests of the dominant class (Gramsci 1977:39–42; Poulantzas 1979a:40–95). In this respect, the Shah was acting as the state (*l'etat c'est mois*), hence preserving the interests of the dominant classes of Iran. In the precapitalist formation, the political economy preserved the interests of the landlords. In the late 1950s, when the precapitalist social formation had been exhausted and the society was ready to transform into a capitalist social formation, the Shah himself led this transformation.

The domination of the society by the state took a new turn after the creation of the Rastakhiz Party in 1975. Rastakhiz was to function as the ideological apparatus of the state and to organize the whole nation under the Shah's banner. The repressive apparatus of the state was tightly controlled by the Shah. The Iranian modern bourgeoisie was also a creation of the state. The oil revenues were used to finance industrialization and the creation of a modern bourgeoisie, so the destinies of the Shah and the modern bourgeoisie were tied together. So long as the Shah could exert his power in the society, the modern bourgeoisie was able to function. As soon as the Shah started losing control of the state, the bourgeoisie disintegrated and fled to Western countries where it could invest its capital safely. By 1976 the Pahlavi state had reached a dead end. Economically, it was suffering from inflation, recession, corruption, decline of the oil revenues, and low productivity (see chapter 6). The modern bourgeoisie was opposed to the domination of the economy by the state and the interference of the Shah in relations between the workers and the entrepreneurs. The modern bourgeoisie was convinced that the mission of the Shah for the creation, protection, and preservation of the capitalist state was over. The *Tehran Economist*, one of the organs of the modern bourgeoisie, suggested that it would be in the best interests of the nation if the state-owned factories were sold to the private sector and the state stayed out of economic activities (June 13, 1966). This class, therefore, struggled with the Shah over assuming the hegemony of the power bloc. The struggle of the Shah and the modern bourgeoisie to get the upper hand in the power bloc made the ruling bloc vulnerable and greatly contributed to the failure of the monarchy.

By 1976, the regime had failed economically, politically, and ideologically. In broad economic terms, the efforts of the Shah for rapid capitalist development had only created a metamorphosis of industrialization. The lack of skilled personnel, an inadequate infrastructure, and the waste of billions of dollars on sophisticated weapons and nuclear reactors had soaked most of the economic resources. According to government officials, by 1978 none of the economic projects of the Fifth Plan was completed (Homayoun 1982:21–50).

Moreover, the rising inflation rate, which widened the gap between poor and rich, plus recession and unemployment widely contributed to popular discontent (Looney 1982:5–6). Politically, by the creation of the Rastakhiz Party, closing of 70 percent of the journals, and increasing the role of SAVAK, the regime had proven that it would not tolerate any opposition. Ideologically, the regime was propagating royal values and Western culture, both of which were alien to the people. Royal values to the majority of the people meant dictatorship, corruption, and plunder. Western culture meant foreign cultural domination. As a result, the ideology of the regime was wholly rejected.

THE EXTERNAL FACTORS

In the mid–1970s human rights organizations and the Western press started a campaign against the violation of human rights in Iran and criticized the Shah for the mistreatment of the political prisoners. In January 1975, the *Sunday Times* of London published a series of articles about the mistreatment of political prisoners and the pervasiveness of SAVAK in the everyday life of ordinary citizens (*Sunday Times*, January 19, 1975). In mid–1975, Amnesty International announced that Iran had one of the worst records in violation of human rights. A year later, the International Commission of Jurists published a pamphlet about the violation of human rights in Iran. The human rights policy of President Carter (and the human rights policy was one of the slogans of the Democratic party during the 1976 presidential campaign), however, played the most significant role in changing the Shah's policy toward the opposition.

The human rights policy of President Carter was taken very seriously by both the opposition and the Shah (Keddie 1981:213; Pesaran 1985:34). For the Shah, liberalization, although undesirable, could be used as a safety valve to overcome the crisis of the state. In the early 1960s, he had resolved the crisis of the state through granting limited liberalization policies, dividing the opposition, reforming the socioeconomic system, and gaining the support of the United States. The Shah was confident that pursuing the same policies would resolve the crisis of the state once again. The result was the announcement of liberalization policies in early 1977.

This policy was immediately put into effect. Between the months of January and March 1977 more than 450 political prisoners were released from jail. In the following months the Red Cross and the International Commission of Jurists were allowed to visit Iranian prisoners. In mid–1977, the Shah allowed the Western media and lawyers to observe the trial of eleven political offenders. The Shah also promised Amnesty International and the Red Cross to improve the conditions of prisons and permit dissidents to participate in the political process. In mid–1977, the Shah ordered the Rastakhiz Party to discuss social issues openly and present constructive criticism. These policies were intended to appease the opposition and buy the support of the United States. Instead they proved catastrophic and provided favorable conditions for the opposition to organize its forces against the regime.

For the opposition, which was aware of the 1960–1963 experience and the influence of the United States on the Shah, the new development was an opportunity which could not be missed. In May 1977, fifty-three lawyers sent a letter to Nasrollah Moinian, the powerful head of the Imperial Bureau of Investigation, protesting against the constant interference of executive power in the judicial process. A month later, forty members of the Association of Iranian Writers, which had been banned since its inception in 1968, wrote an open letter to the then premier Amir Abbas Hoveyda, demanding recognition of their association and permission of the "free exchange of views in the society." On June 12, three prominent leaders of the National Front, Karim Sanjabi, Shahpur Bakhtiar, and Dariush Foruhar, wrote an open letter to the Shah in which they criticized the arbitrary use of power by him and demanded freedom of speech, press, and assembly; freedom of all political prisoners; respect for human rights; and the dissolution of the Rastakhiz Party (Green 1982:65).

Since none of the authors of the above-mentioned letter were imprisoned or harassed, many others were encouraged to join the struggle against the regime. The liberalization policies allowed the opposition to come into the open and express its grievances against the regime and challenge it with all its power. Alexis de Tocqueville argues that political liberalization following a long period of repression results in social upheavals and revolution.

It is not always by going from bad to worse that a society falls into revolution. It happens most often that a people, which has supported without complaint ... most oppressive laws, violently throws them off as soon as their weight is lightened.... Only great genius can save a prince who undertakes to relieve his subjects after a long repression. The evil, which was suffered patiently as inevitable, seems unendurable as soon as the idea of escaping from it is conceived. (Tocqueville 1955:178)

The comments of Tocqueville must be read with caution. Contrary to what he argues, liberalization policies do not result in revolutions; they simply provide the conditions for the opposition to organize itself effectively against the regime. If the economic contradictions in the society are at their heights, there is a nationwide political organization supported by the majority of the people, there is effective leadership, and the popular discontent is widespread, the liberalization policy will pave the way for revolution. In the case of Iran, the power bloc was in the process of disintegration, the state was facing a crisis of authority, and class conflict was at its peak. Based on these factors, liberalization policies helped the grievances against the state to come to the surface. In the absence of a nationwide political organization, the network of 80,000 mosques run by 180,000 mollahs played a crucial role in mobilizing the masses against the regime.

In the next few months several political organizations including the National Front, the Freedom Movement of Iran, and the Radical Movement of Iran (the latter group was founded by Rahmatollah Moghaddam Maraghei) started their political activities (*Iran Times*, February 3, 1984). Following this new development, some new groups were created to defend the rights of political prisoners and publicize the dehumanizing methods used by the security forces against the political prisoners. The Iranian Group for Protection of Human Rights founded by Bazargan and Hassan Nazih (a lawyer), The Society of Iranian Lawyers (led by Bazargan and lawyer Abdol Karim Lahiji) were the most prominent human rights groups created in 1977. Besides these human rights groups, writers and publishers started openly criticizing the regime and demanding respect for human rights and denouncement of the dictatorial measures used against the opposition and also demanding freedom of speech, assembly, and association. Among the latter groups, the Writers' Association of Iran (founded and banned in 1967) and the Group for Books and Thoughts (created by Iranian publishers) are worth mentioning.

CHANGE OF THE GOVERNMENT

The paralyzing crisis of the state made the Shah ponder the future of his throne. During the 1960–1963 period, the Shah found the solution to the crisis in sacrificing his close associates, dividing the opposition, and ensuring U.S. support. If Eqbal and some of the conservative generals were sacrificed in 1960, this time it was the prime minister, Amir

Abbas Hoveyda, several other ministers, and top government officials who were sacked to protect the Shah's position. Hoveyda was dismissed in August 1977 and replaced by the technocrat Jamshid Amouzgar. Amouzgar was minister of interior and the former secretary general of the Rastakhiz Party. As an economist, Amouzgar found the solution in dealing with the economic problems first. Ironically, these measures resulted in more discontent and mobilized the masses against the regime.

In general, Amouzgar's policy was to fight inflation, reduce government overspending, tighten monetary policies, stop construction works, establish a price control commission, pressure the bazaaris through the Chambers of Guilds, and reduce the budget of the religious institutions (Green 1982:59–60; Parsons 1984:62). The deflationary measures and cutting government overspending resulted in recession, unemployment, and more popular discontent (Stemple 1981:80–90). The group which was hit harder than the others was the construction workers, who were in the majority of rural migrants. This group "had nothing to lose but their chains" and as a result shouldered most of the burden of the sacrifices in the struggle against the monarchy.

To make the situation worse, the Amouzgar government decided to level the shanty towns of southern Tehran and evict the rural migrants from their squalid shacks. On August 23, 1977, the government sent bulldozers to destroy the shanty towns in southern Tehran. The squatters refused to leave their homes and put up stiff resistance against the police and SAVAK agents. About nineteen squatters were killed and over one hundred were wounded in this incident (Stemple 1981:84). When the news of the fighting broke out, many students rushed to the area to support the squatters. Faced with fierce resistance by the rural squatters and the students, the security forces withdrew and the plan for the destruction of the squatter areas was shelved. This incident emboldened many to resist the regime and challenge it with all their power (Massaly 1982:7).

INTENSIFICATION OF THE CRISIS

Political activities against the regime intensified when the universities reopened in September 1977 after three months of recession. Students demonstrated against closing the university libraries and lack of academic and political freedom on campuses. Many university professors supported the students' demands and went on strike to show their solidarity with them (Nateq 1982:30). Despite the concerted efforts of students and professors, their demands were not met. Instead, students were attacked by the security forces, and the universities were closed down. This event showed how shallow the liberalization policy was, and the Shah lost the last remnant of his credibility—if any still existed—with the people. As much as the Shah was losing credibility and showing signs of inconsistency in his policies, the opposition was growing stronger and more unified.

November was a crucial month for the revolution. The events of this month put the Shah on the defensive, showed the shallowness of President Carter's human rights policy (hence discrediting liberal and middle-class forces who were counting on the U.S. factor), and eventually gave an opportunity to the militant mollahs to emerge as a major political force. These developments could be categorized as follows: First, Khomeini's son Mostafa died mysteriously in Najaf (Iraq). Many blamed SAVAK for this incident. Mostafa Khomeini's death was commemorated throughout the country, and these commemorations resulted in clashes between the mourners and the police.

Second, the Shah left Iran on November 13 for his twelfth visit since 1941 to the United States. While President Carter was giving a reception for the Shah on November 15 in the White House, a group of 8,500 Iranian students demonstrated against the monarch (Albert 1980:19). The Iranian embassy in Washington had also mobilized about 1,500 "pro-Shah" demonstrators who were paid $100 for their participation. The clash between the demonstrators and counterdemonstrators made the police use tear gas to disperse the feuding parties. The wind carried the tear gas across the White House lawn, causing the eyes of the Shah and President Carter to water. President Carter's lavish praise for the Shah made many Iranians realize that they could not rely on United States goodwill to pressure the Shah to end repression in Iran. This development embarrassed the Freedom Movement and the National Front, which were counting on President Carter's pressure on the Shah to humanize his policies.

To make the situation worse, President and Mrs. Carter spent New Year's Eve with the Shah in Iran. Toasting the Shah, President Carter admired him this way: "Iran under the great leadership of the Shah is an island of stability in one of the most troubled areas of the world. This is a great tribute to you, your majesty, and to your leadership, and to the respect, admiration, and love which your people give to you." The lavish praise of President Carter for the Shah intensified the anti-American sentiments of Iranians.

Third: In early November, the Iranian Writers' Association held ten nights of poetry reading in the Iranian-German Cultural Institute. Between ten thousand and fifteen thousand people participated in each of these sessions (Nima 1983:56). These meetings were highly political, and the poets exposed the dictatorial nature of the Shah's regime and the mistreatment of the political prisoners. On the tenth night of poetry reading, Saiid Soltanpour, a poet and playwright who had been released from jail three months before, praised the armed struggle and the People's Fedaii Guerrilla Organization (Nateq 1982:32). At the end of the meeting, the participants marched to the streets chanting anti-Shah slogans. Police clashed with the students, killing several of them and wounding many others. During these clashes workers announced their support for the students and the Writers' Association (Nateq 1982:32). Following this event, students throughout the country held demonstrations to protest police brutality and the violation of human rights in Iran.

By the end of November, demonstrations and political meetings were growing rapidly throughout the country. The regime's response at this conjuncture was to continue its selective liberalization policies while trying to intimidate the opposition through the creation of covert terrorist groups. SAVAK and the Rastakhiz Party created two terrorist groups from SAVAK agents, police, and the army to harass the opposition. These two groups were called the Underground Committee of Revenge and the Resistance Corps. They attacked several political meetings and demonstrations held by the National Front, students, and the Writers' Association. The Underground Committee of Revenge and the Resistance Corps were also responsible for beating two members of the Iranian Writers' Association, Homa Nateq and Nemat Mirzazadeh, and exploding bombs in front of the houses and offices of the leaders of human rights committees and the National Front, such as Abdolkarim Lahiji, Ali Asghar Hadj Seyyed Javadi, Dariush Foruhar, Karim Sanjabi, and Hedaytollah Matin Daftari (Fischer 1980:193; Nima 1983:61).

EMERGENCE OF THE RELIGIOUS OPPOSITION

The death of Mostafa Khomeini was a turning point in the Iranian revolution. People in general held the Shah responsible for his death. This incident brought the name of Khomeini to the fore once again. During the commemoration people started chanting anti-Shah and pro-Khomeini slogans. The Shah, afraid of Ayatollah Khomeini's charisma, tried to defuse the situation by preventing commemoration of the fortieth day of Mostafa Khomeini's death. This was followed by the publication of an anti-Khomeini article in the semi-official newspaper *Ettella'at*. According to the then Minister of Information, Dariush Homayoun, this article was written by the Shah. It attacked Khomeini as a reactionary mollah who was trying to obstruct the Shah's reforms. The consequence of the publication of this article was devastating. The bazaar closed in protest, and four thousand Talabehs in Qom demonstrated against the regime (see chapter 3). This demonstration was violently broken by police. As a result of the police attack, seventy Talabehs were killed and some four hundred were injured.

Appalled by this incident, Ayatollah Shariatmadary announced that it was the religious duty of people to participate in the commemoration of the fallen Talabehs. By pronouncing the commemoration of the dead a religious duty, Shariatmadary put an Islamic stamp on the revolution. After the Qom incident, the movement took a religious form. Consequently, Islam became the ideology of the revolution and Khomeini its most prominent leader. In the next few months, the secular opposition lost ground to the Shiite hierarchy, and all social classes accepted the hegemony of Khomeini.

After the Qom incident, each death was commemorated throughout the country with religious symbolism and Shi'a-style militancy against the oppression (Zolm). The traditional third, seventh, and fortieth commemoration of the dead played a crucial role for organizing the masses against the regime (see chapter 3). The fortieth commemoration of the fallen Talabehs was held in twelve major cities. These commemorations, however, took the form of a popular uprising in Tabriz (capital of Azerbaijan). The commemoration of Tabriz was held in more than sixty cities. The mourners in Tehran, Ahwaz, Isfahan, and Shiraz attacked government offices, the Rastakhiz headquarters, liquor stores, and movie theaters that were showing explicit sex films.

A question must be raised about the religious context of the revolution and the popularity of Ayatollah Khomeini, Why did the mollahs, who did not have a formal political organization, monopolize the leadership of the revolution? The next question is, Why was Khomeini able to dominate the movement and organize people under his banner? Several factors led to this development. First, a long period of political repression had resulted in the destruction of the political organizations. As a result, people were deprived of political education. Those who constituted the motor of the revolution were rural migrants and the urban poor. These groups were highly religious and could easily identify themselves with the populist slogans of Islam about equality and justice.

Second, in the absence of strong nationwide political organizations, the hierarchy of Shi'a mollahs was able to mobilize the masses against the regime (Parsons 1984:70–72; Zabih 1982:24). In this respect, the religious institutions, collectively known as Haya'at, functioned as the party, mollahs as its cadres, and the masses as disciplined party members. Moreover, Shiism, with its emphasis on martyrdom and resistance against oppression and tyranny (Zolm), provided the ideological basis for the revolution. It was very easy for people to understand and follow the antiregime slogans in familiar Islamic terms (Keddie 1981:23), hence the effectiveness of the Islamic ideology for the mobilization of the masses against the regime.

Third, religious ceremonies such as Rowz-e Khani, Noh-e Khani, Seene-e Zani, and Zanjir Zani provided conditions for the organization of the masses with limited effort (see chapter 3). The mollahs and other religious cadres had learned how to mobilize masses through leading prayers and groups of Seen-e Zans and Noh-e Khans. The only difference was that during the revolution, they were asking people to repeat anti-Shah rather anti-Yazid slogans.

Fourth, the monopolization of the leadership by Ayatollah Khomeini is worth considering. The question is, What happened in 1978 and 1979 to make Khomeini the sole leader of the movement? To start with, Khomeini had gained legitimacy as an opponent of the Shah through his uncompromising position toward him. This, however, did not make him leader of the revolution, especially if we consider that until December 1978, the antiregime strikes and demonstrations were organized by the middle class, bazaaris, intellectuals, and students (Mirzazadeh 1983). The movement at this point lacked any central leadership. Eqbal Ahmad and Homa Nateq note that the Shah's direct attack of Ayatollah Khomeini made him the de facto leader of the revolution (*Iranshahr*, April 22, 1983; Nateq 1983:12).

Fifth, in class terms, the question is, Why did the traditional petty bourgeoisie assume the leadership of the revolution? The answer lies in the fact that the bourgeoisie and the working class were not self-conscious and did not have their own political organizations. The Rastakhiz Party was a multiclass party that was imposed on society from the top and had no mass base. The National Front and the Freedom Movement, which until the early 1960s represented the interests of the bourgeoisie of the bazaar and the national bourgeoisie, had ceased operating since 1963 and as a result had lost contacts with their supporters. The Tudeh Party and small Marxist groups that emerged in the 1960s and 1970s had little connections (if any) with the workers. The traditional petty bourgeoisie, on the contrary, was both class conscious and organized. The political organization of the traditional petty bourgeoisie was the network of the 80,000 mosques and 180,000 mollahs. Its ideology was Islam and its leader was Khomeini.

As a result, when the paralyzing crisis of the state and the crisis of hegemony started in 1976 and 1977, this class organized itself effectively and quickly. The bourgeoisie of the bazaar was the first class to accept the hegemony of the traditional petty bourgeoisie (represented by the militant mollahs). Later, the rural migrants, urban poor, and construction workers joined the coalition. Eventually, the middle class, intellectuals, and the industrial working class accepted the leadership of Khomeini. Thus, the weakness of the Iranian bourgeoisie, the pervasiveness of the petty bourgeoisie, and political repression took a heavy toll. The lack of political education was so great that all of the social classes saw their ideals in an Islamic government. Both the workers and the bourgeoisie of the bazaar thought that Ayatollah Khomeini had no intention of running the government. The oil workers of Abadan Refinery were quoted as saying that Khomeini would take over the power from the Shah and would hand it to them.

Lastly, the hegemony of Ayatollah Khomeini can be explained in relation to the social conditions of Iran. That is, political repression had taken such a heavy toll in the political organizations that the masses looked for a superman, a hero, a "great man." The following passage from Gramsci's *Prison Notebooks* shows why Ayatollah Khomeini was able to attract the broad masses to his cause.

At a certain point in their historical lives, social classes become detached from their traditional parties. In other words, the traditional parties . . . are no longer recognized by their classes. . . . When such crises occur, the immediate situation becomes delicate and dangerous because the field is open for violent solutions, for the activity of unknown forces represented by charismatic men of destiny. (Gramsci 1971:210)

TURNING POINT

The movement was growing stronger every day. By the summer of 1978 all social classes except the modern bourgeoisie and groups had joined the struggle against the monarchy. The crisis of state was at its peak and the regime had lost its legitimacy. The ruling bloc was also in total disarray and was suffering from internal friction. The situation had become so critical that some members of the ruling bloc started criticizing the Shah for mishandling the crisis. Some Majlis deputies such as Ahmad Bany Ahmad and Rahmatollah Moghaddam Maraghei left the Rastakhiz Party in protest. The vacillation of the Shah between repression and liberalization also disheartened the power bloc. The army generals had apparently demanded that the Shah either send the soldiers back to the barracks or allow them to "clear" the streets of demonstrators. Both requests were rejected by the Shah (Sullivan 1981:212; Homayoun 1982:67). Despite this, the situation was not totally out of hand. The opposition was still calling for the implementation of the 1906 Constitution, the demonstrations were fairly peaceful, and there was no call for the overthrow of the monarchy. Two incidents in late summer changed the situation and made the demonstrators call for the overthrow of the monarchy. First, there was the so-called Rex Cinema, and second, the Black Friday incident.

On August 19, 1978, the Rex Cinema in the oil city of Abadan was set on fire. As a result of this incident more than four hundred people were burned alive. The government blamed the "fanatics" (i.e. the religious opposition) for the arson, but Ayatollah Shariatmadary strongly rejected the claim (*Newsweek*, September 4, 1978). The timing of the fire (during the day when people were inside), the location of the movie theater (in a poor neighborhood), and the content of the movie (an antigovernment film called *Deers*) made many people believe that it was the work of SAVAK. Another factor that reinforced this belief was the Shah's speech the night before the incident, in which he had reiterated: "We promise the Great Civilization and they (the opposition) promise great terror." Regardless of the truth of the matter, this incident made the opposition more determined in the struggle against the monarchy. Following the Rex Cinema arson, slogans such as "We Will Burn the Shah Alive" were heard for the first time (Nima 1983:65). A week later, Amouzgar was dismissed and replaced by Ja'afar Sharif Emami.

Second, there was the Jaleh Square massacre known as Black Friday. On September 4 and 7, demonstrations were held in several cities demanding an immediate investigation by the government regarding the Rex Cinema incident. The government's only reaction was the imposition of martial law in Tehran and eleven other cities. On Friday, September 8, about 5,000 people without encouragement from mollahs or any other political organization disregarded the martial law and gathered in Jaleh Square, where they chanted Death to the Shah slogans. A few minutes later the military governor of Tehran, General Gholam Ali Oveisi (the man responsible for the June 1963 massacre) sent soldiers to disperse the demonstrators. When the demonstrators refused to go away, the soldiers opened fire on them. According to government sources about three hundred people were killed. The opposition claimed, however, that the number of the dead was around three thousand (Shivers 1980:71). This incident further increased the militancy of the opposition and radicalized the movement. Slogans for the overthrow of the monarchy became more frequent, and even former Prime Minister Ali Amini suggested that the Shah must resign.

INTENSIFICATION OF THE CRISIS

Sharif Emami, who had served as prime minister in 1960, took the job again. His religious background and his family ties with the mollahs were expected to appease the mollahs. Sharif Emami called his cabinet the Government of the National Reconciliation and tried to defuse the situation by granting freedom of speech, press, and assembly; abolishing the Rastakhiz Party, changing the Imperial calendar back to the Hejira one; and closing the casinos and liquor stores (Irfani 1983:188). Sharif Emami, however, was a poor choice for the job. As the Shah's last prime minister, Shahpur Bakhtiar, notes, Emami was implicated in court corruption, and as the chairman of the Pahlavi Foundation was in charge of running the casinos (*Iran Times*, January 22, 1982).

Besides that, the revolution had not started simply to close down the casinos. Rather, it was intended to bring about radical social changes in society. As a result, the government's concessions did not satisfy the opposition. On September 7, more than 500,000 people demonstrated in Tehran demanding release of the political prisoners, the return of Khomeini to Iran, and the abolition of the monarchy. This demonstration frightened the Shah to such an extent that he ordered the imposition of martial law in twelve major cities, including Tehran. It was the first day of martial law that the Black Friday massacre occurred.

Black Friday was the turning point in the Iranian revolution. This incident made any compromise with the government impossible and alienated the moderate opposition. The Committee for the Defense of Democratic Rights and the Lawyers' Association called for the imposition of martial law illegal. Certain elements within the ruling bloc started criticizing the government for resorting to such measures against unarmed civilians. The situation was so desperate that former Prime Minister Ali Amini, who was now trying to create a power base of his own, called for the Shah's resignation (Abrahamian 1982:517). In desperation and incapable of demoralizing the opposition, the government imposed censorship on the mass media once again. The government also started searching for the hideouts of the secular opposition leaders such as Sanjabi, Matin Daftari, Foruhar, and Bazargan.

Following Black Friday, workers and government employees started six-month strikes against the government. These strikes, which were the longest and the most effective ones in history, eventually brought down the Pahlavi regime. On September 8, seven hundred workers in the Tehran oil refinery went on strike for higher wages as well as for the release of political prisoners. On September 11, oil workers in Abadan, Isfahan, Tabriz, and Shiraz also went on strike. On September 12, the workers and employees of two leading Iranian newspapers, *Keyhan* and *Ettella'at*, followed suit in order to protest the Black Friday massacre and the imposition of martial law and censorship. Within two weeks strikes spread throughout the country. Workers and employees in both public and private sectors went on strike for higher pay, an end to martial law, the release of political prisoners, and the return of Khomeini. Faced with mounting opposition and failing to divide or discourage the demonstrators and strikers, the Shah started making more concessions to the opposition. During October and November, one thousand political prisoners were released and the striking workers were given a 25 percent raise. At the request of Ayatollah Shariatmadary, Sharif Emami extended the concessions by announcing that all of the political exiles, including Khomeini, were allowed to return to Iran (Madany 1981:1234). This gesture failed to attract anyone and emboldened the opposition further. In response to this new development, Khomeini announced that he would go back to Iran only after the Shah had left the country.

THE MILITARY GOVERNMENT

The Shah's failure to divide the movement made him decide to intimidate the opposition while making concessions. This policy, which reflected the Shah's inconsistency and vacillation, was detrimental to the morale of the power bloc and especially to the army. On November 6, he dismissed the Sharif Emami government and replaced it with a military government under the chief of staff, General Gholam Reza Azhari. Even in choosing a military government, the Shah showed signs of vacillation and indecisiveness. It was not clear why the Shah did not choose more hawkish military commanders such as General Manouchehr Khowsrowdad (commander of the Air Force), General Hossein Rabii (commander of the paratroopers), or General Gholam Ali Oveisi (the man responsible for the June 1963 and September 1978 massacres) for this job. These generals had apparently told the Shah to give them permission to "level Tehran."

The answer lies in the fact that, first, the Shah wanted to mend fences with the opposition, and second, he did not want an ambitious and strong general in power. He chose instead the old, moderate, and timid Azhari to do the job. In a dramatic speech delivered on November 6, he announced that he had chosen a military government to restore law and order and to protect the interests of the majority of the people. He also admitted the "errors" committed in the past and promised to correct them and fight against injustice and corruption.

I commit myself to make up for past mistakes, to fight corruption and injustice and for the formation of a national government to carry out free elections.... Your revolutionary message has been heard. I am aware of everything that you have given your lives for. (*Newsweek*, November 20, 1978)

This speech further showed the inconsistency of the Shah both in repression and liberalization. This move, which was intended to appease the opposition, failed but had a negative effect on the power bloc. A great number of the industrialists, high-ranking government officials, and some army generals left the country following the Shah's speech. A report published by the striking employees of the Central Bank of Iran shows that the power bloc transferred more than $2 billion abroad between the months of November and December (Madany 1981:345).

While the Shah was resorting to contradictory policies and constantly vacillating, Ayatollah Khomeini was gradually emerging as the undisputed leader of the movement. In order to ward off the danger of Khomeini's popularity, the Shah decided to remove him from Iraq. One month before the imposition of a military government, the Shah requested the Iraqi president, Saddam Hossein, to expel Khomeini from Iraq. On October 7, Khomeini was asked by Iraqi authorities to leave Iraq. After an unsuccessful attempt to go to Kuwait, Khomeini flew to Paris, where he was welcomed by two of his disciples, Abol Hassan Bani-Sadr and Sadegh Qotb Zadeh. Later, Ebrahim Yazdi, who was residing in the United States, joined Khomeini. These three men created astonishing public relations for him. Instead of living in the remote and gloomy city of Najaf, Khomeini was now in Paris, where he had easy access to international media. From his residence in Neuphle-le Chateau outside Paris, he sent messages to Iran asking the people to continue their struggle against the Shah until the overthrow of the monarchy.

Upon assuming his post, Azhari warned the demonstrators that he would restore "law" and "order" at any price (*Newsweek*, November 20, 1978). On Azhari's orders, on several occasions soldiers opened fire at demonstrators. The army was also sent to the oil city of Abadan to force the workers to go back to work. The workers went back to work only after 30 of them were killed, 100 wounded and between 80 and 160 of them arrested. Although the workers were present at their workplaces, they refused to work. As a result of this strike, oil production went down from 6 billion barrels a day to 750,000, paralyzing the economy.

Azhari also followed a policy of campaigning against corruption in order to appease the opposition. Investigation into the corruption of top government officials started on November 8. The Pahlavi family, however, was excluded from these investigations. The first victim of this policy was former premier Hoveyda. Later, Nassiri (former chief of SAVAK), Dariush Homayoun (former minister of information), and Abdol Azim Valian (former governor of Khorasan) were arrested. The warrant was sent to sixty former government officials, but thirty of them managed to leave the country (Stemple 1981:133).

In early November, Karim Sanjabi, the prominent National Front leader, flew to Paris to make an alliance with Khomeini. The two men signed an agreement according to which they pronounced the monarchy illegitimate and called for the creation of a national government. Mehdy Bazargan, leader of the Freedom Movement of Iran, had already signed the same agreement with Khomeini in late October. On November 11, two National Front leaders, Karim Sanjabi and Dariush Foruhar, were arrested. The bazaar closed for two weeks to protest this measure. By November 25, demonstrations and strikes resumed throughout the country. On November 26, the employees of Central Bank circulated names of those who had withdrawn large sums of money from their accounts. Among these people many top government officials were implicated. On November 27, 1978, the oil workers started a wildcat strike that crumbled the economy. The holy month of Moharram fell on December 2. Moharram provided the best opportunity for the militant mollahs to organize the masses against the regime. The Yazid-Hossein analogy was used repeatedly to expose the nature of the Shah's regime. The Yazid-Hossein analogy, the Noh-e Khani, the Seen-e Zani, and the Zanjir Zani provided conditions for the speedy mobilization of the people (see chapter 3). The oil workers also started the above-mentioned wildcat strike against the regime, which brought the government to its knees. In December, the employees of radio and television stations, and newspapers went on strike once again. Azhari threatened that the government would not pay the salary of the striking workers. The strike funds set up by the bazaaris were the best guarantee that the strikers would not suffer economically.

The strikes paralyzed the government. Street clashes between demonstrators and soldiers became frequent. Gradually some soldiers deserted the military and joined the revolutionaries. On December 17, three soldiers in Levizan garrison opened fire at their commanders and killed several high-ranking generals. Since the antiregime slogans were directed against the Shah, some factions of the ruling bloc started pushing the Shah to resign or leave the country (Fischer 1981:206).

By the middle of the month the military regime had proven itself ineffective. Azhari had a heart attack and could not run the government. In desperation, the Shah invited the National Front leaders such as Karim Sanjabi and Gholam Hossein Seddighi to assume the premiership. They, however, did not reach an agreement. Eventually Shahpur Bakhtiar, another National Front leader, was consulted for the job. Without conferring with the National Front, Bakhtiar accepted the offer—and was expelled from the Front immediately.

Bakhtiar inherited a government that had ceased functioning and an army that was paralyzed by mutiny and lack of discipline. The army was unwilling to cooperate with him, the opposition mistrusted him for attempting to salvage the monarchy, and his old colleagues within the National Front regarded him as a traitor (Madany 1982:187). Even the U.S. ambassador to Iran, William Sullivan, doubted the effectiveness of Bakhtiar, whom he ridiculed as "Don Quixote," and suggested to the White House that the United States negotiate with Khomeini about the future of Iran (Sullivan 1980:176).

When Bakhtiar, in an attempt to bring the moderate opposition to his side, announced the majority of religious leaders were on his side, several moderate mojtaheds, such as Ayatollah Shariatmadary, Ayatollah Golpaigani, and Ayatollah Hassan Qomi, denounced this claim and called his government illegitimate (*Ettella'at*, January 19, 1979). Bakhtiar's last attempt to save his government was organizing the bourgeoisie, the army, and the royalists to support the Constitution. A demonstration organized by these groups attracted about 100,000 in Tehran. This, however, was the last show of force by the old regime.

On February 1, Khomeini arrived in Tehran and received a huge and emotional welcome. On the same day, he delivered a speech in the Behesht-e Zahra cemetery in which he asked the people to oppose Bakhtiar's regime with all their power. Four days later, he announced the establishment of the Provisional Revolutionary Council (PRG) with Bazargan as its prime minister. Bazargan tried to convince Bakhtiar to resign and join the revolution. Bakhtiar, however, rejected this offer by arguing that he had assumed the duty of protecting the Constitution and such action would mean the betrayal of his duties.

THE ROLE OF THE UNITED STATES

The United States until mid-January 1978 consistently supported the Shah. During the Shah's visit to Washington, D.C. in November 1977 and President Carter's visit to Iran in January 1978, President Carter supported the Shah very strongly. Even after Black Friday and the establishment of the military government, the White House expressed total support for the Shah. By December 1978, U.S. policy had changed somehow. That is, some American policymakers started thinking again about the long-term interests of the United States in Iran. On the one hand, George Ball and William Sullivan believed that the monarchy could not be saved and that long-term U.S. interests should precede any other consideration; hence, they suggested close cooperation with the religious leaders for a peaceful transition to the moderate opposition. Brzezinsky, on the other hand, favored saving the monarchy regardless of its consequences (Milani 1988:217). In his informative article about the role of the United States in this period, William Sullivan notes that Brzezinsky was behind all of the hawkish recommendations for Iran. He even suggested that the United States encourage the Shah to use the military against the opposition in order to save the monarchy (1980:179).

General Robert Huyser, commander of NATO forces in Europe, was sent to Iran in mid-January to keep the army together and encourage it to support Bakhtiar's government. Although Sullivan personally disagreed with the latest White House move, he went along with it and encouraged the Freedom Movement and the National Front to cooperate with him. Huyser arranged some meetings between the military generals and members of the PRG for possible cooperation between the two. One of the major consequences of Huyser's mission was that the military decided to remain neutral in the dispute between the PRG and the Bakhtiar government, a factor which facilitated a speedy erosion of the old regime (Hussain 1985:130).

THE OVERTHROW OF THE MONARCHY

The mutiny within the army had become alarming. Many of the soldiers and junior officers were sympathetic to the revolutionaries. Even some high-ranking military officers had started negotiating with the mollahs about the future of the country. By mid-January, the Air Force cadets (Homafars) had joined the revolution. On February 5, they marched in front of Khomeini's residence in order to show their allegiance to the movement. This new development frightened the military commanders. In order to reverse the situation, the Special Forces, which were the most disciplined and loyal division of the armed forces, decided to strike back at the Homafars.

On February 11, while the Homafars were watching the film of Khomeini's return to Iran, the Special Forces attacked them. Some of the Homafars were able to escape and ask for help. Guerrilla forces of the Mojahedin and Fedaii organizations along with many people who were armed attacked the Special Forces and pushed them back. The Air Force personnel opened the arsenal to the people. The armed masses attacked all of the military garrisons. In an effort to keep the military apparatus intact, the commanders of the armed forces announced the neutrality of the military. The fighting, however, continued for three days and ended only after all of the military garrisons were disarmed. This was the end of the monarchy. For the Shah, who had no support base but the army, it was the end of his dreams.

8 Toward the Creation of a Theocracy

The popular movement of 1977–1979 was a political revolution which resulted in the overthrow of the Shah's dictatorship. The class structure of the society remained intact and the mass upheaval of 1977–1979 failed to develop into a social revolution. The Iranian revolution ended the supremacy of the alliance of the comprador-bureaucratic bourgeoisie. A new power bloc emerged that was composed of the bourgeoisie of the bazaar, remnants of the national bourgeoisie (liberal bourgeoisie), and the traditional petty bourgeoisie (Paknejad 1985:110–115). Within two years, the petty bourgeoisie was able to overpower the liberals and provide the conditions for the creation of a theocracy in Iran.

After the overthrow of the monarchy, the Islamic Revolutionary Council (IRC) and the Provisional Revolutionary Government (PRG) replaced the royal apparatus. The IRC was a fifteen-member body dominated by fundamentalist mollahs (i.e., proponents of the creation of theocracy). The names of its members were kept secret for several months. Among the clerical members of the council Ayatollah Mohammad Hossein Beheshti, Ayatollah Mahmud Taleghany, and Ayatollah Morteza Mottahari are worth mentioning. The most prominent nonmollah members of the council were Mehdy Bazargan, Abol Hassan Bani-Sadr, and Sadegh Qotbzadeh. The council therefore was composed of liberal Islamic personalities and fundamentalist mollahs. The only nonfundamentalist mollah within the Revolutionary Council was Ayatollah Mahmud Taleghany, who had ties with the leftist forces and liberals.

The Provisional Government was dominated by the secular and religous liberals. Prime Minister Mehdy Bazargan was the leader of the Freedom Movement of Iran. His close associates in the Freedom Movement occupied several ministerial positions. Ibrahim Yazdee and Abbas Amir Entezam were vice-premiers; Nasser Minachian, minister of Islamic guidance; and Ali Akbar Moinfar, minister of oil. From the National Front, Karim Sanjabee and Dariush Foruhar were given the ministries of foreign affairs and labor, respectively. Assadollah Mobasheri, a judge and a close associate of the National Front, became the minister of justice.

POLITICAL PARTIES AND ORGANIZATIONS

The overthrow of the monarchy provided the conditions for the emergence and growth of political parties. The old and new social classes created or reorganized their political parties in order to influence the transformation of the state. The legal political parties of the post–White Revolution were excluded from political participation, and their leaders fled abroad to escape persecution. These parties represented the comprador-bourgeoisie, and supported the monarchy. As a result, the political parties of the postrevolution period represented all social classes except the comprador-bourgeoisie. The legal political parties after the February uprising represented the traditional and national bourgeoisie, the petty bourgeoisie, and the working class.

These political parties can be categorized into fundamentalist Islamic, liberal, and radical. Fundamentalist Islamic parties were those which aimed to create an Islamic regime based on the *Velayat-e Faghih* (of Ayatollah Khomeini). Three political organizations fell within this category: the Islamic Republican Party, Sazman-e Mojahedin-e Enghelab-e Islami, and the Fedayan-e Islam.

One week after the overthrow of the monarchy, the Islamic Republican Party (IRP), or Hezb-e Jomhoury-e Islami, was created. The IRP came into being as the result of the outgrowth of the Society of the Militant Mollahs founded by Ayatollah Mohammad Hossein Beheshti in 1976. The Society of Militant Mollahs was composed of pro-Khomeini mojtaheds and Talabehs. Five junior mojtaheds, Hojjatol Islam Javd Bahonar, Ayatollah Hossein Beheshti, Hojjatol Islam Ali Khamenei, Ayatollah Ali Akbar Moussavi Ardebily, and Hojjatol Islam Ali Akbar Hashemi Rafsanjani, founded the IRP. The Islamic Republican Party, as a result, had the support of the pro-Khomeini mollahs and did not have much difficulty gaining control of the mosques and other religious institutions.

The IRP rapidly reorganized and unified the Islamic Associations (Anjomanhay-e Islami) under its banner (Mansouri 1985:216). The Islamic Associations were widespread throughout the country and had branches in almost all of the factories, workplaces, and educational institutions. The mosques also fell under the supporters of the IRP. Moreover, Ayatollah Khomeini chose the Friday prayer leaders (Imam Jomeh) mainly from among IRP members and supporters, hence giving his tacit approval to the IRP. Friday prayers are a combination of regular prayers and speeches (Khotbeh) about the recent development of the Islamic community given by Friday prayer leaders in each city.

After the revolution, the Fedayan-e Islam Group was reorganized by Hojjatol Islam Shajouni and Abd-e Khodaii. Its members were from the petty bourgeoisie of the bazaar and Talabehs. The third viable fundamentalist Islamic political organization was the Sazman-e Mojahein-e Enghelab-e Islami, or Organization of the Crusaders of the Islamic Revolution. Its leader, Behzad Nabavi, was a former Marxist who became a fundamentalist moslem while in prison in the 1970s.

Liberal forces composed of the National Front, the Freedom Movement of Iran, and the Radical Movement of Iran represented the interests of the middle class and the remnants of the national bourgeoisie. The National Front was in favor of a secular constitution and the protection of free enterprise. The National Front was weakened and discredited to some extent because of the defection of Bakhtiar and his supporters during the revolution. Although the National Front had three ministers in Bazargan's cabinet, it was in no position to influence the trend of events. As a result of this, the leader of the National Front, Karim Sanjabee, resigned as minister of foreign affairs.

The Freedom Movement, however, was in a better position, but eventually lost ground to the fundamentalist mollahs. The religious background of the leaders of this organization, their close association with Ayatollah Khomeini and his aides such as Ayatollah Mottahari and Hojjatol Islam Rafsanjani, had made this group less vulnerable than the National Front.

Moghaddam Maraghei and some pro-Shariatmadary mojtaheds such as Hojjatol Islam Sadr Balaghi and Hojjatol Islam Reza Golsorkhi founded the Moslem People's Republican Party (MPRP) in April 1979. The party was created in order to counterbalance the Islamic Republican Party. The MPRP called for strengthened private enterprise and a secular constitution. The main base of support of the MPRP was in Azerbaijan, where the majority of the followers of Shariatmadary lived (Rouhani 1983:175).

The radical political organizations were the political parties that favored a social revolution and represented the interests of the working class (or at least claimed to do so). These political organizations were divided into secular and Islamic groups. Major secular radical organizations included the Tudeh Party, the Fedaii Organization, the Peykar Organization, the Democratic Party of Kurdistan, and the Organization of Komeleh. There were also several small Marxist organizations that actively participated in the political process. Among these groups were Ettehad-e Chap (the Unity of Left), Ettehadieh-e Komunistha (the Association of Communists), Hezb-e Ranjbaran (the Toilers Party), Sazman-e Rah-e Kargar (the Organization of the Workers Path), and Sazman-e Vahdat-e Komunistee (the Organization of the Communist Unity). The radical Islamic groups were composed of the Mojahedin-e Khalq Organization, the Movement of the Militant Moslems (Jonbesh-e Mosalmanan-e Mobarez), the Islamic Organization of Shora (Sazman-e Islami-e Shora), the Organization of the Immigrants of the Iranian People (Sazman-e Mohajerin-e Khalq Iran), and the Revolutionary Movement of the Moslem People of Iran (JAMA).

The Tudeh Party was discredited for its conciliatory policies toward the Shah's regime and its dependence on the Soviet Union. As a result, it did not have much appeal for the younger generation, and its main base of support was among the old party members. The policy of the Tudeh Party following the revolution was total support for Ayatollah Khomeini and the Islamic Republican Party. The secretary general of the Tudeh Party, Nourod-Din Kianouri, was the grandson of the protheocracy Sheikh Fazlollah Noori (see chapter 3). Because of the support of Kianouri for the Islamic government, many ridiculed him by calling him Ayatollah Kianouri. The Tudeh Party requested that the other radical organizations support the regime and branded the opposition political parties agents of imperialism. For, example, the Democratic Party of Kurdistan and the Komeleh, which were leading the autonomy movement, were accused of being lackeys of U.S. imperialism. The party also urged the workers not to go on strikes because it would only benefit the United States. In general, the Tudeh Party called for the nationalization of the major industries, banks, and foreign trade (Atighpour 1979:20–54). It also suggested that the victory of the revolution was possible only through establishing close ties with the Soviet bloc and severing ties with the United States.

The Fedaii Organization, contrary to the Tudeh Party, was very popular among youth and industrial workers. Within two months after the overthrow of the monarchy, Fedaiis were able to mobilize as many as 200,000 people for their demonstrations. Despite its popularity, the organization was not ideologically united and was following contradictory policies. The failure of guerrilla tactics to mobilize the masses against the Shah's regime and the nature of the new power bloc were dividing issues among the Fedaii cadres (Moghadam 1988:31). The majority of the members rejected the armed struggle, criticized their former tactics as "militaristic," and argued that they should have paid more attention to working among the masses. They also lent critical support to the new regime, which they called the "government of national bourgeoisie."

A small minority of Fedaii members led by two of the original members of the Fedaii Organization, Ashraf Dehghani and Mohammad Hormati

Pour, argued that the armed struggle was the correct tactic for organizing workers and seizing the state power. This group emphasized that despite the overthrow of the monarchy, the regime represented the interests of the comprador-bourgeoisie and should be overthrown through armed struggle. The Dehghani-Hormati group split from the Fedaii Guerrilla Organization in July 1979.

The Fedaii Organization was opposed to the composition of the Islamic Revolutionary Council and called for the creation of a revolutionary council composed of representatives of the workers, peasants, and soldiers. The Fedaiis actively participated in the creation of peasant councils in the Torkoman Sahra (in northern Iran) and clashed with the Pasdaran, who were dispatched by the government to dismantle these councils (Afshar 1985a:75). By the end of the spring, the Fedaii Organization had to go underground. Its overt organizations, such as Vanguard Students (Danehjouyan-e Peeshgam) and the Progressive Workers (Kargaran-e Peeshrow), linked the organization to the people.

The Organization of Peykar (Struggle) for the Liberation of the Working Class, popularly known as Peykar, was a Maoist offshoot of the Mojahedin-e Khalq Organization. It was more militant than the Fedaii Organization. Peykar regrded the whole power bloc as reactionary and called for the unity of all radical forces against the regime and the creation of a socialist state in Iran.

A new radical organization, the Democratic National Front, was created in April 1979. This organization was founded by Hedayatollah Matin Daftari (Mossadegh's grandson and a prominent civil rights activist), Shokrollah Paknejad (a prominent Marxist and the founder of the Palestine Group in 1969), Nasser Pakdaman (a leftist economist), and Dr. Manouchehr Hezarkhanee (a leftist physician and an essayist). Because of its emphasis on cooperation between radical and liberal forces, some of the leftist organizations branded the Democratic National Front a liberal political organization, a claim which was strongly denied by the leadership of this organization (Matin Daftary 1983; Paknejad 1985:12). The aim of the Democratic National Front was to create unity among the democratic and leftist forces against the Islamic regime (Matin Daftari 1983).

In Kurdistan there were two mass-based radical organizations. The Democratic Party of Kurdistan (KDP), which was disbanded after 1946, emerged during the revolution again. The KDP was a pro-Soviet party that called for the autonomy of Kurdistan. Its main slogan was Autonomy for Kurdistan and Democracy for Iran (Qasemlou 1980:4–5). The Komeleh Organization was founded by Kurdish and non-Kurdish intellectuals and workers in the 1970s. It was a Maoist group and had close ties with the Peykar Organization. Unlike the KDP, the aim of the

Komeleh was not confined to seeking autonomy for Kurdistan. It was also struggling for the creation of a socialist state in Iran (Alizadeh 1983:6).

The Mojahedin-e Khalq was reorganized a few weeks before the overthrow of the monarchy. Its radicalism, its armed struggle against the Shah's regime, and its new interpretation of Islam attracted many young university students and other intellectuals. The organization also had great appeal among the workers and was able to organize the workers' councils in some factories. It also demanded the reorganization of the army, nationalization of the major factories, and distribution of land among peasants.

The fundamentalist Islamic groups staunchly opposed Mojahedin as heretics and called them hypocrites (Monafegh). Monafegh in Qoran refers to those groups who pretend to be Moslem but in fact intend to divide the Islamic community. Mojahedin in turn referred to these groups as reactionary. Mojahedin kept the main body of the organization underground but created overt organizations through which they established contacts with the people. Among these groups were the Youth Organization of Mojahed, the Moslem Student Societies, and the National Movement of Mojahedin. Mojahedin's official organ, *Mojahed*, appeared in August 1979. The circulation of the paper by 1980 was about 500,000 (Irfani 1983:124).

The other radical Islamic groups, the Movement of the Militant Moslems, JAMA, the Islamic Organization of Councils, and the Organization of the Immigrants of the People, closely cooperated with Mojahedin. They all called for the creation of a government based on councils, the reorganization of the armed forces, and socialization of the means of production. Among these groups, the Movement of Militant Moslems soon started taking a pro-Khomeini stance and argued that the political philosophy of Ayatollah Khomeini was anti-imperialist and revolutionary. Through its weekly journal, *Ommat* (The Islamic Community), the Movement of the Militant Moslems discussed these principles as the line of Imam (Khomeini). This new policy of the Movement of the Militant Moslems caused friction among the radical Islamic groups. In late 1979, it broke with Mojahedin and the other radical Islamic groups and joined the fundamentalist parties.

THE STATE

The overthrow of the monarchy did not result in the total destruction of the machinery of the state. The structure of the army, police, and the bureaucracy remained mostly intact. Despite this the fear of a military coup made the fundamentalist mollahs start a massive purge of the army. The Islamic Revolutionary Council and the Provisional Government were also created by Ayatollah Khomeini to replace the royal apparatus.

Most of the ministerial jobs were occupied by members of the Freedom Movement. The National Front received three posts. From Radical Islamic Groups, Kazem Sami (of JAMA) became minister of health. Sami, however, soon resigned in protest to the "nonrevolutionary" nature of the Provisional Government. The Provisional Government was the government of the bourgeoisie and was planning to reorganize the bureaucracy of the old regime under an Islamic name (A'aza-e Sazman-e Mojahedin-e Khalq 1979:4).

The IRC was a fifteen-man coalition of the Freedom Movement (including such figures as Mehdy Bazargan, Ebrahim Yazdi, and Abbas Amir Entezam), some former associates of the Freedom Movement (Abol Hassan Bani-Sadr and Sadegh Qotb Zadeh), and pro-Khomeini mojtaheds (such as Ayatollah Morteza Mottahari and Ayatollah Hossein Beheshti). The only independent personality within the revolutionary council was Ayatollah Seyyed Mahmud Taleghany. The IRC was acting as the legislative body in the absence of the Majlis. It was the organization of the traditional bourgeoisie and the petty bourgeoisie and was dominated by the militant mojtaheds. Because of its structure, the IRC was the scene of clashes between Bazargan and Ayatollah Beheshti.

A few days after the overthrow of the monarchy, Ayatollah Khomeini announced that the aim of the revolution was the creation of an Islamic state in Iran. He quarreled with Bazargan over the official name of the new regime. Khomeini emphasized that the only suitable name for the new regime was the Islamic Republic of Iran, and rejected Bazargan's suggestion to change the name of the new regime to the Democratic Islamic Republic of Iran (*Raygan,* October 14, 1988). In March 1979, a plebiscite was called to determine the name of the new order. The people were asked to choose between the Islamic Republic and the monarchy. More than 97 percent of the 20 million people who participated in the plebiscite voted for the Islamic Republic. All of the secular leftist organizations except the Tudeh Party boycotted the referendum.

Within a week after the overthrow of the monarchy, the Revolutionary Committees (Komiteh) and the Revolutionary Guards (Pasdaran) were created. Komitehs were composed of the committees which were created in the mosques during the revolution for the distribution of oil and food among the poor (Parsons 1984:124). The Pasdaran were created after the revolution from the urban poor, who had total allegiance to Ayatollah Khomeini (Hiro 1985:110–15; Nima 1983:96). The Mojahedin-e Enghelab-e Islami were in charge of training the Pasdaran. Both the Pasdaran and the Komitehs were created in order to protect the new state from a military coup or a military showdown by the left.

The Pasdaran were totally controlled by the IRP (Arjomand 1988:165). The Komitehs, however, were not very well centralized or disciplined. In Kurdistan, they were organized by the landlords and Sunni mollahs. In Azerbaijan, the Komitehs were run by pro-Shariatmadary mollahs and the MPRP. It took the IRP more than two years to take control of the Komitehs and purge nonfundamentalist elements from them.

THE STRUGGLE FOR THE CONSOLIDATION OF POWER

After the overthrow of the monarchy a coalition of fundamentalist mollahs and liberal forces came to power. The fundamentalist mollahs represented the traditional bourgeoisie and petty bourgeoisie composed of merchants and shopkeepers of bazaar and the urban poor. The liberals, on the other hand, represented the interests of the middle class and the remnants of the national bourgeoisie.

Ayatollah Khomeini was the leader of the revolution and the final arbiter of the differences within the power bloc (Hooglund 1987:5–6). Bazargan and his associates in the Provisional Government tried to gain a hegemony within the power bloc, but failed. This was mainly due to the weakness of the national bourgeoisie and its failure to present an alternative to the populism of the fundmentalist mollahs. Liberals regarded the revolution as a political struggle against the Shah and believed that with minor adjustments the machinery of the state could be rebuilt and the business of the government could be resumed (Stemple 1981:215–20). Bazargan had reportedly complained to the media, "We expected rain, but we ended up with flood," implying that the situation had become more radicalized than he and his associates had expected (*Rahaii*, May 23, 1980).

The first task of the new regime was to preserve its existence and neutralize its enemies. Here a difference arose between Bazargan and Ayatollah Khomeini. Bazargan believed that the armed forces must be strengthened and trusted as the protector of the new order. Ayatollah Khomeini and his associates argued that although the army could be preserved, it should be balanced by loyal military forces, hence the creation of the Pasdaran and Komitehs (Bernstein 1986:149). The most staunch supporters of the Shah in the armed forces and SAVAK were purged or executed in order to remove the fear of a military coup.

The autonomy movement became a hot issue after the overthrow of the monarchy. Arabs, Baluchis, Kurds, and Torkomans vied for autonomy in their regions. The aim of the autonomy movement was the creation of favorable conditions for the national minorities and the recognition of their cultural identities (Higgins 1986:174–80; KDP 1981:41–49). It also demanded a more equitable share of the oil revenues in these areas. In Khuzistan, the Arabs were organized by the Cultural Committee of the Arab People, composed of the Arab intellectuals and some religious leaders such as Sheikh Shobeir Khaghani. The Baluchis were led by Marxist intellectuals and Sunni mollahs.

In Kurdistan and Torkoman Sahra, the autonomy movement was accompanied by the land question. In these two areas, the peasants seized lands from the big landlords and created peasant councils. In Torkoman Sahra, the peasants were organized by the Fedaii Organization. The Kurdish peasants, on the other hand, were organized by the Democratic Party of Kurdistan and the Komeleh Organization. The secular leftist organizations (except the Tudeh Party) also participated in the social revolution in the rural areas of Kurdistan. The autonomy movement in Khuzistan, Baluchistan, and Torkoman Sahra was suppressed easily. The Kurdistan, however, remained out of the reach of the government and became the main base of the opposition in Iran.

Despite the growth of the workers' councils, they failed to develop into effective labor unions because they were isolated from each other and there was no attempt to unify them. Moreover, each radical organization wanted to create its own power base in the workplaces instead of organizing the workers into strong trade unions. The failure of the leftist organizations to unify the workers' councils allowed the government to organize Islamic Associations in the factories as support bases of the regime. By late 1980, the government was able to create the Islamic Workers' Councils to replace the independent workers' councils (Nima 1983:80) .

Realizing that a constituent assembly might produce a secular constitution, Ayatollah Khomeini pushed for an "Assembly of Experts" composed of theologians and "committed Moslems." The election for the Assembly of Experts was scheduled for mid-August. In order to show its opposition to the Assembly of Experts, the Democratic National Front organized more than 200,000 people in favor of a constituent assembly. The progovernment mobs known as Hizbollahis attacked demonstrators with clubs, knives, and broken bottles. A few days later, the Democratic National Front was disbanded and its leaders went underground.

Ayatollah Khomeini asked his associates to nominate themselves for the Assembly of Experts and encouraged the people to vote for them (Bernard and Khalilzad 1984:109; *Rahaii*, April 2, 1980). Ayatollah Shariatmadary, the national minorities, the Democratic National Front, and the MPRP boycotted the election. As was anticipated, the IRP members gained the majority of the seventy-five–member Assembly of Experts.

On the inauguration day of the Assembly of Experts, Ayatollah Khomeini announced that the Constitution should be based on Islamic laws (*Ettella'at*, August 19, 1979). The liberal faction of the power bloc tried to dissolve the Assembly of Experts. The plan, however, failed because of Bazargan's vacillation (*Iranshahr*, July 11, 1980). The IRP representatives, who had an absolute majority in the Assembly of Experts, implemented Khomeini's interpretation of an Islamic government in the draft of the Constitution. The *Velayat-e Faghih* (the Government of Jurisprudence) was reflected in Articles 5, 107, and 110 of the Constitution.

According to Article 5, during the occultation of the Twelfth Imam (Mahdy), the Islamic community must be guided and run by foghaha (theologians). Article 107 recognized Ayatollah Khomeini as the faghih of the present time. Article 110 asserted the pervasiveness of the power of the faghih. According to this article, the faghih is the commander-in-chief of the armed forces, he chooses 50 percent of the members of the Council of the Guardians (a twelve-member body that supervises the laws to ensure that they do not contradict the Shari'a), and he evaluates the competence of the presidential candidates. The faghih also has the right to dismiss the president.

By the end of the summer, the situation had become volatile. More than 2 million were unemployed, there was great controversy about the Constitution, the autonomy movement in Kurdistan was growing stronger, and leftist forces were spreading roots throughout the country. The fundamentalist and liberal forces were skirmishing over control of state power, peasants were holding on to the lands they had occupied, and the workers were continuing their struggle for higher wages and control of management in the factories. In general, a great number of people had become disillusioned with the new regime and had become alienated from it.

The hostage crisis mobilized the masses and created mass support for the regime again. On November 4, 1979, about four hundred pro-Khomeini students calling themselves the Moslem Student Followers of the Imam (Khomeini's) Line (hereafter called Moslem Students) took over the American embassy in Tehran and took American diplomats and military personnel hostage. They announced that they would release their hostages only after the Shah (who was then receiving medical treatment in the United States) was handed over to Iran and the $24 billion he had allegedly amassed in the United States was returned to Iran.

The embassy takeover gave a boost to the IRP and Ayatollah Khomeini. The foreign enemy and the danger of an imminent U.S. attack were utilized to rally the masses behind the regime. This took the thunder away from the left and provided the conditions for the mollahs to call for radical slogans; discredit the opposition, both liberal and radical; and ask for a speedy ratification of the Constitution (Irfani 1983:191). The embassy takeover also caused confusion among the leftist forces. Some regarded it as a genuine anti-imperialist struggle tht would result in the radicalization of the society. Some others simply supported this action to relieve themselves from the accusation of complicity with the United States.

The hostage crisis allowed the fundamentalist mollahs to disarm the left and strengthen their position vis-à-vis liberals (Taheri 1986:268). Bazargan resigned after the embassy takeover and all of his duties were entrusted to the IRC (of which Bazargan was a member). The embassy takeover allowed the IRP leaders to organize workers, peasants, and the leftist forces around anti-American slogans. The Moslem Students took the side of the IRP leaders against the liberals. Documents from the U.S. embassy were presented to the people to prove that the liberal forces had connections with the American officials in Iran (Ioannides 1984:66). Moghaddam Maraghei of the MPRP and Bazargan's former deputy prime minister, Abbas Amir Entezam, were accused of having connections with the U.S. embassy (*Iran Times*, January 12, 1981, February 3, 1984). Bazargan was chastised for having met General Huyser and Brzezinski.

Supporters of Ayatollah Shariatmadary, who felt that these documents were mainly used to discredit him, quarrelled with Khomeini supporters in Qom. Clashes between pro- and anti-Shariatmadary demonstrators in Qom angered his supporters in Azerbaijan. The MPRP organized strikes and demonstrations in Azerbaijan to protest against these incidents. The Komitehs joined the demonstrations and occupied government offices and radio and television stations. These turmoils lasted about a month and were eventually suppressed by Pasdaran. The MPRP was dissolved and eleven of its leaders were executed. After this incident Shariatmadary and some of his associates such as Grand Ayatollahs Hassan Qomi and Shirazi were silenced (Bashirieh 1984:157; Nima 1983:106).

Having isolated the radical and liberal forces as well as moderate Ayatollahs and organized the people around anti-American slogans, the IRP leaders mobilized their forces for the presidential election. In nominating their candidate, Jalal od-Din Farsi, for president, the IRP leaders committed a tactical error. Farsi's father was from Afghanistan, and he could not meet the requirements for the presidency and subsequently was disqualified. In total disarray, the IRP nominated its theoretician, Hassan Ayat, and the French-educated Hassan Habibi for the job. Bani-Sadr, who at the time was very close to Khomeini, also nominated himself. The Mojahedin Organization nominated Rajavi. Mojahedin's candidate gained the support of the leftist forces except the Tudeh Party. The Tudeh Party lent its support to Hassan Habibi, one of the IRP candidates. Another popular candidate was Admiral Ahmad Madany, the governor of Khuzistan.

The Mojahedin candidate was disqualified by Ayatollah Khomeini on the grounds that he had not voted for the Constitution. Consequently, Mojahedin and other leftist forces (except the Tudeh Party) boycotted the election. Bani-Sadr was able to get about 75 percent of the votes, which accounted for 11 million votes. Madany was second in rank with about 4 million. The IRP candidates together could not pull more than 800,000 votes.

The failure of the IRP leaders to take over the presidency made them dedicate all their energy to the parliamentary election. In the meantime, the party started massive propaganda against the liberals including Bani-Sadr. The Moslem Students' documents helped the IRP's propaganda tremendously. To nobody's surprise, the IRP's candidates achieved the majority in the parliamentary election. One of the founders of the IRP, Hojjatol Islam Akbar Hashemi Rafsanjani was elected speaker of the Majlis. Leftist forces could not send any deputy to the Majlis. With this new development, the IRP was in a strong position and was ready to launch a massive attack against Bani-Sadr and the left.

The election for the Majlis was completed by May 1980. It gave an absolute majority to the IRP and left Bani-Sadr at the mercy of the Islamic Republican Party. This also showed how feeble the power base of the liberals was. By 1980, the fundamentalist mollahs had asserted their hegemony in the power bloc, which was reflected in the monopolization of the Majlis, the court system, the Pasdaran, the Komitehs, radio and television, the Foundation of the Poor, the Construction Crusade, and the mosques by the Islamic Republican Party. The only political institution that was not occupied by the IRP was the presidency. The next step of the IRP was to occupy that office as well.

Bani-Sadr tried to improve his position by choosing a nonfundamentalist prime minister. He first nominated Ahmad Khomeini (Khomeini's son) who at that time had close ties with him. Ayatollah Khomeini rejected his son's nomination by arguing that he did not want members of his family to be directly involved in politics (*Iranshahr,* July 12, 1980). Bani-Sadr's second and third choices were Admiral Ahmad Madany (former governor of Khuzistan) and Hossein Mir Salim (deputy minister of the interior). The Majlis rejected both candidates and instead selected an IRP supporter, Mohammad Ali Rejaii (Hiro 1985:162). Rejaii, who was Bazargan's minister of education, was a fundamentalist and a protégé of Beheshti. Rejaii's premiership weakened the position of Bani-Sadr further (Bill 1988:267–68). This meant that the IRP now had a hold on the executive power as well. Realizing that in the absence of a political organization he would not be able to hold on to the power much longer, Bani-Sadr turned to Mojahedin for support. Mojahedin lent their active support to Bani-Sadr and participated in demonstrations in his favor. Some small Maoist groups such as Ettehadeih-e Komunistha and Ranjbaran also supported Bani-Sadr against the IRP.

By May 1980, the struggle between the IRP and Bani-Sadr had reached its climax. Attacks against liberals (who were branded as the agents of imperialism) were frequent. The Tudeh Party and the Movement of

Militant Moslems provided theoretical and ideological support for the IRP against Bani-Sadr and other liberals. Having orchestrated their efforts against the liberals, the IRP and the students proposed a "cultural revolution" to purify the universities from the "pernicious" influence of the East and the West. The reasons for the "cultural revolution" were to close down the universities, to purge nonconformist elements from the institutions of higher education, and to turn them into Islamic centers. In early June, Hojjatol Islam Nasser Makarem Shirazi, in a seminar in Qom, suggested that the government close the universities for the time being (*Iranshahr*, June 6, 1981). The universities were officially closed in July 1980.

The summer of 1980 witnessed the growing power of fundamentalist forces and the outright attack of Ayatollah Khomeini against liberal and radical forces. In a speech in June 1980 he criticized himself for choosing Bazargan and "nonrevolutionary" elements for the Provisional Government. He also attacked Bani-Sadr for not acting in an Islamic and revolutionary manner to apply Islamic principles in the society. A week later, Ayatollah Khomeini attacked Mojahedin for causing tension in the society. Mojahedin members, who were aware that this speech was the beginning of skirmishes between their supporters and Hizbollahis, closed their offices throughout the country in order to avoid such clashes.

Fundamentalist forces scored more victories following a split within the Fedaii Organization in early July (*Iranshahr*, June 132, 1980). The majority of the central committee members of the Fedaii Organization formed a coalition with the Tudeh Party and announced their total support of the IRP (Taheri 1986:255). This faction was renamed the Fedaii Organization (majority). The minority of the central committee, on the other hand, argued that the ruling bloc was reactionary and must be overthrown. This faction was called Fedaii Guerrilla Organization (minority). This new development weakened the leftist forces further and gave a boost to the IRP.

While Bani-Sadr and the IRP were engaged in a fierce power struggle, a group of royalist officers were getting ready to overthrow the regime through a militry coup. The plot, however, was unveiled, many officers were arrested, and several of them were executed. This new development encouraged the Iraqi army to invade Iran in the hope of overthrowing the Islamic regime.

Several factors made the Iraqi leadership decide to invade Iran. First, the Iraqi regime was afraid of the ideological impact of the Iranian revolution in the Shi'a population of Iraq. Second, the constant call of the fundamentalist forces to export the Iranian revolution had terrified Iraq and the other Persian Gulf countries (Bahraini 1987:4; Mohammadi 1987:36–44). By early 1980, several fundamentalist Islamic groups had been created in Iraq that had allegiance to Iran. These groups wanted to create an Islamic regime in Iraq. By heading off the revolution in Iran, the Iraqis believed, the danger of an Islamic revolution would be eliminated in Iraq. Third, Saddam Hossein was planning to "liberate" the oil-rich province of Khuzistan that he called "Arabistan" in order to enhance his influence in the region (Ramazani 1986:66). Fourth, defeating Iran would boost the power and prestige of the Iraqi president, Saddam Hossein, in the Arab countries, and he could assume the leadership of the Arab world (Cottam 1986:235).

Following the Iraqi invasion, the Iranian army was reorganized under Bani-Sadr, which initially strengthened his position vis-à-vis his fundamentalist opponents. This, however, was short-lived, and the army failed to push the Iraqi troops back (Taheri 1986:271). The IRP managed to mobilize the masses against the Iraqi army. The Iraqi invasion changed the situation drastically on behalf of the fundamentalist mollahs. The people were asked to join the revolutionary guards and the army to defend the "Islamic homeland." A new miiltary organization named Basij-e Mos taz'afin (the Mobilization of the Oppressed) was created to increase the war efforts of Iran against Iraq. Basij, which was strictly composed of volunteers, played a crucial role in pushing Iraqis beyond the international borders (Chubin and Tripp (1988:44–46).

In the meantime, the IRP through its handpicked prime minister, Mohammad Ali Rejaii, started a campaign for the release of the American hostages. The powerful Majlis speaker Hashemi Rafsanjani arranged for a resolution for the release of American hostages (Saunders 1985:292). Bani-Sadr tried to make political gain out of this development by calling the solution of the hostage crisis a total sellout, but he failed.

March 7, 1981, witnessed the climax of the power struggle between Bani-Sadr and the IRP. On that day Bani-Sadr was addressing a rally in Tehran University on the occasion of the commemoration of Mossadegh's death. A group of Hezbollahis slandered Mossadegh and attacked the demonstrators (Zabih 1986:34). Mojahedin members who had participated in the rally disarmed the Hezbollahis and handed them over to the security forces of the president. The IRP counterattacked by accusing Bani-Sadr of using force against the defenseless followers of Khomeini.

Following this incident, Ayatollah Khomeini completely broke with Bani-Sadr and started openly supporting the IRP against him. Bani-Sadr, on the other hand, was encouraged by Mojahedin's support and called for a referendum on the future of the country. Bazargan and Mojahedin supported Bani-Sadr's proposal, while the fundamentalist groups rejected it, and the secular leftist forces (except the Tudeh Party) called for a constituent assembly.

Bani-Sadr had become expendable now, and Ayatollah Khomeini decided to do away with him once and for all. On June 10, he dismissed

Bani-Sadr as the commander-in-chief of the armed forces. He also threatened to crush Bani-Sadr if he did not cooperate with the Majlis. Without referring to Bani-Sadr, Ayatollah Khomeini announced:

If there are some people who deliver speeches and their speeches cause turmoil. I will destroy them regardless of who they are. . . . I will do the same thing with them, that I did with Mohammad Reza (Shah). (*Iranshahr*, May 23, 1981)

Three days later, the IRP deputies voted for the removal of Bani-Sadr from the presidency (*Jomhoury-e Islami*, June 13, 1981). Bani-Sadr therefore was dismissed on June 19, 1981. This was followed by a huge demonstration organized by Mojahedin and the leftist forces on June 20. The fundamental mollahs took this incident very seriously and decided to destroy the opposition once and for all. The Pasdaran and Hizbollahis broke the demonstrations violently. Several demonstrators were killed by the Hizbollahis and Pasdaran, and many of those who were arrested were executed.

With the dismissal of Bani-Sadr, the liberal opposition lost its last hope to assume the hegemony within the power bloc. After June 1981, the stage was prepared for the creation of a theocracy in Iran.

9 State and Theocracy in Iran

The fall of Bani-Sadr stripped the liberals of their stake in the executive power and resulted in the total domination of the state by the fundamentalist forces. The Islamic Republican Party, which had struggled for two years to create a theocracy based on Khomeini's *Velayat-e Faghih*, dominated the government. This new power bloc was composed of the traditional bourgeoisie, the petty bourgeoisie, and a new bureaucratic bourgeoisie. After the fall of Bani-Sadr the regime achieved greater internal cohesion. This allowed the ruling bloc to reorganize its forces and assert its authority in the society. At this stage, three sets of challenges were posed against the regime: the threat of the radical opposition, the economy, and the war. The relative success of the regime in regard to these issues allowed it to survive these challenges and stabilize itself.

The elimination of the radical oposition was the major obsession of the regime. The winning card of the regime was that it could still count on its intellectual and moral leadership among the broad masses and depend on their support (Gramsci 1971:57–58). Consequently, it was in a position to impose the conditions of war on the opposition, a factor that allowed the government to suppress the opposition within a few months. Although the Mojahedin, the Fedaiis (minority), Peykar, the Kurdish Democratic Party, and Komeleh had a de facto coalition for the overthrow of the government, they were not able to unify their forces and coordinate their activities against the regime. This gave an opportunity to the regime to destroy these organizations one after another.

The Mojahedin and the Fedaiis mobilized their forces for a military showdown with the government. In a series of bombings, Mojahedin succeeded in eliminating the top leadership of the Islamic Republican

Party including Ayatollah Beheshti (secretary general of the party), Mohammad Ali Rejaii (the new president), and Javad Bahonar (prime minister) (Bill 1988:270–71). The regime retaliated by starting a manhunt for the arrest of the opposition leaders. During the summer and fall of 1981, several political organizations including Peykar and Ranjbaran were virtually wiped out. The Fedaiis also suffered such heavy casualties that they put aside their projected tactic of "red terror." Instead, they called for general strikes and mobilization of the masses for the overthrow of the regime (*Kar*, August 9, 1981; *Kar International*, November 1981). Ettehadieh Communistha organized its forces in the northern city of Amol in February 1982. These guerrillas took the control of the city for seventy-two hours, but they were decimated when Pasdaran forces that had arrived from Tehran surrounded them and recaptured the city (Zabih 1986:163). The Mojahedin were the most serious threat to the regime, hence the regime organized all its forces to uproot them once and for all (Afkhami 1985:202). Several hundred Mojahedin supporters and members were executed and many more were arrested during the summer and fall of 1981. Mojahedin's heaviest casualties occurred in February 1982 when some of its top leadership, including Mousa Khiabani (second in rank after Rajavi) and Ashraf Rabii (Masoud Rajavi's wife), were gunned down by Pasdaran.

The failure of Mojahedin to mobilize the masses against the regime or to build a united front with the secular radical forces made them enter into an official coalition with Bani-Sadr. This coalition, the National Resistance Council (NRC) was announced in Paris in August 1981 upon the flight of Mojahedin's leader Mosoud Rajavi and Bani-Sadr to France. The NRC called for the creation of the Democratic Islamic Republic of Iran. The program of the NRC had Islamic and social democratic flavors. The NRC asked all of the opponents of the regime except the monarchists and Tudeh Party to join the coalition. Many secular leftist organizations including Peykar, the Fedaiis, and the Organization of Communist Unity refused to join the NRC because they argued that it was a coalition of the liberal bourgeoisie (i.e., Bani-Sadr and his supporters) and the petty bourgeoisie (i.e., Mojahedin). Some small leftist organizations, such as Shoray-e Mottahed-e Chap Baray-e Democracy va Esteghlal (the United Council of Left for Democracy and Independence) as well as the Democratic National Front and the Democratic Party of Kurdistan, joined the NRC. Despite the optimism of Bani-Sadr and Rajavi, the NRC failed to mobilize the masses against the regime. Because of differences among the members of the council over strategy toward the regime, relations with Iraq, and cooperation with other political forces, Bani-Sadr and his supporters, the KDP, and Shoray-e Mottahed-e Chap left the NRC.

By late 1982 the opposition was weakened to such an extent that the regime did not feel an immediate threat from them. Consequently, the

Iranian leaders felt secure enough to relax the repression. On December 15 Ayatollah Khomeini issued his famous Eight-Point Decree for liberalizing the political system and reducing pressure on entrepreneurs and managers of the factories. A few months later, the universities that were purged of the radical elements were reopened.

After the elimination of the radical opposition, the regime turned against the Tudeh Party. Several factors led to this new development. First, until 1982 the regime needed the Tudeh Party to justify suppression of the radical opposition, which the Tudeh Party labeled as the agents of imperialism. The Tudeh Party had developed a theory according to which opposition to the Imam Line (see chapter 8) would only benefit imperialism (*Peyam-e Azady*, April 1983). With the elimination of the radical opposition there was no need for the services of the Tudeh Party. Second, the regime was alarmed by the infiltration of the Tudeh Party members in the army and the bureaucracy (*Iranshahr*, May 27, 1983). A factor that enhanced these fears was the defection of a Soviet diplomat in Tehran, Vladimir Kuzichkin, to England. Kuzichkin gave the details of Soviet involvement in Iran and the infiltration of the Tudeh members in the army and the other government institutions. The British government informed the Iranian government about this new development (Chubin and Tripp 1988:210–11). Last but not the least was the reaction of the Tudeh Party to the invasion of Iraq by Iran. When Iranian troops pushed Iraqi forces beyond the international borders and entered Iraqi territory in 1982, the Soviet Union and naturally the Tudeh Party attacked this new development and announced that the continuation of the war would only benefit the United States. These combined factors made the Islamic leaders determined to do away with the Tudeh Party.

In early April 1983 the massive arrest of Tudeh Party members started. The prosecutor general of the Islamic regime, Ayatollah Abdol Karim Ardebili, accused the Tudeh Party members of spying for the Soviet Union and infiltrating the army and the bureaucracy. The leaders of the Tudeh Party such as Secretary General Nourod-Din Kianoori; the party's theoretician, Ehsan Tabari, and many other top-ranking Tudeh members admitted these charges and revealed the involvement of the Soviet Union in the internal affairs of Iran (*Iranshahr*, May 6, 1983; Milani 1988:304; Zabih 1986:40–45). These confessions were skillfully utilized by the regime, which branded the left in general as agents of foreign powers.

Having eliminated the Tudeh Party, the Iranian leaders launched an offensive against their conservative clerics organized in the Hojjatieh. The Hojjatieh group was founded by Sheikh Mahmud Halaby in the late 1950s. It is a conservative and anti-Bahaii group that believes in the sanctity of private property and opposes the involvement of Ulema in politics. Hojjatieh believes that only Imam-e Zaman should rule and any government during the occultation period is illegitimate. Conservative

Ulema such as Ayatollah Hassan Qomi, Ayatollah Mohammad Reza Golpaigani, Ayatollah Abolqasem Khoii, and Ayatollah Shahab od-Din Marashi share these views with the Hojattieh group (Bayat 1985:27). The IRP leaders started a massive propaganda warfare against the Hojjatieh group and accused them of deviating from the "Imam Line." Realizing that this propaganda might be the beginning of the massive purge of his supporters from the government, Sheikh Mahmoud Halaby suspended all of the activities of Hojjatieh in late 1983.

On the economic front, the regime had a major task ahead. The most pressing issues were the limitation of private property and the role of the state in economic planning. According to Article 44 of the Constitution, the economy is composed of three sectors: private, state, and cooperative. The state is to run the major industries, infrastructure, radio and television, and foreign trade. The cooperative sector was to distribute goods and services in both urban and rural areas. Small industries, commerce, agriculture, and animal husbandries were to be run by the private sector.

The immediate problem before the economic planners was the question of private property (Behdad 1988a:118; Razavi and Vakil 1984:113). In January 1982, Taghi Banki, head of the PBO, announced that without making a clear decision about the definition and limits of private property, economic planning would be impossible (*Iran Times* January 22, 1982). Rafsanjani also indicated that there was disagreement among the Majlis deputies, members of the Council of Guardians, the cabinet, and the leading mojtaheds over the problem of private property. He played down the importance of this issue by arguing that the real disagreement was over the percentage of the economy that should be run by the state and the percentage that should be run by the private sector (*Iran Times*, February 3, 1983).

The land question was yet another issue that haunted the fundamentalist forces. After the overthrow of the monarchy, many peasants started seizing land throughout the country (Najmabadi 1987:201). On most occasions, the government evicted the peasants. Gradually the Iranian leaders realized that by alienating the peasants it could not survive. Right before the hostage crisis, Ayatollah Khomeini ordered the creation of seven-member land commissions in the provinces to deal with the land question and supervise the distribution of land among the peasants. Reza Isfahani, vice-minister of agriculture, played a crucial role in this regard. Like Hasan Arsanjani twenty years before, Isfahani was in favor of creating a strong peasantry as the support base of the regime. This time, because the hegemonic faction of the power bloc led by Ayatollah Khomeini and radical wing of the Islamic Republican Party were in favor of such initiative, the government sided with the peasants in the rural areas. In postrevolutionary Iran, peasants and rural migrants constituted the backbone of support for the regime. Big landlords and conservative mollahs opposed land distribution as non-Islamic and felt it should be stopped immediately. Despite the opposition of these groups, by 1981, 185,000 hectares of land were distributed among the peasants throughout the country and another 60,000 hectares of land were dedicated to the Organization of Development for Agricultural Production (Ashraf 1982:33).

The Construction Crusade (Jahad-e Sazandegi), which was created in June 1979, played a crucial role in restructuring the rural areas. From the beginning, the Islamic Republican Party was able to monopolize this organization. Members of the Construction Crusade were originally the dedicated Islamic volunteers who were in favor of radical changes in the rural areas. Jahad gradually became a very important organization of economic planning in the rural areas and its members became the official employees of the government. By 1983, the budget of this organization was over $1 billion. According to Ali Reza Afshar, a leading member of the Jahad-e Sazandegi, by late 1982 this organization had built 400 bridges, distributed electricity to more than 1,000 villages, and constructed 9,374 miles of road in rural areas (*Iran Times*, March 5, 1983). Ali Zangeneh, minister of the Jahad-e Sazandegi, also indicated that by 1988 Jahad-e Sazandegi had provided drinking water to 31 percent of villages (*Ettella'at*, June 18, 1988).

Another economic organization created by the new regime was Foundation of the Poor, or Mostazafan Foundation. This organization took over the Pahlavi Foundation and the lands and factories of the royal family and those entrepreneurs who had fled abroad. According to Mehdy Tabatabaii, one of the chief administrators of the foundation, it owns 15 percent of all of the factories and all of the big agricultural corporations. The Mostazfan Foundation is also the largest landowner, with land value of about $10 billion (*Iran Times*, February 24, 1984). This organization is gradually emerging as the most powerful economic foundation of the country and is providing the conditions for a state capitalist system in Iran.

In order to increase state control over the economy, the Majlis approved the nationalization of foreign trade in November 1980. This initiative was opposed by the big merchants and the Council of Guardians, who found it contrary to the principles of Islam (Akhavi 1987:55). Ayatollah Khomeini attacked the council for its shortsightedness and asked the Majlis to disregard the recommendation of the councils.

Despite the disagreement of the different factions of the power bloc about economic planning, which had made economic development virtually impossible, the oil sector kept the economy from collapse. The oil sector, which accounted for 97 percent of the total merchandise export, declined to 95 percent by 1980. However, it went up again and by 1984 totalled about 99 percent of exports (Karimi 1986:40). The oil revenues are about $18 billion a year, which enabled the government to fund the development plans and the distribution of welfare among the poor and victims of the war, hence securing their support.

Another problem that had preoccupied the regime was the war with Iraq. Contrary to what the Iraqi regime, the royalist opposition, and some radical forces had anticipated, it helped the regime tremendously (Hooglund 1989:4; Tagavi 1985:67). Saddam Hossein, who was counting on an uprising among the Arab population of Khuzistan, was surprised by the support of Arabs for the government. Radical forces such as Peykar, the Fedaiis, and Komeleh, which—based on the experience of the Russian Revolution—were pushing for transforming the Iran-Iraq War into a civil war, only discredited themselves in the eyes of the broad masses, who regarded this tactic as cooperation with the foreign enemy. The Mojahedin also fell in the same trap, and by seeking sanctuary in Iran in 1986, lost much of their following in Iran.

There were some other factors that helped the regime to turn the war in its favor. First of all, the war allowed the regime to stabilize itself and mobilize the masses for the defense of the Islamic homeland (Heller 1987:20; Hooglund 1984:33–36). Second, it kept the army busy so that it was not involved in the political process. Third, the war allowed the regime to train the Pasdaran for a possible civil war in the future. Fourth, the regime was able to turn the war into an ideological struggle against Iraq, which it referred to as an atheistic state, hence helping to Islamize the society through mobilizing the masses against the Iraqi regime. In 1983 Prime Minister Hossein Moosavi announced that in its war with Iraq, Iran was fighting against international atheism (*Iranshahr*, September 29, 1983). Ayatollah Khomeini also emphasized that Iran was engaged in a holy war (Jihad) against the enemies of Islam and that the overthrow of Saddam was the first step toward an everlasting peace in the region (Anthony 1984:112; Chubin and Tripp 1988:161).

The combined forces of Pasdaran, the army, and the Basij were able to push the Iraqis back by the summer of 1982 (Entesar 1988:67). The battle of Fathol-Mobin not only resulted in the repulsion of Iraqis but also in capturing some Iraqi lands. Following this new development, the Iranian leaders announced that the war would end only after the overthrow of Saddam Hossein (Chubin and Tripp 1988:165; Rafsanjani 1984:42–43).

On July 12, 1982, the Iranian armed forces invaded Iraq and were able to penetrate ten miles inside Iraqi territory (Hiro 1984:10). The Iraqis succeeded in repulsing the Iranian offensive. Iran was able to capture more territories in the next offensives but was not able to defeat Iraq; hence the war continued for the next seven years. Despite the cautions of many inside Iran and international mediators including the United

Nations, the Arab League and the PLO Iranian leaders insisted that without punishing Saddam Hossein the war would not end (Anthony 1984:112). Iraq reacted by bombing Iranian cities and using chemical weapons against Iranian civilians (Chubin and Tripp 1988:59–60). Until July 1988, the position of Iran remained unchanged. The war, however, drained the Iranian economy and cost at least 160,000 lives and about $450 billion in property damage (Hooglund 1989:4–8). Iran was spending 40 percent of its budget on the war with Iraq (Renner 1988:189). This had resulted in uncontrollable inflation (Behdad 1988b:7–12). The cost of a twenty-inch color television set was more than $8,000, and the price of one pound of beef was over $5.00. This most be viewed in light of the low salaries in Iran. A schoolteacher makes less than $1,000 a month. The cooperatives (4,000 throughout the country) somehow were able to alleviate the burden by selling some of the basic goods and foodstuffs at a reasonable price. For example, one pound of sugar could be purchased for 15¢ in the cooperatives versus $9.00 in the free market. The supply of goods was very limited, and the goods were black-marketed, which made many dissatisfied with the government. This made some of the Iranian leaders concerned about the future of the regime. Pragmatists such as Rafsanjani were in favor of ending the war. Ayatollah Khomeini might have reached the same conclusion by early 1988, when he started giving more power to Rafsanjani. When Rafsanjani became the acting commander-in-chief of the armed forces on June 2, 1988, it was clear that the situation was moving toward a solution. Iran had suffered several military setbacks in the winter and spring of 1988. This might have convinced the Iranian leaders that there was no way to win the war. Eventually, on July 19, 1988, Ayatollah Khomeini announced that despite his opposition to ending the war, he had accepted the recommendations of his aides tht Iran should accept the 598 United Nations Resolution (*Ettella'at*, July 19, 1988). This resolution called for an immediate cease-fire, withdrawal of all forces behind the international borders, and negotiations for a lasting peace. With the acceptance of this resolution, Iran and Iraq started negotiating to reach a settlement through United Nations' mediators.

THE POWER STRUGGLE AND THE FUTURE OF THE ISLAMIC REPUBLIC OF IRAN

The Islamic Republic of Iran is a populist state based on Islamic ideology. The power bloc is composed of the traditional bourgeoisie, the petty bourgeoisie, and a new bureaucratic bourgeoisie. The term "new" bureaucratic bourgeoisie is utilized here to distinguish it from its old counterpart, since it fled abroad following the revolution. The new bureaucratic bourgeoisie recruits its members from the ranks of leaders of the Construction Crusade and Mostazafan Foundation. The pro-Khomeini mollahs have the hegemony within this power bloc.

The regime mobilizes the Mostazafin or Mostazafan (oppressed) against the Mostakberin (powerful and wealthy) (*Kayhan,* July 8, 1988). Mostazafin are composed of the poorest strata of the society, mainly rural migrants, poor peasants, and the urban poor. The members of Pasdaran and Komitehs are mostly recruited from this socially disadvantaged group. The Mostazafan, as a result, see their ideals in the success of the regime and lend their active support to the government. The regime has succeeded in organizing the workers and peasants in Islamic councils throughout the country. These councils are closely associated with Pasdaran, hence linking the poorest strata of the society to the state.

Among the Iranian leaders two tendencies can be identified. A radical faction led by Meshkini, Moosavi Ardebili, Prime Minister Hossein Moosavi, Hashemi Rafsanjani, and President Ali Khamenei is in favor of the domination of the economy by the state and restriction of big capital. Conservative religious leaders such as Ayatollah Ali Kany, Ayatollah Abolghasem Khazali, Ayatollah Jannati, Safi, Imami Kashani, and Momen are in favor of private property and oppose nationalization and land redistribution (Akhavi 1986:68). They are close to the Hojjtieh group and wealthy bazaaris.

Ayatollah Khomeini, who had anticipated a devastating power struggle following his death, handpicked Montazeri as his successor. In 1983, he called for the convention of the Assembly of Experts to decide about the future Valy-e Faghih. According to the Constitution, if a Faghih does not emerge he could be appointed by the Assembly of Experts. As was expected, the assembly picked Montazeri in November 1985 (Hooglund 1987:6). This was opposed by Ayatollah Qomi who argued that Montazeri did not qualify for the position. Despite this, Ayatollah Khomeini reconfirmed Montazeri as his successor in December 1985.

Through his aide and brother of his son-in-law, Mehdy Hashemi, Montazeri was able to connect the Islamic as well as the secular liberation movements in an anti-American direction. Hashemi's bold statement about the export of revolution made more pragmatic leaders of the regime, such as Rafsanjani, and Minister of Foreign Affairs, Ali Akbar Velayati, concerned about the consequences of such propaganda. Hashemi was arrested in early 1986 on charges of several murders, confiscation of arms from the Pasdaran, and creating a secret intelligence service.

There was yet another reason for Hashemi's arrest. He was against the establishment of ties with the United States that Rafsanjani was advocating. The reason that made Rafsanjani favor establishing relations with the United States was that he believed that Iran badly needed

American technology and weapons for reorganizing the economy and enhancing its war efforts against Iraq. The United States also was searching for a new opening with its former ally because of Iran's logistic importance and its influence on the Hizbollah group who had taken several Americans hostage (Armstrong et al. 1987; Chomski 1988:180; Sick 1987:703). Although this policy did not bring the desired results for either party, it showed the potential in both quarters for future cooperation.

This new development known as "Iran-Gate" and the "Iran-Contra Affair" was revealed by the supporters of Mehdy Hashemi who thought it would weaken the position of Rafsanjani. They had concluded that this new development would result in the release of Hashemi and his emergence as a leading radical. Contrary to what Hashemi and his supporters had thought, this revelation did not hurt Rafsanjani who had masterminded this initiative. Rafsanjani emerged from this crisis stronger than ever before and was able to weaken the position of his rivals such as Ayatollah Montazeri and Ali Akbar Mohtashemi.

Since the fall of 1988, when the health of Ayatollah Khomeini started deteriorating, Ayatollah Montazeri decided to strengthen his position vis-à-vis his rivals and to establish himself as the most powerful man of the country next to Ayatollah Khomeini. His constant call for respecting individual rights and fair treatment of political prisoners reminded many of Bani-Sadr's futile efforts (1980–1981) to gain popular support against the Islami Republican Party. At that time, Rafsanjani frustrated Bani-Sadr's ambitions and masterminded his removal from the presidency. Eight years later, Rafsanjani was still in a position to do away with a potentially powerful rival. He was eventually able to convince Ayatollah Khomeini that Montazeri would harm the Islamic Republic should he remain in his position as Khomeini's successor. Montazeri's removal in April 1989 showed Rafsanjani's talent in outmaneuvering his rivals and establishing himself as the real power broker in Iran.

Having ousted a potentially powerful rival, Rafsanjani prepared himself for the presidential election of 1989. He easily won the support of the Association of the Militant Mollahs (see chapter 8). President Khamenei, whose term would expire in 1989 and who would not be eligible to run again, also recommended his ally Rafsanjani for the position. Since nobody else had been nominated, Rafsanjani's election was mostly guaranteed. Rafsanjani's next step was to push for an amendment to the constitution that would change the structure of the executive power. His main goals were to eliminate the post of prime minister and combine its duties with those of the president and to reduce the power of Ayatollah Khomeini's successor to that of a figurehead.

Ayatollah Khomeini approved the recommendation and selected a committee to make necessary changes. Before the completion of the mission of the committee, Ayatollah Khomeini died on June 3, 1989. The Assembly of Experts immediately appointed Khamenei as Ayatollah Khomeini's successor and granted him the position of Ayatollah. Khamenei owes his position to Rafsanjani who reportedly supported his appointment (*Keyhan Havai*, June 14, 1989).

With the domination of the political leadership by pragmatists, the situation seems to be more predictable for the future. In the post-Khomeini era, Rafsanjani is the most powerful man of the country. He has the total support of the Assembly of Experts, the Society of Militant Mollahs, and the Majlis. Khamenei has also expressed his confidence in Rafsanjani and has confirmed him in his position as the acting commander-in-chief of the armed forces. Rafsanjani's initiatives such as ending the war with Iraq, relaxing tough government policies toward women who do not observe head-to-toe veiling, and opening relations with the Western powers have been very popular. He is the sweetheart of the middle class for moderating the government's policies regarding social issues. Ayatollah Khomeini's death increased the power of Rafsanjani and he has been able to handle the more radical mollahs led by minister of interior, Ali Akbar Mohtashemi, easily.

Trends of events are in favor of Rafsanjani. The post-war economy requires huge investments mostly provided by Western investors. More than 500 firms have negotiated with the Iranian regime for the reconstruction of the country. This in turn gives more power to the technocrats and middle class who support Rafsanjani. The opposition is too weak and fragmented to pose a serious threat against the regime. Stability of the regime will depend on its overall policies to reorganize the political economy and neutralize its radical and conservative clerics. Despite this, it is difficult to predict anything about the future of a country which has puzzled millions of people throughout the world. Iran—a country in the midst of huge changes—might still surprise social scientists and political observers.

Glossary

AYATOLLAH   "Sign of God"; a high ranking religious leader

AYATOLLAH OL-OZMA   Grand Ayatollah

BAZAAR   Traditional Iranian marketplace

BAZAARI   An Iranian shopkeeper or merchant

BONEH   Pre-land-reform cooperative system that existed in the Iranian villages for the management of agricultural production

FAGHIH   Jurisprudence

FATWA   Declaration; an opinion on a religious matter expressed by a mojtahed

GAVBAND   Oxen owner

GHAIBAT   Occultation of the Twelfth Imam Mahdy

HADITH   Quoting from the prophet, Imams, and their close associates

HOWZEH-E ELMIEH   A center for learning Islamic laws

IMAMATE   Political and religious leadership of the Islamic community

KADKHODA   Village headman

KHALESEH   State land

KHOMS   A religious tax to support the poor descendents of the prophet and the religious institutions

KHORDEH MALEKI   Small landownership

KHOSHNESHINS   Landless Iranian peasants, rural artisans, money lenders, and gavbands

MAJLIS   Parliament

MALEKKIAT-E-ARBABY   Private landownership

MALEKKIAT-E-DEGHANI   Peasant landownership

MARJ'A-E TAGHLID   Literally, the source of imitation; highest ranking Shi'a religious leader

MOBASHER   Landowner's overseer in the villages

MOGHALID   Imitator; someone who follows the rulings of a mojtahed

MOJTAHED   Scholar of Islamic law who uses his independent judgment for the interpretation of the Islamic law

MOLLAH   Iranian clergy, regardless of rank

MOSHA'A   A piece of land owned communally

NASAGH   Sharecropping system

OMMAT   The Islamic community

QANAT   Underground aqueduct

ROWZ-E KHAN   Preacher; the one who narrates the tragedy of Karbala and sufferings of other Imams

SHARI'A   Islamic Law

TAGHIEH   Dissimulation

TA'AZIEH   Passion play

TOYOUL   Land assigned to the individuals by the monarchs in lieu of salary or service

ULEMA   See Mojtahed

VELAYAT-E FAGHIH   Government of Jurisprudence; the theory of Islamic government developed by Ayatollah Khomeini. According to this theory, religious hierarchy should directly rule in the society

WAQF (pl. OUGHAF)   Charity endownments

ZAKAT   Another religious tax paid by the faithful to Mojtaheds

Bibliography

A'aza-e Sazman-e Mojahedin-e Khalq. *An Analysis of Seizing the Spying Center of the United States*. Tehran: n.p., 1979.

Abrahamian, E. "Structural Causes of the Iranian Revolution." *MERIP Reports* 10, no. 4, (May 1980): 21–26.

———. *Iran Between Two Revolutions*. Princeton, N.J.: Princeton University Press, 1982.

———. "The Crowds in Iranian Politics, 1905–53." In *Iran: A Revolution in Turmoil*, edited by H. Afshar. Albany: State University of New York Press, 1985.

Abrahamian, E., and Farahad Kazemi. "The Nonrevolutionary Peasantry of Iran." *Iranian Studies* 11 (1978): 259–304.

Adamyyat, F. *The Ideology of the Constitutional Movement in Iran*. Tehran: Peyam Press, 1976.

Adamyyat, F., and H. Nateq. *Social, Political, and Economic Thoughts in Unpublished Literature of Qajar Period*. Tehran: Agah Publishing House, 1977.

Afkhami, G. R. *The Iranian Revolution: Thantanos on a National Scale*. Washington, D.C.: The Middle East Institute, 1985.

Afshar, H. "An Assessment of Agricultural Development Policies in Iran." In *Iran: A Revolution in Turmoil*, edited by H. Afshar. Albany: State University of New York Press, 1985a.

———., ed. *Iran: A Revolution in Turmoil*. Albany: State University of New York Press, 1985b.

Ahmadzadeh, M. *Armed Struggle: Both a Strategy and a Tactic*. New York: Support Committee for the Iranian People's Struggle, 1977.

Akhavi, S. *Religion and Politics in Contemporary Iran: Clergy-State Relations in the Pahlavi Period*. Albany: State University of New York Press, 1980.

———. "Clerical Politics in Iran since 1979." In *The Iranian Revolution and the Islamic Republic*, edited by N. Keddie and E. Hooglund. Syracuse, N.Y.: Syracuse University Press, 1986.

———. "Institutionalizing the New Order in Iran." *Current History* (Spring 1987): 53–56.

Alavi, H., and F. Halliday, eds. *State and Ideology in the Middle East and Pakistan*. New York: Monthly Review Press, 1988.

Albert, D., ed. *Tell the American People: Perspectives on the Iranian Revolution*. Philadelphia: Movement for a New Society, 1980.

Al-e Ahmad, J. *Westoxication*. Tehran: Ravaq Press, 1980.

———. *On the Services and Disservices of the Intellectuals*. Tehran: Ravaq Press, 1981.

Algar, H. *Religion and State in Iran: 1785–1909, the Role of the Ulema in the Qajar Period*. Berkeley and Los Angeles: University of California Press, 1969.

———. "The Oppositional Role of Ulema in the Twentieth-Century Iran." In *Scholars, Saints, and Sufis*, edited by N. Keddie. Berkeley and Los Angeles: University of California Press, 1972.

Alizadeh, E. "A Conversation with Ebrahim Alizadeh." (*Iranshahr's* interview with Ebrahim Alizadeh, a leading member of the Political Bureau of the Komeleh Organization.) *Iranshahr* (June 3, 1983): 8–15.

Alvandi, M. "About the Division of Products Based on Five Inputs." In *Land and Peasant Questions*. Tehran: Agah Publishers, 1982.

Amirahmadi, H., and M. Parvin. *Post-Revolutionary Iran*. Boulder, Colo.: Westview Press, 1988.

Amirsadeghi, H., and R. Ferrier, eds. *Twentieth-Century Iran*. London: Heinemann, 1977.

Amouzgar, J., and M. A. Fekrat. *Iran: Economic Development under Dualistic Conditions*. Chicago and London: University of Chicago Press, 1971.

Anthony, J. D. "Regional and Worldwide Implications of the Gulf War." In *The Iran-Iraq War: An Historical, Economic and Political Analysis*, edited by M. S. El Azhary. London and Canberra: Croom Helm, 1984.

Apter, D. *The Politics of Modernization*. Chicago and London: The University of Chicago Press, 1965.

Arfaʿ, H. *Under Five Shahs*. London: Murray, 1964.

Arjomand, S. A. *The Shadow of God and the Hidden Imam: Religion, Political Order and Societal Change in Shiʿite Iran from the Beginning to 1890*. Chicago and London: The University of Chicago Press, 1984.

———. *The Turban for the Crown: The Islamic Revolution in Iran*. New York: Oxford University Press, 1988.

Armstrong, S. et al. *The Chronology*. New York: Warner Books, 1987.

Ashraf, A. "Historical Obstacles to the Development of a Bourgeoisie in Iran." *Iranian Studies*, 2, no. 2–3 (Spring 1969): 54–79.

———. "Iran, Imperialism, Class and Modernization from Above." Ph.D. dissertation, New School for Social Research, 1971.

———. *Historical Obstacles to the Development of Capitalism in Iran*. Tehran: Payam Press, 1980.

———. "Peasants, Land, and Revolution." In *Land and Peasant Questions*. Tehran: Agah Publishers, 1982.

———. "Bazaars and Mosques in Iran's Revolution." (Ervand Abrahamian's interview with Ahmad Ashraf.) *MERIP Reports* (March–April 1983): 16–18.
Atighpour, M. *The Bazaar and Bazaaris in the Iranian Revolution.* Tehran: Kayhan Publishers, 1979.
Avery, P. *Modern Persia.* New York: Praeger, 1965.
Avery, P., and J. B. Simmon. "Persia on the Cross of Silver." *Middle East Studies* 10, no. 13 (October 1974): 259–86.
Bahraini, P. "The Iran-Iraq War: Is There a Settlement?" Unpublished paper, 1987.
Baktash, M. "Ta'azieh and Drama in Iran." In *Ta'azieh, Rituals, and Drama in Iran,* edited by P. Chlkowski. New York: New York University Press, 1974.
Baldwin, G. *Planning and Development in Iran.* Baltimore, Md. The Johns Hopkins University Press, 1967.
Banani, A. *The Modernization of Iran: 1921–1941.* Stanford, Calif. Stanford University Press, 1961.
———. "Reflections on the Social and Economic Structure of Safavid Persia at its Zenith." *Iranian Studies* 11 (1978): 83–116.
Bank Markazi. *The Annual Report and Balance Sheet.* Tehran: Bank Markazi, 1977.
Baraheni, R. *What Has Happenend and What Will Happen in the Iranian Revolution?* Tehran: Zaman Publication Company, 1979.
Bashirieh, H. *The State and Revolution in Iran.* London and Canberra: Croom Helm, 1984.
Banuazizi, A., and M. Weiner, eds. *The State, Religion, and Ethnic Politics: Afghanistan, Iran, and Pakistan.* Syracuse, N.Y.: Syracuse University Press, 1986.
Bayat, M. "Shi'a Islam as a Functioning Ideology in Iran: The Cult of the Hidden Imam." In *Iran Since the Revolution: Internal Dynamics, Regional Conflict, and the Superpowers,* edited by B. Rosen. New York: Columbia University Press, 1985.
Behdad, S. "The Political Economy of Islamic Planning in Iran. In *Post-Revolutionary Iran,* edited by H. Amirahmadi and M. Parvin. Boulder, Colo. Westview Press, 1988a.
———. "Foreign Exchange Gap, Structural Constraints, and the Political Economy of Exchange Rate Determination in Iran." *International Journal of Middle East Studies* 20, no. 1 (February 1988b): 1–21.
Bergsten, C. et al. *American Multinationals and American Interests.* Washington, D.C.: The Brookings Institution, 1978.
Bernard, C., and Z. Khalilzad. *The Government of God: Iran's Islamic Republic.* New York: Columbia University Press, 1984.
Bernstein, A. "Iran's Low-Intensity War against the United States." *ORBIS* 30, no. 1 (Spring 1986): 149–68.
Bharier, J. *Economic Development in Iran: 1900–1970.* London and New York: Oxford University Press, 1971.
Bill, J. *The Politics of Iran: Groups, Classes, and Modernization.* Columbus, Oh.: Merrill, 1972.

———. "Power and Religion in Revolutionary Iran." *The Middle East Journal* 36, no. 1 (Winter 1982): 22–47.

———. *The Eagle and the Lion: The Tragedy of American-Iranian Relations.* New Haven and London: Yale University Press, 1988.

Brinton, L. *The Anatomy of Revolution.* New York: Vintage Books, 1952.

Brown, B. *The Fiscal Influence on Economic Development.* Unpublished dissertation, University of Wisconsin, 1959.

Browne, E. *The Persian Crisis of December 1911.* London: Cambridge University Press, 1912.

———. *The Persian Revolution of 1905–1909.* London: Cambridge University Press, 1966.

Brun, T., and R. Dumont. "Imperial Pretensions and Agricultural Dependence." *MERIP Reports* 8, no. 8 (October 1978): 15–20.

Cahen, C. "L'evolution de l'Iqta de IX au XIII Siecle." *Annales Economie, Societe, Civilization* (1953): 25–52.

Castells, M. *The Urban Question.* Cambridge, Mass.: MIT Press, 1979.

Chomsky, N. *The Culture of Terrorism.* Boston: South End, 1988.

Christensen, A. *L'Iran Sous Les Sassanides.* Copenhagen: Ejnar Munksgaard, 1944.

Christopher, W., and P. Kreisberg, eds. *American Hostages in Iran: The Conduct of a Crisis.* New Haven and London: Yale University Press, 1985.

Chubin S., and C. Tripp. *Iran and Iraq at War.* Boulder, Colo.: Westview, 1988.

Cohan, A. S. *Theories of Revolution: An Introduction.* London: Wheaton & Company, 1975.

Cottam, R. *Nationalism in Iran.* Pittsburgh, Penn.: University of Pittsburgh Press, 1979.

———. "Iran and Soviet-American Relations." In *The Iranian Revolution and the Islamic Republic,* edited by N. Keddie and E. Hooglund. Syracuse, N.Y.: Syracuse University Press, 1986.

Curzon, G. *Persia and the Persian Question.* 2 vols. London: Longmans, 1966.

Danesh, H. *An Introduction to a Theory of Irregular Rural to Urban Migration: A Case Study in Iran.* Tehran: Plan and Budget Organization, 1984.

Davies, J. "Toward a Theory of Revolution." *American Sociological Review* 27 (1962): 3–19.

de Villiers, D. G. et al. *The Imperial Shah, an Informative Biography.* Boston and Toronto: Atlantic Monthly, 1976.

Diba, F. *Mossadegh: A Political Biography.* London: Croom Helm, 1986.

Djamalzadeh, M. A. *The Plentiful Treasure.* Berlin: Kaveh, 1956.

Dobb, M. *Studies in the Development of Capitalism.* New York: International Publishers, 1947.

Draper, H. *Karl Marx's Theory of Revolution.* New York: Monthly Review, 1978.

Dunn, J. *Modern Revolutions: An Introduction to the Analysis of a Political Phenomenon.* London: Cambridge University Press, 1972.

Eagleton, W. *The Kurdish Republic of 1946.* London and New York: Oxford University Press, 1963.

Eden, A. *Full Circle.* Boston: Houghton Mifflin, 1960.

El Azhary, M. S., ed. *The Iran-Iraq War: An Historical, Economic, and Political Analysis.* London and Canberra: Croom Helm, 1984.

Elwell-Sutton, E. A. *Persian Oil.* London: Lawrence and Wishart, 1955.

Engler, R. *Politics of Oil: A Study of Private Power and Democratic Direction.* New York: Macmillan, 1961.
Entessar, N. "The Military and Politics in the Islamic Republic of Iran." In *Post-Revolutionary Iran,* edited by H. Amirahmadi and M. Parvin. Boulder, Colo.: Westview, 1988.
Etemad-os Saltaneh, M. H. *Memoires of Etemad-os Saltaneh.* Tehran: Amir Kabir Publications, 1971.
Falk, R. "One of the Great Watersheds of Modern History." *MERIP Reports* 9, no. 2–3 (March–April 1979): 9–12.
Fashahi, M. "Les Causes economiques et Sociales de la Revolution Bourgeoise de 1900–1912 en Iran ou fin de Production Asiatique et la Naisance des Raports Capitalistes en Iran (1796–1921)" Doctoral thesis, Sorbonne University, Paris, 1979.
Fateh, M. *The Economic Position of Persia.* London: P. S. King & Great Smith Street, 1926.
Fatemi, F. S. *The USSR in Iran.* South Brunswick and New York: A. S. Barnes and Company, 1980.
Feierabend, I. K. et al. *Anger, Violence, and Politics.* Englewood Cliffs, N.J.: Prentice-Hall, 1972.
Fekrat, M. A. "Economic Growth and Development in Iran." In *Iran: Past, Present and Future,* edited by J. Jacqz. New York: Aspen Institute for Human Studies, 1976.
Ferdows, A. "Shariati and Khomeini on Women." In *The Iranian Revolution and the Islamic Republic,* edited by N. Keddie and E. Hooglund. Syracuse, N.Y.: Syracuse University Press, 1986.
Fischer, M. "Persian Society: Transformation and Strain." In *Twentieth-Century Iran,* edited by H. Amirsadeghi and R. Ferrier. London: Heinemann, 1977.
———. *From Religious Dispute to Revolution.* Cambridge, Mass.: Harvard University Press, 1980.
Fraser, J. *Narrative of a Journey into Khorasan in the Years 1821 and 1822.* London: Longmans and Green, 1825.
Gorouh-e Ettehad-e Communistee. *Problems and the Questions of the Movement.* Np.: Gorouh-e Ettehad-e Communistee, 1977.
———. *What Is Not to Be Done? A Critique of the Past and a Guide for the Future.* Np.: Gorouh-e Ettehad-e Communistee, 1978.
Graham, R. *Iran: The Illusion of Power.* London: Croom Helm, 1980.
Gramsci, A. *Selections from the Prison Notebooks.* Edited by Q. Hoare and G. Smith. New York and London: Lawrence & Wishart, 1971.
———. *Selections from Political Writings (1919–1920).* New York: International Publishers, 1977.
Green, G. *Revolution in Iran: The Politics of Countermobilization.* New York: Praeger, 1982.
Gurr, T. R. "Psychological Factors in Civil Violence." *World Politics* 20 (January 1968): 245–78.
———. *Why Men Rebel.* Princeton, N.J.: Princeton University Press, 1970.
———. "Psychological Factors in Civil Violence." In *Anger, Violence, and Politics: Theories and Research,* edited by Feierabend, I. et al. Englewood Cliffs, N.J.: Prentice-Hall, 1971.

———. "A Causal Model of Civil Strife: A Comparative Analysis Using New Indices." In *Anger, Violence, and Politics*, edited by Feierabend, I. et al. Englewood Cliffs, N.J.: Prentice-Hall, 1972.

———. ed. *Handbook of Political Conflict, Theory and Research*. London: The Free Press, 1980.

Haeri, A. H. "Sheikh Fazlollah Noori's Refutation of the Idea of Constitutionalism." *Middle East Journal* 13, no. 3 (October 1977): 327–39.

Halliday, F. *Iran: Dictatorship and Development*. New York: Penguin, 1979.

———. *After the Shah*. Washington, D.C.: Institute for Policy Studies, 1980.

———. "Iran's New Grand Strategy." *MERIP Reports* 17, no. 1 (January–February 1987): 7–8.

———. "The Iranian Revolution: Uneven Development and Religious Populism." In *State and Ideology in the Middle East and Pakistan*, edited by H. Alavi and F. Halliday. New York: Monthly Review Press, 1988.

Hanaway, W. L. "Stereotype Imagery in the Ta'azieh." In *Ta'azieh, Rituals, and Drama in Iran*, edited by P. Chlkowski. New York: New York University Press, 1979.

Heller, M. "The War Strategy of Iran." *Middle East Review*, 19, no. 4 (Summer 1987): 17–24.

Hershlag, Z. Y. *Introduction to the Modern Economic History of the Middle East*. Leiden, Netherlands: E. J. Brill, 1980.

Higgins, P. J. "Minority-State Relations in Contemporary Iran." In *The State, Religion, and Ethnic Politics*, edited by A. Banuazizi and M. Weiner. Syracuse, N.Y.: Syracuse University Press, 1986.

Hilton, R. ed. *The Transition from Feudalism to Capitalism*. London: New Left Books, 1976.

Hiro, D. "Chronicle of the Gulf War." *MERIP Reports* 14, no. 6–7 (July–September 1984): 3–15.

———. *Iran Under the Ayatollahs*. London, Melbourne, and Hinley: Routledge & Kegan Paul, 1985.

Hobsbawm, E. "From Feudalism to Capitalism." In *The Transition from Feudalism to Capitalism*, edited by R. Hilton. London: New Left Books, 1976.

Homayoun, D. *Yesterday and Tomorrow: Three Discourses about the Revolutionary Iran*. N.p., 1982.

———. "Mollahs and the Revolution. (Author's interview with Dariush Homayoun, former minister of information and tourism.) Washington, D.C., July 1984.

Hooglund, E. "The Khoshneshinan Population of Iran." *Iranian Studies* 6 (Autumn 1973): 29–245.

———. *Land Reform and Revolution in Iran, 1960–1980*. Austin: University of Texas Press, 1980.

———. "Iran's Agricultural Inheritance." *MERIP Reports* 11, no. 7 (September 1981): 15–20.

———. "The Gulf War and Islamic Republic." *MERIP Reports* 14, no. 6–7 (July–September 1984): 31–42.

———. "Iran 1980–1985: Political and Economic Trends." In *The Islamic Republic and the Iranian Revolution*, edited by N. Keddie and E. Hooglund. Syracuse, N.Y.: Syracuse University Press, 1986.

———. "Search for Iran's Moderates." *MERIP Reports* 17, no. 1 (January–February 1987): 5–6.
———. "The Islamic Republic at War and Peace." *MERIP Reports* 19, no. 1 (February 1989): 4–12.
Hosseiny. A. T. *Notes and News of the Constitution and the Iranian Revolution.* Tehran: Amir Kabir, 1972.
Hosseiny, G. "Asiatic Mode of Production in Iran." (Author's interview with the Iranian sociologist Ghaffar Hosseiny.) Paris, France, June 1983.
Hosseiny, S. A. "A Dictatorship under the Name of Islam." (Fred Halliday, interview with Sheikh Ezzodin Hosseiny.) *MERIP Reports* 13 no. 3 (March–April 1983) 9–10.
Hoveyda, F. *The Fall of the Shah.* New York: Simon and Shuster, 1979.
Huntington, S. *Political Order in Changing Societies.* New Haven, Conn.: Yale University Press, 1970.
Hussain, A. *Islamic Iran: Revolution and Counterrevolution.* New York: St. Martin's Press, 1985.
Hussain, J. *The Occultation of the Twelfth Imam.* Cambridge: Cambridge University Press, 1982.
Huyser, R. *Mission to Iran.* London: Andre Deutsch, 1986.
Ioannides, C. *America's Iran: Injury and Catharsis.* New York and London: University Press of America, 1984.
Iran Almanac and Book of Facts. Tehran: Echo of Iran, 1963.
———. Tehran: Echo of Iran, 1973.
Irfani, S. *Iran's Islamic Revolution.* London: Zed Books, 1983.
Issawi, C. *The Economic History of Iran, 1800–1914.* Chicago: University of Chicago Press 1971.
Jacqz, J. W., ed. *Iran: Past, Present, and Future.* New York: Aspen Institute, 1976.
Jafri, S.H.M. *Origin and Early Development of Shiʿa Islam.* London and New York: Longmans, 1979.
Jazani, B. *Armed Struggle in Iran: The Road to Mobilization of the Masses.* n.p.: Iran Committee, 1974.
———. *The Sociology and the Foundation of the Strategy of the Revolutionary Movement in Iran.* Tehran: People's Fedaii Guerrilla Organization of Iran. 1978.
———. *Capitalism and Revolution in Iran.* London: Zed Press, 1980.
Johnson, C. *Revolutionary Change.* Stanford, Calif.: Stanford University Press, 1982.
Kambakhsh, A. *An Overview of the Workers' and Communist Movement in Iran.* Stockholm: Tudeh Press, 1972.
Karimi. S. "Economics, Policies, and Structural Changes since the Revolution." In *The Iranian Revolution and the Islamic Republic,* edited by N. Keddie and E. Hooglund. Syracuse, N.Y.: Syracuse University Press, 1986.
Kasravi, A. *A History of the Constitutional Revolution of Iran.* Tehran: Amir Kabir, 1983.
Katouzian, M. A. "Land Reform in Iran: A Case Study in Social Engineering." *Journal of Peasant Studies* 1, no. 2 (1974): 220–239.
———. *The Political Economy of Modern Iran: 1926–1979.* New York: New York University Press, 1981.

Kazemi, F. *Poverty and Revolution in Iran.* New York and London: New York University Press, 1980.
Kazemzadeh, F. *Russia and Britain in Persia, 1864–1914.* New Haven, Conn.: Yale University Press, 1968.
Keddie, N. *Historical Obstacles to Agrarian Change in Iran.* Claremont, Calif.: Asian Studies, 1960.
———. *Scholars, Saints, and Sufis.* Berkeley: University of California Press, 1972.
———. *Roots of Revolution.* New Haven, Conn., and London: Yale University Press, 1981.
Kermany, A. *History of the Iranian Constitutional Revolution.* Isfahan: Isfahan University Press, 1972.
Kermany, N. *History of the Awakening of Iranians.* 2 vols. Tehran: Farhang Press, 1967.
Keshavarz, F. *I Accuse the Tudeh Party of Iran.* Tehran: Ravaq Press, 1982.
Key Ostovan, H. *The Policy of the Negative Equilibrium in the Fourteenth Majlis.* Tehran: Taban Press, 1948.
Khameii, A. *The Great Missed Opportunity.* Tehran: Hafteh Publications, 1983.
Khomeini, R. *Unveiling of Secrets.* Qom, Iran: Mostafavi, 1943.
———. "An Exile's Dream for Iran." (*Le Monde,* interview with Ayatollah Rouhollah Khomeini.) In *Iran Erupts,* edited by A. R. Nobari. Stanford, Calif.: Iran American Documentation Group, 1978.
———. *Selected Messages and Speeches of Imam Khomeini.* Tehran: The Ministry of National Guidance, 1979.
———. "Khomeini's New Year's Speech." *MERIP Reports* 10, no. 5 (June 1980): 22–25.
———. *Islam and the Revolution.* Translated by Hamid Algar. Berkeley, Calif.: Mizan, 1981.
Khosrawi, K. *Systems of Landownership in Iran from the Sassanids to Saljukids Periods.* Tehran: Shabgar Publishers, 1977.
———. *The Peasant Community of Iran.* Tehran: Payam Publishing Company, 1979.
Klare, M. "Arms and the Shah." In *Tell the American People,* edited by D. Albert. Philadelphia: Movement for a New Society, 1980.
Kostiner, J. "Counterproductive Meditations: Saudi Arabia and the Iran Arms Deal." *Middle East Review* 19, no. 4 (Summer 1987).
Kurdish Democratic Party of Iran (KDP). *Report of the Central Committee of the Democratic Party of Kurdistan.* N.p.: Publication du Parti Democratic Du Kurdistan D'Iran, 1981.
Kuznetsova. "Urban Industry in Persia During the Eighteenth and Nineteenth Century." *Central Asiatic Review* 11, no. 3 (1963): 308–21.
Laing, M. *The Shah.* London: Sidgwick & Jackson, 1977.
Lambton, A.K.S. *Landlords and Peasants in Persia.* London: Oxford University Press, 1953.
———. "Persia Today." *The World Today* 17, no. 2 (February 1961): 76–87.
———. "Reconsideration of the Position of Maraj' Taghlid and the Religious Institutions." *Studia Islamica* 20 (1964): 115–35.
———. "The Evolution of Iqtaʿ in Medieval Iran." *Journal of Persian Studies* 5 (1967): 41–50.

———. *The Persian Land Reform, 1962–1966*. Oxford: Clarendon Press, 1969.
———. "The Case of Hajji Abd al-Karim: A Study on the Role of the Merchants in the Mid-Nineteenth Century." In *Iran and Islam*, edited by G. E. Bosworth. Edinburg: Edinburg University Press, 1971.
Limbert, J. W. *Iran at War with History*. Boulder, Colo.: Westview, 1985.
Looney, R. *The Economic Development of Iran: A Recent Survey with Projections to 1981*. New York: Praeger, 1973.
———. *Iran at the End of the Century*. Lexington, Mass.: D. C. Heath, 1977.
———. *Economic Origins of the Iranian Revolution*. New York: Pergamon Press, 1982.
Lotz, J. "Problems and Proposal for the First Seven-Year Plan." *The Middle East Journal* 4, no. 1 (January 1950): 102–5.
McLachlan, K. S. "Land Reform in Iran." In *The Cambridge History of Iran*. Vol. 6. Cambridge: Cambridge University Press, 1968.
———. "The Iranian Economy, 1960–1976. In *Twentieth Century Iran*, edited by H. Amirsadeghi and R. Ferrier. London: Heinemann, 1977.
McNaugher, T. "The Iran-Iraq War: Slouching Towards Catastrophe." *Middle East Review* 19, no. 4 (Summer 1987).
Madany, J. *The Political History of Iran*. Vol. 1. Tehran: Islamic Publications, 1981.
———. *The Political History of Iran*. Vol. 2. Tehran: Islamic Publications, 1982.
Mahdavy, H. "The Coming Crisis of Iran." *Foreign Affairs* 44, no. 1 (October 1965): 135–46.
Malcolm, J. *History of Persia*. London: Murray, 1892.
Mansouri, J. *Twenty-Five Years of Domination of Iran by the United States*. Tehran: n.p., 1985.
Marlowe, J. *Iran: A Short Political Guide*. London: Pall Mall, 1963.
Marx, K. *A Contribution to the Critique of Political Economy*. Chicago: Charles H. Kerr & Company, 1911.
———. *Pre-Capitalist Economic Formations*. (Edited with an introduction by Eric J. Hobsbawm.) New York: International Publishers, 1965.
———. *On Colonialism and Modernization*. (Edited with an introduction by S. Avinieri.) Garden City, N.Y.: Doubleday, 1969.
Marx, K., and F. Engels. *Manifesto of the Communist Party*. New York: International Publishers, 1983.
Massaly, H. "We Should Struggle to Save Iran from Political and Social Decay." *Iranshahr* (October 29, 1982): 7–9.
———. "A Conversation with Hassan Massaly." *Iranshahr* 5, no. 11 (May 27, 1983): 5–9.
Matin Daftari, A. "Foundation of the National Democratic Front." (Author's interview with Ahmad Matin Daftari, a founding member of the National Democratic Front.) Paris, France, August 1983.
Mazdak. The Profiles of Mossadegh and the Tudeh Party. Florence, Italy: Mazdak, 1982.
Milani, M. *The Making of Iran's Islamic Revolution: From Monarchy to Islamic Republic*. Boulder, Colo., and London: Westview, 1988.
Milliband, R. *The State in Capitalist Society*. New York: Basic Books, 1969.
Millspaugh, A. C. *Americans in Persia*. Washington, D.C.: The Brookings Institutions, 1946.

Mirzazadeh, N. "Mollahs, Poor, and the Revolution." Author's interview with the Iranian poet Nemat Mirzazadeh. Paris France, June 1983.
Moghadam, V. "The Left and the Revolution in Iran: A Critical Analysis." In *Post-Revolutionary Iran*, edited by H. Amirahmadi and M. Parvin. Boulder, Colo.: Westview, 1988.
Mohammadi, M. *The Principles of the Foreign Policy of the Islamic Republic of Iran*. Tehran: Sepehr, 1987.
Mohsen, S. "Defense of Said Mohsen." In *Published Documents of Mojahedin-e Khalq*. Wilmette, Ill.: Organization of the Iranian Moslem Students, 1978.
Mojahedin-e Khalq. *The Administration of President Carter*. Tehran: Mojahedin, 1979a.
———. *The Establishment and the History of the Mojahedin-e Khalq from 1965 to 1971*. Tehran: Mojahedin, 1979b.
Momeni, B. *The Land Question and the Class Struggle in Iran*. Tehran, n.p., 1978.
———. "Land and Revolution in Iran." (Author's interview with Bagher Momeni.) Paris, France, June 1983.
Motamedi, N. *The Necessity of Industrialization or Increasing the National Productivity*. Tehran: Economist, 1971.
Mottahari, M. *About the Islamic Revolution*. Qom, Iran: Islami Publisher, 1982.
Najmabadi, A. *Land Reform and Social Change in Iran*. Salt Lake City: University of Utah Press, 1987.
Nashat, G. *The Origins of Modern Reform in Iran, 1870–80*. London and Chicago: University of Illinois Press, 1982.
Nasr, S. H. "Religion in Safavid Persia." *Iranian Studies* 7 (1974): 271–86.
Nateq, H. "A Conversation with Dr. Homa Nateq. (*Iranshahr* interview with Homo Nateq, Iranian historian.) *Iranshahr* 3, no. 44 (January 22, 1982): 12–14.
———. "Saiid Soltanpour in the Student Movement." *Soosialism Va Enghelab* (November 23, 1983).
Nejati, G. *The Oil Nationalization Movement and the 1953 Coup*. Tehran: Enteshar, 1986.
Nikpay, G. *A Report of the Meetings of the Economic Council in Presence of His Imperial Majesty, Shahanshah Aryamehr*. Tehran: Farhang va Honar, 1969.
Nima, R. *The Wrath of Allah*. London: Pluto Press, 1983.
Nirumand, B. *Iran: The New Imperialism in Action*. Translated by L. Mins. New York and London: Monthly Review Press, 1969.
Nobari, A. R., ed. *Iran Erupts*. Stanford, Calif.: Iran-American Documentation Group, 1978.
Nomani, F. *The Evolution of Feudalism in Iran*. Tehran: Sepehr, 1979.
Noori, F. *Treatises, Announcements, Writings, and Newspapers of the Martyred Sheikh Fazlollah Noori*, Edited by M. Torkoman. Tehran: Rasa Cultural Institute, 1984.
Pahlavi, M. R. *Mission for My Country*. New York: McGraw Hill, 1961.
———. *The White Revolution*. Tehran: Bank Melli, 1966.
———. *Answer to History*. Briarcliff Manor, N.Y.: Stein and Day, 1980.
Paknejad, S. "Kurdistan, the Arm of the Iranian Revolution." (Atefeh Gorgin, interview with Shokrollah Paknejad.) *Daf tarhay-e Azadee* 1 (1985): 110–15.
Parsa Benab, Y. *Independence and Dependence: Struggle between Two Lines in the Political History of Iran*. 2 vols. New York: Azar, 1982.

Parsons, A. *The Pride and the Fall: Iran 1974–1979*. London: Jonathan Cape, 1984.
Parvin, M., and M. Taghavi. "A Comparison of Land Tenure in Iran under Monarchy and under the Islamic Republic." In *Post-Revolutionary Iran*, edited by H. Amirahmadi and M. Parvin. Boulder, Colo.: Westview, 1988.
Pesaran, M. H. "Economic Development and Revolutionary Upheavals in Iran." In *Iran: A Revolution in Turmoil*, edited by H. Afshar. Albany, N.Y.: State University of New York Press, 1985.
Pigulovskaya, N. et al. *A History of Iran from Ancient Times to the End of the Eighteenth Century*. Translated from Russian by K. Keshavarz. Tehran: Entesharat-e Payam, 1975.
Plan and Budget Organization. *The Agricultural Indicators of 1974*. Unpublished paper, Tehran, 1975.
Poulantzas, N. *Classes in Contemporary Capitalism*. London: New Left Books, 1979a.
———. *Fascism and Dictatorship: The Third International and the Problem of Fascism*. Verso edition. London: New Left Books, 1979b.
Qasemlou, A. "Kurdish People Do Not Want to Fight with Their Brothers." (Kayhan, interview with Abdolrahman Qasemlou, the leader of the Democratic Party of Kurdistan.) *Iranshahr* (May 8, 1980): 4–5.
Rafsanjani, H. "Timing of the Next Offensive." *MERIP Reports* 14, no. 6–7 (July–September 1984): 42–43.
Rahaii. *Fadayan-e Islam*. N.p.: Supporters of the Organization of the Communist Unity in Europe, 1982.
Rah-e Kargar. "Stages of the Iranian Revolution." (Author's interview with "Comrade Ahmad" from the Organization of Rah-e Kargar.) Paris, France, June 1983.
Ramazani, R. *Revolutionary Iran: Challenge and Response in the Middle East*. Baltimore, Md., and London: Johns Hopkins University Press, 1986.
Razavi, H., and F. Vakil. *The Political Economy of Economic Planning in Iran, 1971–1983: From Monarchy to Islamic Republic*. Boulder, Colo., and London: Westview, 1984.
Rejai, M. *The Comparative Study of Revolutionary Strategy*. New York: David McKay Company, Inc., 1977
Renner, G. "A Comparison of Land Tenure in Iran under Monarchy and under the Islamic Republic." In *Post-Revolutionary Iran*, edited by H. Amirahmadi and M. Parvin. Boulder, Colo., and London: Westview, 1988.
Rezun, M. "Reza Shah's Court Minister: Teimour Tash." *International Journal of Middle East Studies* 12, no. 2 (1980): 119–37.
Roosevelt, K. *Countercoup: The Struggle for the Control of Iran*. New York: McGraw Hill, 1979.
Rossen, B. M., ed. *Iran since the Revolution: Internal Dynamics, Regional Conflict, and the Superpowers*. New York: Columbia University Press, 1985.
Rouhani, H. *A Review and Analysis of Imam Khomeini's Movement in Iran*. N.p., 1977.
———. *Shariatmadary in the Court of History*. Qom, Iran: n.p., 1983.
Rubin, B. *Paved with Good Intentions: The American Experience and Iran*. New York and Oxford: Oxford University Press, 1980.

Saedi, G. H. "A Conversation with Dr. Gholam Hossein Saedi." *Iranshahr* 5, no. 8 (May 1983): 9–10.
Safavi, R. *The Economy of Iran*. Tehran: Ettehadieh, 1929.
Safinejad, J. *Boneh*. Tehran: University of Tehran Press, 1977.
Saikal, A. *The Rise and the Fall of the Shah*. Princeton, N.J.: Princeton University Press, 1980.
Sanghavi, R. *The Shah of Iran*. New York: Stein and Day, 1966.
Sarjehpeyma, H. *The Economic Impact of Internal Migration: Iran as a Special Case*. Doctoral diss. Norman: University of Oklahoma, 1984.
Saunders, H. "The Beginning of the End." In *The American Hostages in Iran: The Conduct of a Crisis in Iran*, edited by W. Christopher and P. Kreisberg. New Haven, Conn., and London: Yale University Press, 1985.
Savory, R. "The Principles of Homostasis Considered in Relation to Political Events in Iran in the 1960's." *International Journal of Middle East Studies* 3, no. 7 (1972): 282–302.
Schwartz, D. "Political Alienation: The Psychology of Revolution's First Stage." In *Anger, Violence, and Politics*, edited by I. Feierabend et al. Englewood Cliffs, N.J.: Prentice-Hall, 1972.
Shafa, S. *The Crime and Punishment: Iran 1979–1986*. Paris: n.p., 1987.
Shafaq, S. R. "The Iranian Seven-Year Development Plan." *The Middle East Journal* 1 (January 1950): 100–102.
Shajii, Z. *Members of the Majlis of National Council during the Twenty-one Legislative Sessions*. Tehran: Tehran University Press, 1965.
Shariati, A. *Martyrdom*. Tehran: Hosseinieh Ershad, 1972.
———. *With a Familiar Audience*. Tehran: Hosseinieh Ershad, 1977.
———. *Return to Oneself, Return to Which Oneself?* Tehran: Hosseinieh Ershad, 1978.
Sharifi, R. "How the National Front was Established." (Author's interview with Rahim Sharifi, the secretary general of the Iran party.) Paris, France, July 1983.
Sheikholeslami, A. R. "From Religious Accommodation to Religious Revolution: The Transformation of Shi'ism in Iran." In *The State, Religion, and Ethnic Politics*, edited by A. Banuazizi and M. Weiner. Syracuse, N.Y.: Syracuse University Press, 1986.
Shekooee, H. *Squatter Migrants of Tabriz: Northern Part of Tabriz*. Tabriz: Azerbaijan University Press, 1975.
Shivers, L. "Inside the Iranian Revolution." In *Tell the American People*, edited by D. Albert. Philadelphia: Movement for a New Society, 1980.
Sick, G. *All Fall Down: America's Tragic Encounter with Iran*. New York: Random House, 1985.
———. "Iran's Quest for Superpower Status." *Foreign Affairs* (Spring 1987): 697–715.
Singh, K. R. *Iran: Quest for Security*. New Delhi: Vikas Publishing House PVT Ltd., 1980.
Sismondi, de Sismonde. *Political Economy and the Philosophy of Government*. New York: Augustus M. Kelley Publishers, 1966.
Skocpol, T. *States and Social Revolutions*. Cambridge: Cambridge University Press, 1979.

Sodagar, M. *An Analysis of the Iranian Land Reform: 1961–1971*. Tehran: Pazand Research Institute, 1979.
Sovani, N. V. "The Analysis of Overurbanization." *Economic Development and Cultural Change* 12, no. 2 (1964): 113–122.
Stemple, J. D. *Inside the Iranian Revolution*. Bloomington, Ind.: Indiana University Press, 1981.
Stookey, R. *America and the Arab States: An Easy Encounter*. New York: John Wiley, 1975.
Sullivan, W. "Dateline Iran: The Road Not Taken." *Foreign Policy* 40 (Fall 1980): 170–86.
———. *Mission to Iran*. New York: W. W. Norton, 1981.
Tabatabaiiᶜ, M. H. *Shiᶜite Islam*. Translated by Hossein Nasr. Albany: State University of New York Press, 1975.
Taghavi, J. "The Iran-Iraq War: The First Three Years." In *Iran since the Revolution*, edited by B. M. Rosen. New York: Columbia University Press, 1985.
Taheri, A. *The Spirit of Allah*. Bethesda, Md.: Adler & Adler, 1986.
Tarzi, S. M. "The Political Economy of American Foreign Oil Policy and the Middle East: The Influence of the Multinationals." Ph.D. dissertation, University of California, Riverside, 1982.
Teimouri, E. *The Boycott of Tobacco: The First Negative Resistance in Iran*. Tehran: Sherkat Sahamy Ketabhay-e Jeebee, 1982.
Tilly, C. *From Mobilization to Revolution*. Reading, Mass.: Addison-Wesley, 1978.
Tilly, C.L. and R. Tilly. *The Rebellious Century, 1830–1930*. Cambridge, Mass.: Harvard University Press, 1975.
Tocqueville, A. de. *The Old Regime and the French Revolution*. Garden City, N.Y.: Doubleday, 1955.
United Nations. "Progress in Land Reform." Fourth Report. Department of Economics and Social Affairs, New York, 1966.
Wallerstein, E. *The Capitalist World Economy*. Cambridge: Cambridge University Press, 1979.
Wilber, D. *Contemporary Iran*. New York: Praeger, 1963.
———. *Riza Shah Pahlavi: The Resurrection and Reconstruction of Iran*. Hicksville, N.Y.: Exposition Press, 1975.
Wittfogel, K. *Oriental Despotism: A Comprehensive Study of Total Power*. New Haven, Conn.: Yale University Press, 1957.
Zabih. S. *Iran's Revolutionary Upheaval*. San Francisco: Albany Books, 1979.
———. *Iran since the Revolution*. Baltimore, Md.: Johns Hopkins University Press, 1982.
———. *The Left in Contemporary Iran: Ideology, Organization and Soviet Connection*. London and Sydney: Croom Helm, 1986.
Zirinski, M. P. "Blood, Power, and Hypocrisy: The Murder of Robert Imbrie and American Relations with Pahlavi Iran, 1924." *International Journal of Middle East Studies* 18, no. 3 (1986): 275–92.
Zonis, M. *The Political Elite of Iran*. Princeton, N.J.: Princeton University Press, 1971.

Index

Abadan, 123
Abbas Mirza, 37
Abrahamian, 97
Afghanistan, 27
Afshar, Ali Reza, 151
Agribusiness, 98
Agricultural corporations, 98
Ahmadzadeh, Masoud, 105–6
Ahwaz, 93
Ala, Hossein, 57–58
Alam, Amir Assadollah, 65, 78
Alamuti, Noor od-Din, 74, 76
Al-e Ahmad, Jalal-e, 39
Ali (First Imam), 33–34
Ameri, Ali, 101
Amini, Ali, 72–73, 77–78; and consortium agreement, 74; and the United States, 74–75, 77
Amin-od-Dowleh, 27
Amin-oz-Zarb, Hadj Hassan, 20
Amin-oz-Zarb, Hadj Hossein, 20
Amir Entezam, Abbas, 137, 141
Amir Kabir, Mohammad Taghi Khan, 22
Amnesty International, 115–16
Amouzgar, Jamshid, 118
Anglo-Iranian Oil Company (AIOC), 57–58

Apter, David, 99
Aramesh, Ahmad, 76
Arfaʿ, General Hassan, 53
Armenia, 26
Arsanjani, Hassan, 85, 150
Ashura, 34
Asiatic Mode of Production (AMP), 9–12
Assembly of Experts, 139
Ayat, Hassan, 141
Azerbaijan Province, 133; autonomy movement in, 47–48; Democratic Party of, 54
Azhari, General Gholam Reza, 126, 127–28

Badi Zadegan, Ali Asghar, 43, 106
Baghaii, Mozaffar, 50
Baghdad Pact, 64
Bahonar, Javad, 148
Bakhtiar, General Teimour, 63; assassination of, 96, 101; chief of SAVAK, 72; military governor of Tehran, 65
Bakhtiar, Shahpur, 73; a leader of the National Front, 116; the Shah's last prime minister, 128–29
Baldwin, James, 86

Ball, George, 129
Bani-Sadr, Abol Hassan, 111, 127, 141; the fall of, 145; a member of the Islamic Revolutionary Council, 131, 137; and National Council of Resistance, 148; struggle against the Islamic Republican Party, 142–44
Banki, Taghi, 150
Bany Ahmad, Ahmad, 123
Bazaaris, 18–22, 24; and mashruteh revolution, 37–38; opposition to the Shah, 72, 75, 106; and Tobacco Movement, 37
Bazargan, Mehdy: a founding member of the Freedom Movement of Iran, 73; member of Provisional Revolutionary Council, 131; relation with Shahpour Bakhtiar, 129; supported Bani-Sadr, 144; vacillation, 139; wanted by the military government, 125
Beheshti, Ayatollah Hossein, 43; assassination of, 148; a founding member of the Islamic Republican Party, 132; and the Islamic Revolutionary Council, 137
Black Friday, 125
Boneh, 17
Bonyad-e Mostazafin, 32
Borujerdi, Ayatollah Hossein, 39–40, 71
Bourgeoisie, 9, 26, 89; modern, 18, 40, 90, 113–14; rural, 17, 81; traditional, 7, 13, 18
Brinton, Crane, 3, 7
Britain, 9, 18; against the oil nationalization in Iran, 57–59; as Iran's major trade partner, 26–28; struggle for domination of Iran, 52
Bureaucracy, 97, 114
Bureaucratic capitalism, 21

Capitalism, 12, 18
Capitalist development, 9–10, 18–19, 86
Carter, Jimmy, 129; and human rights policy in Iran, 115, 119

Caspian Sea, 26
Caucasia, 26
Central Intelligence Agency (CIA), 1, 60, 62
Central Treaty Organization (CENTO), 64
Chamran, Mostafa, 111
Civil society, 22
Class, 2–4
Class struggle, 5
Constitution, 129
Constitutional Revolution. *See* Mashruteh Revolution
Construction Crusade, 32, 151
Council of the Guardians, 150–51
Curzon, Lord, 14

Darakhshesh, Mohammad, 74
D'Arcy, William Knox, 27; concession, 23
Dashti, Ali, 49
Davies, James, 3, 27
Dehghani, Ashraf, 134–35
Democratic National Front, 139
Democratic Party of Kurdistan, 43, 133, 135, 148
Despotism, 11, 39
Dulles, Allen, 62
Dulles, John Foster, 64

Ebtehadj, Abolhassan, 66
Edalat Khaneh, 38
Egypt, 31
Engels, 10–11
Eqbal, Manouchehr, 25, 39, 65–67, 71, 101, 117; and Open Door Policy, 25, 66, 69
Ershad, Hosseinieh, 42
Etemad-os Saltaneh, 20
Europe, 18, 26

Faizieh seminary, 40–41
Falk, Richard, 103
Farsi, Jalal od-Din, 141
Fath Ali Shah, 37
Fedaii Organization. *See* People's Fedaii Guerrilla Organization
Fedayan-e Islam, 42, 50, 62, 133

Feudalism, 9–10, 12, 18
Fischer, Michael, 42
Foreign capital, 14, 19, 26
Foruhar, Dariush, 116, 125
Foundation of the poor, 142, 151
France, 26, 31
Fraser, James, 16, 19
Freedom Movement of Iran, 73, 116

Gavband, 16–17, 82, 119, 132, 136–37
Georgia, 26
Germany, 26
Golistan Treaty, 26
Golpaigani, Ayatollah Mohammad Reza, 128, 150
Golsorkhi, Reza, 133
Graham, Robert, 92, 95, 106
Gramsci, Antonio, 2, 6, 114, 123
Guilan, 20
Gurr, Robert Tedd, 3–5

Hadith, 35
Hadj Abdul Karim, 27
Hadj Rezaii, Tayyeb, 62
Hadj Seyyed Javady, Ali Asghar, 101
Hagh Shenas, Jahangir, 49–50
Hakeem, Ayatollah Mohsen, 40
Halaby, Sheikh Mahmud, 149–50
Halliday, Fred, 90, 108, 111
Hanif Nejad, Mohammad, 43, 106
Harriman, Averell, 59
Hashemi, Mehdy, 154–55
Hassan Askari, (Eleventh) Imam, 35
Hegemony, 2, 5
Henderson, Loy, 62
Hezarkhanee, Manouchehr, 135
Hitler, Adolf, 99
Hobsbawm, Eric, 26
Hojjatieh, 149–50
Homayoun, Dariush, 92, 127
Hormati Pour, Mohammad, 134–35
Hossein, (Third) Imam, 34, 41
Hossein, Saddam, 126, 152
Hostage crisis, 140–41, 144
Hoveyda, Amir Abbas, 7, 102, 117–18
Hoveyda, Fereidoun, 96
Huntington, Samuel, 99
Huyser, General Robert, 129

Ideology, 6
Imam-e Zaman, 36, 149
Industrial development, 85–86
Intellectuals, 38
International Court of Justice (ICJ), 58–59, 61
International Monetary Fund (IMF), 67
Iran, 9, 18–19, 25–26, 53, 149, 154; and national minorities, 53; political economy of, 9, 12–13; social formation of, 81
Iran-Gate, 155
Iran Novin Party, 98
Iran Party, 49–50, 55
Iraq, 41, 143, 149
Isfahani, Reza, 150
Isfahani, Seyyed Jamal od-Din, 39
Islam, 1, 3, 43, 106
Islamic Republican Party (IRP), 132–33; and the Assembly of Experts, 138–40; control of the Revolutionary Committees, 137–38; and domination of the Majlis, 142; struggle against Bani-Sadr, 142–45
Islamic Revolutionary Council (IRC), 131, 137, 139, 141–42

Jahad-e Sazandegi, 32, 151
JAMA (Revolutionary Movement of the Iranian People), 42, 134–37
Jazani, Bijan, 50, 105–6
Johnson, Chalmers, 4–5

Kadkhodas, 15
Kambakhsh, Abdol Samad, 50–51, 57
Kany, Ayatollah Ali, 154
Karbala, 34
Kashani, Ayatollah Abol Qasem, 50, 57, 75, 62
Katouzian, Homa, 23, 51, 91
Keddie, N., 10, 2
Kennedy, John, 73–74, 77
Keshavarz, Feridoun, 50
Khaghani, Sheikh Shobeir, 138
Khaleseh, 13–14
Khalil, Maleki, 50–51
Khameii, Anwar, 50–51

Khamenei, Ayatollah Ali, 100, 132, 154, 156
Khiabani, Mousa, 148
Khoii, Ayatollah Abolqasem, 150
Khomeini, Ahmad, 142
Khomeini, Ayatollah Rouhollah, 7; appoints a new government, 129, 132, 137–38; attack on opposition forces, 143–46; Eight Point Decree of, 149; and formation of the Islamic Republic of Iran, 129, 136–37; and Iran-Iraq War, 152–56; and leadership of the Revolution, 120–21, 123–26; opposition to the Family Protection Law, 44; opposition to the White Revolution, 40–41; return to Iran, 128; and *Velayat-e Faghih*, 44, 140, 147
Khomeini, Mostafa, 44–45, 119
Khoms, 35
Khonji, Mohammad Ali, 73
Khorramshahr, 93
Khoshneshinan, 16, 84
Khowsrowdad, General Manouchehr, 126
Khuzistan Province, 152
Kianouri, Nourod-Din, 50–51, 57, 134, 149
Komeleh, 133, 135–36, 139, 147
Komiteh. *See* Revolutionary Committees
Kurdistan Province: autonomy movement, 47–48, 139–40; Democratic Party of (KDP), 54, 133, 139, 147
Kuzichkin, Vladimir, 149

Lambton A.K.S., 27, 40
Landlords, 22–23, 25, 38, 84
Landownership, 13; land reform, 81–86; large, 15; small, 15
Liberalization policies. *See* Political liberalization

Madany, Admiral Ahmad, 141–42
Mahallati, Ayatollah Hossein, 40
Mahdy, (Twelfth) Imam, 33, 140
Majidi, Abdol Majid, 101

Majlis, 20–21, 52, 56, 70, 75, 142, 145, 151, 156
Makarem Shirazi, Nasser, 143
Makki, Hossein, 62
Maqam, Qaem, 22, 37
Marashi, Ayatollah Shab od-Din, 150
Mardom Party, 66, 98, 101
Marj'a-e Taghlid, 36
Martyrdom, 33
Marx, Karl, 4–5, 10, 12
Marxism, 42, 106
Marxist, 2, 10
Marxist-Leninist, 105
Mashru'eh, 38
Mashruteh Revolution, 20, 22, 27–28, 37–38
Matin Daftari, Hedayatollah, 125, 135
Maximov, Alexander, 53
Mellioun Party, 66
Meshkini, Ayatollah Ali, 154
Middle class, 108
Milani, Ayatollah Mohammad Hadi, 41
Milliband, Ralph, 1
Millspaugh, Arthur, 29, 52–53
Minachian, Nasser, 132
Mir Salim, Hossein, 142
Mirzazadeh, Nemat, 120
Mismanagement, 91–92
Mobasher, 15, 17
Mobasheri, Assadollah, 132
Mode of Production, 4, 6, 11
Modernization, 22
Moghaddam Maraghei, Rahmatollah, 123, 141
Mohammad Ali Shah, 39, 51
Moharram, 34
Mohsen, Saiid, 43, 106
Mohtashemi, Ali Akbar, 156
Moinfar, Ali Akbar, 132
Moinian, Nasrollah, 116
Mojahedin-e Khalq, 42–43; as base of support, 106; intensify their activities, 141–44; participation in the revolution, 130; reorganized after the fall of the Shah, 134–36; struggle for the overthrow of the regime, 147–48, 152

Mojahein-e Enghelab-e Islami, 133
Mojtahed, 35, 38
Montazeri, Ayatollah Hossein Ali, 43, 100, 106, 154–55
Moosavi, Hossein, 154
Moosavi Ardebili, Ayatollah Abdol Karim, 149, 154
Mosha'a, 15
Moslem People's Republican Party (MPRP), 133, 141
Mossedegh, Mohammad, 21, 25, 29; and the economy without oil program, 60, 86; as a Majlis deputy, 49, 52; and negative equilibrium, 53; as prime minister, 58–62; and second National Front, 72; and the student movement, 110
Mosque, 18
Motavali, 15
Mottahari, Ayatollah Morteza, 43, 106, 131, 137
Movement of the Militant Moslems, 42, 134, 136, 142–43
Mozaffar-od-Din Shah, 20, 38
Multinational corporations, 83

Nabavi, Behzad, 133
Nader Shah of Afshar, 14–15
Nasagh-holders, 16, 81
Nasser-od-Din Shah, 20
Nasser-ol-Molk, Hassan Khan, 20
Nassiri, Nematollah, 62, 96, 127
Nateq, Homa, 120
National bourgeoisie, 21, 132
National Front, 41, 50, 57–58, 62, 72, 78, 103, 105, 110–11, 127, 132–33; and opposition to Amini's government, 77; and the student movement, 110–11
National Iranian Oil Company, 58
Naus, Monsieur, 27
Nehzat-e Azadi-e Iran. *See* Freedom Movement of Iran
Nikpay, Gholamreza, 114
Nixon, Richard, 109; Doctrine, 96
Noori, Sheikh Fazlollah, 39, 51, 134
North Atlantic Treaty Organization (NATO), 129

Occultation, 33, 35
Oriental Despotism (Karl Wittfogel), 11
Ouqaf, 13, 15
Oveisi, General Gholam Ali, 124, 126

Page, Howard, 64
Pahlavi Foundation, 151
Pakdaman, Nasser, 135
Paknejad, Shokrollah, 135
Pakravan, General Hassan, 96
Parsons, Anthony, 104
Party of the Iranian People, 50
Pasdaran. *See* Revolutionary Guards
Peasants, 15–17, 84
Peeshevary, Ja'far, 54
People's Fedaii Guerrilla Organization, 105–6, 133–35; participation in the revolution, 130; Peykar, 135, 147; popularity of, 133–35; split within, 143; struggle against the regime, 147–48
Persian Gulf, 92, 96, 143
Plan and Budget Organization (PBO), 31, 66, 90, 99, 150
Plan Organization. *See* Plan and Budget Organization
Poles of development, 98
Political economy, 9, 12, 27
Political liberalization, 6–7, 71, 105
Poulantzas, Nicos, 1, 114
Pouyan, Amir Parviz, 105
Power bloc, 2, 22, 24–25, 29, 48, 52, 70, 114, 126, 131
Private property, 24
Provisional Revolutionary Council (PRG), 129, 131

Qajar dynasty, 36
Qanat, 11
Qarani, General Valyollah, 74
Qavam-os-Saltaneh, Ahmad, 24, 48, 52, 55–56, 61
Qazi, Mohammad, 54
Qom, 40–41, 45, 120–21
Qomi, Ayatollah Hassan, 41, 100, 104, 128, 141
Qoran, 35

Qotb Zadeh, Sadegh, 112, 127, 131, 137

Rabii, Ashraf, 148
Rabii, General Hossein, 126
Radmanesh, Reza, 51
Rafsanjani, Ali Akbar, 43; acting commander-in-chief of the armed forces, 153; and the economic policies of the government, 150; and the Islamic Republican Party, 132; as the Majlis speaker, 142–44; and the power struggle in Iran, 155–56; prisoned by the Shah, 100
Rajavi, Masoud, 141, 148
Rastakhiz Party, 98–100; and anti-Shah opposition, 116, 120–21; and the Shah's dictatorship, 102
Razm Ara, General Hadji Ali, 56–57
Red Army, 29, 48; and the autonomy movements in Iran, 54–55
Rejaii, Mohammad Ali, 142, 144
Reuter, Baron Julius de, 27
Revolution, 1, 4; French, 3; Iranian, 1; theories, 2–5, 7
Revolutionary Committees, 137–38, 152
Revolutionary Guards, 137–38, 152
Rex Cinema, 123
Reza, (Eighth) Imam, 15
Reza Shah, 12, 21–23, 28–29, 39, 47–48, 54; abdication of, 49–51; ruling bloc (*see* Power bloc)
Rezaii, Ali, 113
Roosevelt, Kermit, 65
Rouzbeh, Khosrow, 62
Rural Cooperatives, 82, 85
Rural Migrants, 95, 108–9; participation in the revolution, 109
Russia, 19, 27–28, 36

Sabet, Hossein, 106
Sahabi, Yadollah, 73
Saleh, Allah Yar, 49, 75
Sanjabi, Karim, 116, 124, 127–28, 132
SAVAK (the Shah's secret police), 43, 65; its chiefs, 96; and intimidation of the opposition, 99–101; members purged, 138; penetration in the anti-regime activities, 110–11; against rural migrants, 118–20; against workers, 90, 111
Schwartz, David, 2
Seddighi, Gholam Hossein, 128
Senegal, 31
Sepah Salar, Mirza Hossein, 20, 37
Shaban the Brainless, 62
Shah, Mohammad Reza Pahlavi, 1, 47, 52; attitude toward bazaaris, 106; and consolidation of power, 65–66; as a constitutional monarch, 48; and great civilization, 101; and land reform, 83; and liberalization policy, 70, 74–75, 115–18; and the military, 95–96; relationship with workers and entrepreneurs, 114
Shariati, Ali, 42–43
Shariatmadary, Ayatollah Kazem, 40–41; as a liberal Ayatollah, 104; and the Moslem People's Republican Party, 133, 141; opinion on Rex Cinema incident, 123; role in the revolution, 45, 125, 128
Shariff Emami, Ja'afar, 75, 124–26
Shi'a, 33–35, 36; rituals in revolution, 128
Shiism, 33–34, 36
Shuster, Morgan, 28
Shwartskopf, General Norman, 29, 62
Siahkal, 106
Sismondi, de Sismonde, 14
Skocpol, Theda, 5
Slavery, 10, 12
Social Class. *See* Class
Social Formation, 1, 9, 11
Social Revolution, 5
Soheili, Ahmad, 52
Soltanpour, Saiid, 119
Sonnis, 33
Soviet Union, 28–29, 59, 87, 134; and autonomy movements in Iran, 53–56; and fall of Mossadegh, 64–65; and obtaining an oil concession in Iran, 51–53
Squatter Migrants. *See* Rural Migrants

State, 12–13, 19, 22–24, 40, 98; relative autonomy, 1–2, 70
Stokes, Richard, 59
Sullivan, William, 101, 104, 128–29
Sur Israfil, Jahangir, 39

Tabari, Ehsan, 149
Tabatabaii, Seyyed Zia'a od-Din, 49, 52
Tabriz, 96, 121
Talbot, Major, 27, 37
Taleghany, Ayatollah Seyyed Mahmud, 43; a founder of the Freedom Movement of Iran, 73; in the Islamic Revolutionary Council, 131, 137; jailed by the Shah, 100; supported Mojahedin, 106
Tash, Teimour, 23
Tehran, 20, 92, 95
Theocracy, 1, 7, 145, 147
Third World, 90
Thornburg, Max, 24
Tilly, Charles, 4, 6
Tobacco Movement, 20, 37
Tocqueville, Alexis de, 3, 6, 116–17
Toiler's Party, 50
Torkoman Tchai, 26
Toyoul, 13, 15, 21–22, 36
Tribal Khans, 23, 47, 52
Truman, Harry, 59
Tudah Party, 29; and assassination of the Shah, 57; creation of, 50–53; disbandment by government, 149; supported the Islamic Republican Party, 142; and labor union, 51; in the Majlis, 49; and the 1953 coup, 63; position toward Mossadegh Goverment, 61–62; and the student movement, 111
Turkey, 41

Ulema, 18, 23, 37–41, 153
United Nations, 96
United States, 29; and the consortium agreement, 64, 116; and oil nationalization movement, 59–60, 62; and the opposition in Iran, 129; pressured the Shah for reform, 71, 74; and Soviet troops in Iran, 55; struggle for domination of Iran, 52–53

Valian, Abdol Azim, 127
Velayat-e Faghih, 140
Velayati, Ali Akbar, 154
Vosough od-Dowlleh, 28

White Revolution, 78–79, 110; sale of the state owned factories, 89
Wittfogel, Karl, 11
Working class, 90, 111, 132; and SAVAK, 111
World Bank, 102

Yazdi, Ebrahim, 127
Yazid, 34
Yeganeh, Mohammad, 100

Zahedy, General Fazllolah, 62–65
Zakat, 35
Zangeneh, Ali, 151
Zarifi, Hassan, 105
Zirak Zadeh, Ahmad, 49

About the Author

MOHAMMAD AMJAD is Assistant Professor of Political Science at the College of Saint Rose, Albany, New York.